About the author

Imogen Tyler is a senior lecturer in sociology and director of the Centre for Gender and Women's Studies at Lancaster University. She specializes in the area of marginal social identities, a topic which brings together research on asylum and migration, borders, sexual politics, motherhood, race and ethnicity, disability, social class and poverty. Her work focuses on representation and mediation and the relationship between social theory and activism. Other recent publications include a special issue of *Feminist Review* (with C. Gatrell) on the theme of 'Birth', a special issue of *Studies in the Maternal* (with T. Jensen) on the theme of 'Austerity Parenting', a special issue of *Citizenship Studies* on the theme of 'Immigrant Protest' (2013) and a book (with K. Marciniak), *Immigrant Protest: Politics, Aesthetics, and Everyday Dissent* (SUNY, forthcoming).

REVOLTING SUBJECTS

SOCIAL ABJECTION AND RESISTANCE IN NEOLIBERAL BRITAIN

Imogen Tyler

Zed Books

LONDON | NEW YORK

Revolting subjects: social abjection and resistance in neoliberal Britain was first published in 2013 by Zed Books Ltd, 7 Cynthia Street, London N1 9JF, UK and Room 400, 175 Fifth Avenue, New York, NY 10010, USA

www.zedbooks.co.uk

Set in Monotype Plantin and FFKievit by Ewan Smith, London NW5
Index: ed.emery@thefreeuniversity.net
Cover design: www.alice-marwick.co.uk
Printed and bound in Great Britain by CPI Group (UK) Ltd, Croydon, CRO 4YY

Distributed in the USA exclusively by Palgrave Macmillan, a division of St Martin's Press, LLC, 175 Fifth Avenue, New York, NY 10010, USA

A catalogue record for this book is available from the British Library
Library of Congress Cataloging in Publication Data available

ISBN 978 1 84813 852 0 hb
ISBN 978 1 84813 851 3 pb

CONTENTS

FIGURES

ACKNOWLEDGEMENTS

I am incredibly grateful to the Leverhulme Trust for awarding me a Research Fellowship (2010/11), as the teaching and administrative relief it afforded made this book possible. I also want to thank my colleagues, students and friends in the Department of Sociology and the Centre for Gender and Women's Studies at Lancaster University, especially Celia Roberts, Maureen McNeil, Lucy Suchman, Vicky Singleton, Anne-Marie Fortier, Gail Crowther, Bülent Diken, Adrian Mackenzie, Rebecca Coleman and Anne Cronin. A special thank-you to the 'feminist knitters' and in particular the queen of the hive, Debra Ferreday, and her bees, including Carla Banks and Natalie Gill. Thanks also to Martin Pedersen, who introduced me to 'the commons', Joe Rigby, who persuaded me to read Jacques Rancière, and my MA and PhD students for everything they have taught me, especially Denise Nicholas, Maja Sager, Brigit Morris Colton and Kate McNicholas Smith.

I owe a debt of gratitude to my Leverhulme referees Bev Skeggs, Margaret Wetherell and Rosalind Gill (who also offered great feedback on the Introduction). Thank you also to Sara Ahmed for inviting me to speak at the Emotion, Culture, Affect conference at Goldsmiths, to Bev Skeggs and the Centre for Gender Studies at Stockholm University for inviting me to speak at the (Un)Making Personhood workshop when I was beginning to formulate this project, and to Lauren Berlant for her feedback on my work in Stockholm and at other key meetings over the years. The inspirational scholarship of Bev, Lauren and Sara has been central in developing the ideas for this project. Thank you also to Alison Mountz for inviting me to speak about *Revolting Subjects* at the CAG conference in Canada when I was finishing the book; your advice was pivotal. I was delighted to be made an honorary member of the Island Detention Project on my visit and to talk about my work with the fabulous Jenna Loyd, Kate Coddington, Emily Mitchell-Eaton, Jennifer Hyndman and Margaret Walton-Roberts. Thanks also to

Sally Hinds and the Centre for Interdisciplinary Gender Studies at the University of Leeds, and to Christina Scharff and LSE Sociology for inviting me to present work from this book.

Pivotal research collaborators during the period of writing this book have included Lena Šimić (and the Institute for the Art and Practice of Dissent at Home), the wonderful Tracey Jensen, and my colleagues Nick Gill, Deirdre Conlon and Ceri Oppen, whom I had the privilege to work with as part of an ESRC-funded project, 'Making Asylum Seekers Legible and Visible: An Analysis of the Dilemmas and Mitigating Strategies of Asylum Advocacy Organisations' (RES-000-22-3928-A). A special mention to my superb US-based collaborator Katarzyna Marciniak, with whom I was working on a related project on 'Immigrant Protest' while I was writing this book; she played a significant part in *Revolting Subjects*.

Two chapters of this book, 'The abject politics of British citizenship' and 'Naked protest: maternal politics and the feminist commons', have appeared in earlier forms in the journal *Citizenship Studies*, and I am grateful to guest editor Cindy Weber and associate editor Peter Nyers for feedback and advice. I am also grateful to *Feminist Theory* and Jackie Stacey for guidance on an earlier piece of work, 'Against Abjection', which informed *Revolting Subjects*, and to the editors and reviewers at *Feminist Media Studies*, particularly Cindy Carter, and also the *European Journal of Cultural Studies*, where I published earlier work.

I am fortunate in having an especially large and loving family and among them I want to say the biggest thank-you to my mum, Jane Kholoud, my dad, John Tyler, Barbara and Richard Bennett, Mohamed Kholoud and Liz Tyler, and all my siblings, Deb, Jim and Taryn, Matt and Anna, Lamia, Ibiti and Gavin. My lovely cousin Rachael Twist died while I was writing this book and I often thought of her as I was typing away. As I wrote I was sustained by the warmth of everyday friendship, most especially that of Fiona Macleod, Maria Piacentini, Bob Kemp, Samantha Brand, Mark Westcombe, Sean Arnold, Abi Mills and Bethan Kitchen; thank you to you all, especially Fiona for the coffee mornings.

I couldn't have completed *Revolting Subjects* without the following people: the interviewees and research participants who gave up their time to talk with me; my editor at Zed Books,

Ken Barlow, who nudged the project forward and gave editorial feedback; Lisa Baraitser, who provided love, encouragement and invaluable advice on draft chapters; Rachel Thomson, whose friendship and sage counsel were vital; Brigit Morris Colton, who proofread and assisted with the challenge of assembling the bibliography; Celia Roberts, who has been a wonderful and supportive friend; my sister, Deb, who provided hugs, ideas, Scrabble, food and wine; my son, Louis, an inspirational artist and a formidable intellect who daily challenged my thinking, and my daughter, Bella, whose joyful spirit, singing and laughter make me happy to be alive.

Finally, I want to thank my partner, the brilliant and tirelessly kind Bruce Bennett, who read and carefully edited the whole manuscript. It was my good fortune in meeting Bruce twenty years ago that enabled me to find my voice, and I dedicate *Revolting Subjects* to him.

INTRODUCTION: REVOLTING SUBJECTS

Revolting

Verb: The action of revolt; apostasy; rebellion, insurrection.
Adjective: That [which] evokes revulsion; repulsive, disgusting.
Noun: That which is revolting; revoltingness.

Abridged from the *Oxford English Dictionary*, 2012

19 October 2011, Dale Farm, Essex, England

The time has come for a final reckoning with this scum
[Gypsies and Travellers] and their bedfellows, the Chavs. We will
NOT allow our country to be held to ransom by these parasites
and their idiotic supporters. [...] Well, my friends, that final
reckoning is near. It is up to every decent, law-abiding, moral
citizen to rid this pestilence and filth from our land and reclaim
this country.

Comment posted on the Dale Farm Solidarity website,
September 2011

On 19 October 2011, an estimated 150 riot police converged on the
largest Gypsy and Traveller site in Europe, Dale Farm near Basildon
in Essex, to enable Basildon Borough Council and the notorious
private bailiff company Constant and Co. Ltd to carry out the largest
forced eviction of British citizens from their homes in living memory.
Around five hundred people (of whom approximately one hundred
were children) had been targeted for eviction from a six-acre plot of
land owned by Irish Traveller families. While one half of the Dale
Farm site had been a Traveller site since the 1960s, and had the
necessary planning permission for the establishment of dwellings, the
second half of the site, developed on a former scrapyard, contravened
local planning laws and was deemed 'illegal'. In what they called
'Operation Cabinet', the Essex police, in full riot gear, employed taser
guns, a battering ram, iron bars, batons, sledgehammers and shields
to enter the site, which had been barricaded by the Travellers and a
significant number of activist allies. A *Guardian* editorial described

the 'stomach-churning scenes' as terrified residents watched while police and bailiffs stormed on to Dale Farm (Editorial 2011). As the eviction unfolded over the subsequent forty-eight hours, broadcast live on rolling news channels, the unruffled speeches of Tony Ball, the leader of Basildon Borough Council, to the gathered international news media jarred with television footage of trampled fences and burning caravans. 'I will never ever forget the children screaming,' said one former teacher who was a legal observer at the eviction. 'There are some things you don't forget' (cited in Troughton 2011). After the eviction, Gypsy Council representative Jo Cowley noted, 'there is this feeling that after Dale Farm, nothing will ever be the same again [...] There is terror in the community' (cited in Topping 2011). Indeed, as I will argue later in this book, the 2011 eviction at Dale Farm was one of the most disturbing and corrosive events in the recent history of British race relations, the consequences of which are still unfolding.

Yet despite the bleakness of the outcome, and the ongoing violent cycles of eviction and occupation that will undoubtedly follow, Dale Farm also marked a significant moment of political revolt in Britain. For this forced displacement of citizens from their land coincided with the emergence of a number of 'space-hacking' social and political movements which variously contest the effects of neoliberal social and economic policies. Activists from networks which included NoBorders, No One is Illegal, the Occupy movement (who were camping outside St Paul's Cathedral in London during the Dale Farm eviction), Climate Camp, trade union representatives and human rights monitors came together to struggle alongside the Gypsy and Traveller community in a historically unprecedented demonstration of solidarity between Traveller and settled communities. The 'revolting subjects' of Dale Farm thus composed a new and vital alliance between the long-stigmatized members of Gypsy and Traveller communities and a diverse cross-class network of concerned, angry and rebellious protesters. Together these 'revolting subjects' constituted a new, if precarious, political collective: a counter-public within the borders of the state which, through their protests, fractured and contested the coercive ideologies, injustices and deepening inequalities of a degraded British democracy. The voices of resistance against the abjectifying logics of neoliberal governmentality are growing louder.

Introduction

Revolting is a powerful word. Within an emotional register, being revolted is an expression of disgust, 'to react or rise with repugnance against something. To turn away with disgust or loathing from something; to recoil from' (OED 2012). We can perceive this meaning of revolt in the visceral loathing of the xenophobic hate-speech against the Gypsy and Traveller community which the Dale Farm eviction provoked. Within a political register, 'revolt' describes acts of protest and rebellion against authority, insurrections and uprisings: 'a movement or expression of vigorous dissent' (ibid.).

Revolting Subjects proceeds from the intersections of these different meanings of revolt(ing) in order to offer an account of 'social abjection' and revolt in contemporary Britain. In weaving together a series of political parables for our time, my concerns are to elaborate a rich account of neoliberal Britain from the bottom up, of the abject forms of inequality and injustice which neoliberalism effects and the resistance and revolt to which it gives rise. Focusing on citizenship, social class and migrant illegality, *Revolting Subjects* restages a series of recent revolts by disenfranchised populations: the protests of migrants in detention and facing deportation, the ongoing resistance of Gypsies and Travellers to eviction from their land and homes, and the riots of young people across England in the summer of 2011 and protests by disability activists against the erosion of welfare support systems. Using these revolts as a guide, the book maps the borders of the state from the inside out, suggesting we look anew at *the state we are in*. Indeed, what drives *Revolting Subjects* is a critical and political concern with thinking about how we might contest both the state(s), *states of being* (human life) and *states of belonging* (political life) which characterize contemporary British life. At its heart, *Revolting Subjects* raises the question of how states are made and unmade – and how we might critically engage with and intervene in this process of making and unmaking (Butler and Spivak 2007). To respond to this question, I have drawn together a diverse body of theoretical scholarship, from feminist theory, sociology, media studies, critical theory, psychosocial studies and political philosophy. *Revolting Subjects* draws this theoretical work together through the conceptual paradigm of *social abjection*.

Combining a theoretical and empirical archive, each of the chapters in *Revolting Subjects* explores the dual meanings of 'abjection' and 'revolt': the processes through which minoritized populations are imagined and configured as revolting and become subject to control, stigma and censure, and the practices through which individuals and groups resist, reconfigure and revolt against their abject subjectification. As a polemic this book also attempts to move us towards revolt – that is, to induce revulsion about the forms of disenfranchisement it describes, as well as to provoke the desire to do something about it. In encouraging revolt in this third sense my book attempts to provoke others to look anew and think differently – to prompt an imaginative engagement with dissent against the neoliberal consensus and 'the politics of disposability' which characterize contemporary Britain (Giroux 2007).

Social abjection

Over the course of the book I develop a rich account of *social abjection* as a theory of power, subjugation and resistance. Julia Kristeva's (1982) seminal psychoanalytic account of abjection has had a considerable influence in arts and humanities disciplines for over two decades. However, there has been no sustained account of abjection as a lived social process, and abjection has received little sustained academic attention within the social sciences. Furthermore, as I detail in Chapter 1, while Kristeva's account of abjection is compelling (at an explanatory level) what is absent from her and many subsequent developments of this concept is an account of what it means to be (made) abject, to be one who repeatedly finds herself the object of the other's violent objectifying disgust (see Tyler 2009a). *Revolting Subjects* argues for a more thoroughly social and political account of abjection through a consideration of the consequences of 'being abject' within specific social and political locales. By drawing upon a substantial archive of empirical materials that include interview data, policy documents, political speeches, artworks, news media reports and other popular cultural materials, I develop *social abjection* as a theoretical resource that enables us to consider states of exclusion from multiple perspectives, including the perspective of those who are 'obliged to inhabit the impossible edges of modernity', those border zones within the state, in which the overwhelming imperative is not transgression, but survival (McClintock 1995: 72). What the conceptual paradigm of social abjection reveals is that if state power relies on the production of abject subjects to constitute itself and draw its borders, the state is also that which it abjects. The critical task, as Ranjana Khanna expresses it, 'is to conceive of forms and categories of political life that will stop the creation of garbage-can populations' (Khanna 2009: 193). The case studies in *Revolting Subjects* take up this challenge, both examining the consequences of 'being made abject' and exploring how abjection is resisted and recuperated in forms of counter-political speech.

Revolting times

We are living through a turbulent period in world history in which several man-made catastrophes, including environmental change, peak oil, terrorism and warfare and global economic recession, are converging with ruinous consequences (see Urry 2010). In the globalized world of the twenty-first century, economic polarization has reached unparalleled depths both in terms of the deepening inequalities within post-industrial nation-states and in terms of the staggering inequalities between the global North and the global South. In countries like Britain, which have ostensibly been the beneficiaries of the epochal shift from industrial to neoliberal modes of capitalism in the 1970s, neoliberal modes of governmentality have been unleashing caustic inequalities for some time – something Danny Dorling revealed in his startling statement that '[i]n Britain today chances in life are now more determined by where (and to whom) they were born as compared to any other date in the last 651 years' (Dorling 2007: 5). Many accounts of neoliberalism concentrate on 'thin economic conceptions of neoliberalism as market rule' (Wacquant 2010: 197). In *Revolting Subjects*, I offer a *thick* social and cultural account of neoliberalism as a form of governance – concentrating in particular on the mechanisms through which public consent is procured for policies and practices that effect inequalities and fundamentally corrode democracy.

In *The Birth of Biopolitics* (2008), Foucault offers a prescient account of the forms of governance that have enabled the kinds of social decomposition which I detail in *Revolting Subjects* to be 'democratically' effected. *The Birth of Biopolitics* is one of several series of lectures which Foucault gave in the late 1970s when the epochal shift to neoliberal capitalism was accelerating in Europe and North America. Foucault argues that, after the Second World War, the horrors of Nazism, and the decomposition of former communist states, a 'state-phobic' consensus emerged (on the political left and the right) which imagined 'the big state' as the primary enemy of human freedom. It was amid this anxiety about the fascistic potential of the big state that the dismantling of centralized state controls (cutting red tape, getting rid of bureaucracy) became the (symbolic) work of national governments as they laboured to create the conditions in which state borders could be most thoroughly penetrated by the 'free market'. Foucault described this process in the following way:

> Instead of accepting a free market defined by the state and kept as it were under state supervision – which was, in a way, the initial formula of liberalism: let us establish a space of economic freedom and let us circumscribe it by a state which will supervise it [...] a state under the supervision of the market rather than a market supervised by the state. (Ibid.: 116)

However, the power of the state wasn't shrunk in this process. Instead, modes of surveillance and control hybridized and multiplied. Power did not shift from state governments to the markets but combined in the form of the neoliberal maxim: 'One must govern for the market, rather than because of the market' (ibid.: 121). Governing for the market entails the tentacles of government extending and dispersing into every stratum of social and cultural life, working tirelessly to unblock impediments to capital, to deregulate resource extraction and to 'securitize' profits within the new global class of the super-rich. As governments have come to govern for the markets they have also come to govern *against* the people. The protections and freedoms which post-Second World War liberal democracies once ostensibly offered citizens in return for their loyalty and labour have been incrementally eroded. Thus, on the one hand, neoliberal political discourses are state-phobic, and on the other hand neoliberalism demands continuous, repressive interventions by the state. As Foucault warned, 'Neo-liberalism should not therefore be identified with *laissez-faire*, but rather with permanent vigilance, activity, and intervention' (ibid.: 132).

Alongside rising levels of social inequality and reversing social mobility, Britain has witnessed a serious erosion of workers' rights, civil liberties and human rights, which are seen to block market competition. The tearing up of the new social contract instituted after the Second World War can be tracked in the period since the 1970s through the rollback of the welfare state and the deproletarianization of labour (and the decomposition of trade unions), as well as the neoliberalization of citizenship. At the same time formal *and* informal modes of democratic protest, epitomized by workers' revolts and the political movements of minority subjects (notably women, black civil rights, queer and disability politics) in the 1970s and 1980s, have been seriously if not fatally undermined (Midnight Notes Collective and Friends 2009: 3). This is manifested in the seeming ineffectiveness of mass protest today, and is epitomized by the inability of the anti-war movement to halt or even slow the invasion of Iraq in 2003 despite some of the largest mass street protests in history. As both the political left and the right share the neoliberal consensus there is effectively no mainstream political opposition to the modes of neoliberal governmentality which have curtailed democratic freedoms, fractured communities, decomposed the fabric of social life and (re)constituted nineteenth-century levels of economic inequalities within the state. This in turn has led to a 'crisis in state-participation' (Berlant 2011: 14) and the dramatic collapse of trust in political, civic and judicial institutions and processes (Kennedy 2005). Indeed, one effect of the neoliberal political consensus is that people's capacity to protest effectively against the state we are in has been eroded as the acceptable means for formal and democratic protest are practically non-existent. As the aggressive policing of recent student protests against austerity measures has revealed, in contemporary Britain protest itself has been incrementally criminalized (Atkins 2007).

'Left melancholia' now suffuses mainstream politics and critical theory today. In Britain, successive post-war governments led the citizenry to believe that neoliberalism would effect a new market-driven egalitarianism. This was epitomized by the New Labour government and the premiership of Tony Blair (1997–2007), who, on taking office, announced the dawn of a new meritocratic and 'classless' society. This political rhetoric has transpired to be a myth. As David Harvey (2005) argues, neoliberalism is itself a *class* project: an ideology which aims to restore and consolidate class power, under the veil of the rhetoric of individualism, choice, freedom, mobility and national security. What characterizes neoliberal states is the creation of 'wasted humans' within and at the borders of sovereign territories (Bauman 2004: 5). Within his studies of the new forms of poverty effected by neoliberalism, Loïc Wacquant (2008) details the three major forms of symbolic and material violence that characterize these processes of human waste production: labour precariousness, which produces 'material deprivation, family hardship, temporal uncertainty and personal anxiety' (ibid.: 24–5); the relegation of people to decomposing neighbourhoods in which public and private resources are dwindling; and heightened stigmatization 'in daily life as well as in public discourse' (ibid.: 24–5).

In *Revolting Subjects* I think through these conditions of disenfranchisement on the ground, focusing in particular on how *stigmatization* operates as a form of governance which legitimizes the reproduction and entrenchment of inequalities and injustices. As will become apparent, one of the concepts that *Revolting Subjects* reformulates is the notion of class struggle. It extends what we ordinarily think of as 'social class' to a broader understanding of social classification and *declassificatory struggles*, in order to think *intersectionally* about modalities of difference and resistance. In focusing on not one but several different categories and groups of people 'laid to waste' by neoliberal economic, political and social policies (including asylum seekers and other unwanted irregular migrants, politically and economically disenfranchised young people, Gypsies and Travellers, people with disabilities), my intention is to produce an intersectional account of marginality and resistance that will deepen critical understandings of the *common* processes and practices of neoliberal governmentality both within Britain and beyond.

Figurative methods

A central argument developed in this book is that a major characteristic of neoliberal 'democracies' is that they function through the generation of consent via fear and anxiety, rather than fidelity to national identity. We can understand this in terms of 'crisis management', in which crises are generated, or, as in the case of the current economic crisis (from 2007 onwards), exploited by governments in order all the more effectively to procure public consent for the marketization of public institutions, goods and services and penal welfare and border-control regimes. This is exemplified by the dramatic acceleration of the privatization of the welfare state in Britain during the current financial economic downturn, in which the election of a Conservative-led coalition 'Austerity' government in 2010 has not only enabled the introduction of penal welfare regimes such as 'workfare', but has allowed previously 'sacred' national institutions, such as the National Health Service, to be fully penetrated by competition and private finance. This tallies with Wacquant's account of neoliberal state-crafting in which he argues that neoliberal governance functions through the generation of *'social insecurity'* in the body politic (2010: 197). This *state of insecurity* is continuously fuelled and orchestrated through the proliferation of fears about border controls and terror threats, as well as economic insecurity and labour precariousness. In such a climate public anxieties and hostilities are channelled towards those groups within the population, such as the unemployed, welfare recipients and irregular migrants, who are imagined to be a parasitical drain and threat to scarce national resources. I call the figurative scapegoats I examine in this book 'national abjects', and they include 'the bogus asylum seeker', 'the illegal immigrant', 'the chav', 'the underclass' and 'the Gypsy'. National abjects function in a similar way to what Homi Bhabha terms the 'discursive strategy of the stereotype' (Bhabha 1983: 18). The national abject is an *analytic of ambivalence* 'in excess of what can be empirically proved or logically construed' (ibid.: 18). This ambivalence is the political currency of the national abject insofar as it permits the endless reconfiguration of abject others 'in changing historical and discursive conjunctures' (ibid.: 18). Drawing upon the work of Frantz Fanon, Bhabha argues that the stereotype is not simply the fabrication of a 'false image' that becomes the scapegoat of discriminatory practice, but a *subjectifying force* (ibid.).

In *Revolting Subjects* I explore how national abjects become enmeshed within the interpellative fabric of everyday life, the impact of the stigmatization effected by these abject figurations, and the forms of resistance to which they give rise. These abject figures are ideological conductors mobilized to do the dirty work of neoliberal governmentality. They are symbolic and material scapegoats, the mediating agencies through which the social decomposition effected by market deregulation and welfare retrenchment are legitimized. Through these figures, existing historical beliefs and prejudices about particular populations coalesce with the current fears and anxieties of precarious populations. The media involved in this process include the various communication arms of government, the public relations industry and the global corporate networks of the mass media, but also, importantly, the run-of-the-mill communication systems of everyday life (Hall et al. 1978). As Stuart Hall and his colleagues elaborated over thirty years ago, the hardening of public opinion into consent relies upon the repetition and accumulation of expressions and beliefs 'on the streets', in 'conversations between neighbours, discussion at street-corners or in the pub, rumour, gossip, speculation' (ibid.: 129). Increasingly in twenty-first-century Britain, 'the street' includes the informal technologies of social media such as blogs, wall posts, text messages and tweets. The national abjects constituted through these process and practices are the border subjects of the neoliberal body politic – those whose lives are deemed worthless or expendable.

In *Revolting Subjects* I use the term 'figure' as both a theoretical concept and as a method to detail the ways in which the populations I examine become fetishistically overdetermined and publicly imagined and represented (that is, figured) in excessive, distorted and/ or caricatured ways (see Tyler 2008). This figurative method involves tracking the fabrication and repetition of abject figures across several different sites – popular culture, news media, policy documents, political rhetoric, academic discourses – and within a range of social spaces including the communicative practices of everyday life. This method makes it possible to ascertain the ways in which national abjects are employed to incite and legitimize 'tough' economic measures and punitive governmental responses, even when these policies frequently curtail the freedoms of all citizens and further impoverish democracy.

Capture and escape

Over several decades feminist, queer and post-colonial theories of embodiment and resistance have been instrumental in developing accounts of how power is lived and the mechanisms through which subjects come to collude with those political and social forces that curtail freedom and reproduce inequalities. Influenced by Foucault, social and political theorists have theorized the realignments of sovereignty, citizenship and subjectivity that have taken place in the transition to neoliberal capitalism in terms of new bio-political technologies of (self-)surveillance and control (see, for example, Rose 1999). The forms of citizenship and subjectivity that neoliberalism gives rise to have been variously described as 'flexible' (e.g. Ong 1999), 'performative' (e.g. Butler 1990), 'mobile' (e.g. Sheller and Urry 2003), 'plastic' (e.g. Žižek 2006) and 'neurotic' (e.g. Isin 2004). These conceptual vocabularies attempt in different ways to capture how neoliberal governmentality regulates social life from within its most intimate interiors, exercising 'a control that extends throughout the depths of the consciousness and bodies of the population' (Hardt and Negri 2000: 24). What many of these accounts of transformations in citizenship and/or subjectivity share is an emphasis upon the ways in which neoliberal governmentality has reconfigured the relationship between individuals and the body politic by inducing and capitalizing on psychic anxiety as a mode of (self-)governance (Molé 2008). However, as Rosalind Gill argues, within this scholarship there is still an incomplete understanding of how 'the social or cultural "gets inside", and transforms and reshapes our relationships to ourselves and others' (Gill 2008: 433). As Gill suggests, the very notion of inside/outside, interior/exterior is contingent; the fabrication of this distinction is an effect of a historical discourse, namely psychoanalysis. Many social and political theorists have been busy 'shaking off' the theoretical vocabularies of subjectivity inherited from psychoanalysis. At the same time, it is unclear (to me, at least) how we think of the changing relations of subjectivity and sovereignty without a psychosocial theory of the subject. That is, without an account of what Butler describes as 'the psychic life of power' (Butler 1997).

This turn away from subjectivity is exemplified by Dimitris Papadopoulos, Niamh Stephenson and Vassilis Tsianos's *Escape Routes: Control and Subversion in the 21st Century* (2008),[1] which troubles the theoretical legacy of concepts such as sovereignty, subjectivity, subjugation and resistance. They argue that 'social transformation is not about reason and belief, it is about perception and hope. It is not about the production of subjects, but about the making of life. It is not about subjectivity, it is about experience' (ibid.: xii). In *Escape Routes,* subversion means eluding sovereign capture by refusing the traps of identity and representation, 'the policing practices of subjectivity', and the statist politics of citizenship and rights, to embrace instead mobile forms of life (ibid.: xvii). As an example we might think of the ways in which irregular migrants employ strategies of clandestinity, such as burning identity papers, obtaining forged papers and multiple passports or removing their fingerprints, to evade capture at state borders, detention and deportation. From this 'autonomy of migration' perspective, Papadopoulos et al. argue that 'becoming imperceptible' is the most effective tool that marginal populations can employ to oppose prevailing forms of geopolitical power. Certainly, invisibility is an important strategy of evasion. As we shall see, it is also the expressed desire of many who find themselves in unbearable states of capture within the borders of the state, such as those 'failed' asylum seekers and Gypsies and Travellers whose visibility and categorization has, as we shall see, led to their immobilization within systems of bureaucracy and penal control. In this way *Escape Routes* makes a rich contribution to our understanding of social transformation. However, it also opens up many questions about what 'autonomy' and 'flight' might mean in, for example, contexts of worklessness, disability, immobility and dependent relations of care (Tyler and Marciniak forthcoming).

For many of the disenfranchised populations I consider in this book, mobility, work and indeed escape are not available possibilities. Indeed, it is their existing *capture* which precisely moves many 'failed citizens' and non-citizens to revolt. Moreover, it is through revolt, and demands for justice and equality, that political agency is exercised, even while demands for recognition often lead to further cycles of punishment and capture. What I have found repeatedly in my empirical research is that, for many, the conditions for a liveable life involve being able to lay down roots, to feel safe, to create a family and home, to belong to a community and to have some sense of a (better) future. Lauren Berlant describes these desires as 'cruel optimism': forms of attachment that feed, fuel and sustain people in the face of precariousness and daily survival (Berlant 2011). What many disenfranchised people actively desire is not *flight* but rather *anchorage*. However cruel the optimism, we nevertheless continue to seek the protections of citizenship and government with regard to access to secure housing, medical care, welfare support and education, even while those very forms of shelter are being incrementally eroded and withdrawn both through processes of neoliberal stratification and the individualistic demands of neoliberal subjectivity. It is for these reasons that I continue to work with and develop richer understandings of the contradictions and ambivalences of subjectivity, subjugation and sovereignty for thinking about the differentials of power and resistance on the multiple scales of both the body and the body politic.

So, while *Revolting Subjects* shares many of the political concerns of *Escape Routes*, it develops along an opposite theoretical axis focusing on moments of capture and revolt. In some ways this involves fetishizing 'the event' by inflating the meaning and potential of protests as moments of political hope for the future. However, as will become clear in the course of this book, it is often not events of protest or resistance themselves, many of which barely register within the public domain or are quickly forgotten or suppressed, but rather the *storying* of revolts – and the forms of aesthetics this affects – which *matters* most. For it is the vitalization and proliferation of political protests and acts of resistance within their many documentary afterlives that allows for the weaving of alternative political imaginaries with which to perceive differently the state we are in. *Revolting Subjects* is thus concerned with the *mediation* of resistance, the reframing of events and the capacity of aesthetic practices of counter-mediation to fracture the neoliberal consensus. In this sense the restaging of protests as *political parables* within *Revolting Subjects* is not about 'the epiphany of events' (Papadopoulos et al. 2008: xii) but about the necessity 'to reinvent, from the scene of survival, new idioms of the political, and of belonging itself' (Berlant 2011: 262).

The structure of *Revolting Subjects*

In Chapter 1, 'Social abjection', I rework existing theories of abjection to explore how states, both states of being and nation-states, are made and unmade through abjection (Butler and Spivak 2007). This chapter draws upon a short essay by Georges Bataille, '*Abjection et les formes misérables*' (Bataille 1993 [1934]), as a point of departure from which to think about these two states, subjectivity and sovereignty, together. At the core of the account of social abjection I develop here is the paradox delineated by Bataille, namely the 'inclusive excluding' logic of human life and political life. This chapter also offers a critical account of Kristeva's exegesis of the concept of abjection. As an unfaithful reader of Kristeva, I am not concerned about remaining obedient to the orthodox psychoanalytic logic and conservative political agenda that inform the development and application of the concept of abjection in her writing. Rather, my intention is to prise abjection out of the theoretical and political frames in which it is positioned in her work. The critical task, as Butler describes it, is to consider abjection not as a 'permanent contestation of social norms condemned to the pathos of perpetual failure', but rather as 'a critical resource in the struggle to rearticulate the terms of symbolic legitimacy and intelligibility' (Butler 1993: 3). In the second half of this chapter, engaging in particular with the work of Judith Butler, Gayatri Chakravorty Spivak and Frantz Fanon, I explore the potential of abjection as a theory of power, subjugation and resistance, focusing not on Britain but the struggles of migrant and post-colonial subjects in France.

In Chapter 2, 'The abject politics of British citizenship', I trace a route through the ugly history of British citizenship. I advance the claim that British citizenship has been redesigned to abjectify specific groups and populations, producing paralysed, dejected and 'deportable' populations of non-citizens within the internal borders of the nation (Butler, in Butler and Spivak 2007: 40). Abjection, I will argue, is a design principle of British citizenship, in the most active and violent sense of the verb, 'to design': to mark out and disqualify from juridical modes of belonging populations that are at the same time contained within the state as an 'interiorized other' (ibid.: 16). This chapter focuses in particular on the 1981 Nationality Act and the violent conflicts between the police and black communities in Brixton that accompanied the passage of the Act through the British parliament. Employing Foucault's concept of state racism (Foucault 2003), I argue that the 1981 Nationality Act marked a pivotal moment in the neoliberal redesign of British citizenship and has operated as the template for a glut of subsequent nationality legislation. I explore some of the consequences of the abolition of birthright citizenship (*Jus soli*) through an account of the experiences of a 'failed asylum seeker' drawn from interview data and from the campaign materials of anti-deportation activists. I argue that British citizenship is a legal, political and social field of intelligibility that abjectifies some people outside of the realm of citizenship altogether, constituting them as illegal but also, paradoxically, fixing, capturing and paralysing them within the borders of the state. Thus immobilized, those designated as abject are transformed into commodities within 'asylum markets', the booming trade in 'illegality' effected by the penetration of the global security industries within the state.

Chapter 3, 'The asylum invasion complex', begins with the protest of a 'failed asylum seeker' against his deportation from Britain. By restaging this protest and its documentary afterlife as a political parable for our times, I examine the constellation of historical, political and economic forces that gave rise to the institution of an 'asylum invasion complex' within the British state. I offer a detailed account of the fabrication of the 'bogus asylum seeker' as a national abject, focusing on the years of the New Labour government. I argue that the fabrication of the category of the asylum seeker was the source of considerable political capital as it enabled the government to be able to claim that they were 'tough on immigration'. At the same time, asylum legislation was designed in ways which would enable the abjection of asylum seekers to be economically capitalized upon by allowing a new global market in asylum determination, detention and deportation to open up within the state. The marketization of asylum has created a precedent for the further outsourcing of previously state-run and state-accountable services and industries. In short, I suggest that asylum seekers were not only political scapegoats but also experimental subjects in a programme of neoliberal economic reform which has marked the decisive end of the post-war social contract in Britain. Finally, I return to the forms of resistance employed by migrants, activists and artists against the neoliberal politics of illegality and deportability to which the asylum invasion complex has given rise, and the efforts made to contest the effects of the politics of disposability.

In Chapter 4, 'Naked protest: maternal politics and the feminist commons', I respond to Silvia Federici's call for a 'feminist commons' as a reaction to the democratic deficits, staggering economic inequalities and laissez-faire violence which have been effected by neoliberal globalization (Federici 2011). In the context of the current upsurge of 'space-hacking' forms of protest against austerity, best illustrated by the wave of pro-democracy revolts in North Africa and the Middle East (the 'Arab Spring') in 2010 and 2011, and the North American and European Occupy movements against austerity that were inspired by these revolts, I consider how we interpret Federici's feminist call for women to mobilize their bodies collectively to take back space. This chapter moves us beyond the shores of Britain to explore practices of 'feminist commoning' on a transnational scale through an examination of three protests: a naked protest by a group of mothers, 'failed' asylum seekers at Yarl's Wood immigration removal centre in England in 2008; the use of the 'naked curse' in protests by indigenous mothers against global oil corporations in the Niger Delta in 2005; and the 'Expose the Naked Truth' protest against the BP oil spill in the Gulf of Texas enacted by the feminist activist network Code Pink in Houston in 2010. Weaving together activist materials, news reports, interviews, documentaries and historical data, I examine these seemingly local and disparate protests together in order to elucidate the transnational connections between them. My aim is to map the common forms of maternal politics which are being mobilized by women in different geopolitical spaces, in their resistance to the gendered architectures of expropriation effected by neoliberalism.

In Chapter 5, 'The Big Society: eviction and occupation', I turn my attention back towards the internal borders of the British state to consider the eviction of Gypsies and Travellers from Dale Farm in Essex, England, in 2011, the single largest forced eviction of citizens from their land and homes within Britain in living memory. This chapter examines the heightened stigmatization of Gypsies and Travellers within news media, political rhetoric, policy and popular culture over the last decade in the context of state decentralization and the institution of localism, epitomized by the Conservative Party's 'Big Society' election manifesto in 2010, and the subsequent Localism Act (2011). The chapter concludes by considering the longer history of the subjugation of Gypsies and Travellers in Britain as a 'tragedy of the commons' (Hardin 1968) effected by the enclosure and privatization of land and property that both made nomadic ways of life increasingly untenable and rendered these populations abject in the eyes of settled communities and the state. Offering an account of the emergence of the Traveller solidarity network, in the wake of the Dale Farm eviction, I highlight the relationship between longer histories of struggle against enclosure by Travellers and the politics of new social movements against neoliberalism, such as the Occupy movement, which draw inspiration from the philosophy of the commons and understand their activism as a *politics of occupation* against capitalist enclosure.

In Chapter 6, 'Britain and its poor', I tell the story of the concerted efforts by New Labour in the 1990s – in concert with some sociologists – to make class a *revolting subject*. This chapter examines how questions of class-based inequalities were repressed, reconfigured and reformulated within sociological and political discourses and, latterly, within wider popular and public culture. It details how the conceptual frame of the underclass, and in particular the popular reconfiguration of the underclass discourses in the figure of 'the chav', functioned as part of wider efforts by the political elites to scour the political vocabulary of class from the public domain. Drawing on the work of Skeggs, it will examine this abjectification of class politics as a form of *class-making* (Skeggs 2005). Turning to Jacques Rancière's (2004a, 2011) formulation of class as *a struggle over names*, and Raymond

Williams's claim that *the masses don't exist* (Williams 1960), I will consider what lessons we might learn from the polarized debates among social commentators, experts and academics around the figure of the chav. My central argument is that without some deeper understanding of the class struggles effected by neoliberalism, it is impossible to understand or theorize the politics of global economic restructuring, urban disinvestment, the intensification of resource extraction and ecological crises, the opening up of state borders to flows of capital and migrant labour, the emergence of a new class of super-rich, the deepening precariousness of all labour, the demise of the post-war social contract and the fraying of the welfare state.

The final chapter, 'The kids are revolting', draws together the central themes of this book: social abjection, citizenship as a regime of governance, xenophobia and state racism, penality and the punishment of the poor, the manufacturing of modes of consent, and the forms of dissensus effected by revolt. It focuses on the meaning and representation of the riots in England in August 2011, considering how the abject conceptual and perceptual frame of the underclass was deployed as a means of both explaining and containing the meaning of the riots as an 'apolitical' event. Tracing the longer revolting history of the underclass and its eugenic origins, this chapter examines how and why this concept has become embedded as the frame through which poverty and inequality are perceived in neoliberal Britain. I will argue that, deployed to contain the meaning of these events, the term underclass legitimized the subsequent exceptional judicial and economic punishments as the riots were used to generate further public consent for the shift from protective liberal forms of welfare to punitive workfare regimes. My central claim in this chapter is that if we want to fight neoliberalism, to *defend society*, it is essential that we prise open and fracture the concept of the underclass (Foucault 2003). Only then can we begin to make sense of the August riots as one part of a deepening global neoliberal legitimation crisis.

Revolting Subjects concludes with a short afterword which attempts to draw together the central theoretical, empirical and political threads developed over the course of the book through a focus on the protests of disability activists in the context of the celebration of disability rights in the London 2012 Paralympic Games and the simultaneous erosion and privatization of welfare systems for disabled people in Britain.

Un/timeliness

This book is the culmination of more than a decade of teaching and research. So, while many of the chapters speak to current tumultuous events, much of the thinking that shapes the analysis prefigured current events. Indeed, when I began to write this book, I couldn't have imagined quite how timely my title, *Revolting Subjects*, would be. On the contrary, for many years the themes my work has centred on, class, gendered and racialized inequalities within the British state, have felt out of time and out of place, out of date and out of fashion in our 'post-ideological', 'post-political' times. Today, what has sometimes felt untimely about my work has now acquired a certain timeliness. Writing on the phenomenon of un/timeliness, Brown stakes a claim for untimeliness as a critical strategy. As she writes:

> To insist on the value of untimely political critique is [...] to contest settled accounts of what time it is, what the times are, and what political tempo and temporality we should hew to in political life. Untimeliness deployed as an effective intellectual and political strategy, far from being a gesture of indifference to time, is a bid to reset time. Intellectual and political strategies of successful untimeliness therefore depend on a close engagement with time in every sense of the word. They are concerned with timing and tempo. (W. Brown 2005: 4)

Revolting Subjects both stages protests and is itself something of an irreverent protest that has emerged from my own political desire to contest neoliberalism as the ideology of our times. Disrupting the fixity of ideologies and technologies of neoliberalism is crucial, in Brown's words, to 'keeping the times from closing in on us' (ibid.: 4). By tracking the forms of disenfranchisement which neoliberal governmentality effects, I hope that *Revolting Subjects* 'unmakes' the state in ways that are redolent of other possible political futures. As austerity measures deepen and public attitudes harden, this collection of political parables and critical essays attempts to make a small contribution to the development of a new political imaginary for these revolting times.

1 | SOCIAL ABJECTION

Along the fault-lines of the world disorder piles of human
waste are rising (Bauman 2002: 47)

The wretched of the earth

In an extraordinary short essay entitled 'Abjection and miserable forms' (Bataille 1993 [1934]), Georges Bataille, writing in the
shadow of Hitler's rise to power, developed the concept of abjection
to explore what he perceived to be the pressing political issues of the
1930s: 'the dehumanization of labour, class struggle, mass fanaticism'
(Lotringer 1993: 3). Bataille argued that abjection is the imperative
force of sovereignty, a founding exclusion which constitutes a part of
the population as moral outcasts: 'represented from the outside with
disgust as the dregs of the people, populace and gutter' (Bataille 1993
[1934]: 9). Whether this marginality is the effect of an inability or
unwillingness to be sucked into proletariat classes of factory workers
and servants, or, in the case of fascist (or colonial) systems of power,
a consequence of perceived racial inferiority, these surplus populations
are disenfranchised to the degree that they are 'disinherited [from]
the possibility of being human' (ibid.: 11). The wretched are those
who are deemed fundamentally unequal, rightless, 'the scum of the
earth' (Arendt 1973 [1951]: 267). These are classes of people who
are, paradoxically, classless, a section of the population that has been
omitted 'from the processes of representation to the point where it
can no longer think of itself as a class' (Krauss 1996: 100).

Yet, while they are excluded, Bataille argued that the waste populations created by sovereign power at the same time intrude at the
centre of public life as objects of disgust: the 'national abjects' I
examine in this book. In this sense all prohibitions are inherently
paradoxical since, in order for a prohibition to function, it must at
the same time be continually transgressed. For example, in order for
a sexual practice to be declared obscene, experienced as disgusting
and regulated accordingly, it must be seen to be practised within the
body politic. Social prohibitions are dependent upon the (re)intrusion

of that object, practice, thing or person which has been constituted as abject, cast out and illegalized. To summarize Bataille's argument, the disciplinary forces of sovereignty, its processes of inclusion and exclusion, produce waste populations: an excess that threatens from within, but which the system cannot fully expel as it requires this surplus both to constitute the boundaries of the state and to legitimize the prevailing order of power. As Stallybrass and White argue similarly, 'The low-Other is despised and denied at the level of political organisation and social being whilst it is instrumentally constitutive of the shared imaginary repertories of the dominant culture' (Stallybrass and White 1986: 5–6). Waste populations are in this way *included through their exclusion*, and it is this paradoxical logic which the concept of abjection describes. As Bataille argues, abjection describes '*the inability to assure with sufficient force the imperative act of excluding abject things* (which constitutes the foundations of collective existence)' (Bataille 1993 [1934]: 10, emphasis added). Within this paradox lies the possibility of resistance to abjection. As Bataille writes: '[i]n the collective expression, the miserable, the conscience of affliction already veers from a purely negative direction and begins to pose itself as a threat' (ibid.: 10). Or as Fanon puts it in *The Wretched of the Earth*, '[h]owever hard it is kicked or stoned it continues to gnaw at the roots of the tree like a pack of rats' (Fanon 2004: 81).

Introduction

> Abjection (noun):
> The action or an act of casting down, humbling, or degrading; an act of abasement.
> That which is cast off or away, esp. as being vile or unworthy; refuse, scum, dregs.
> The state or condition of being cast down or brought low; humiliation, degradation; dispiritedness, despondency.
>
> Abridged from the *Oxford English Dictionary*, 2012

At the heart of *Revolting Subjects* is the question of how states – *states of being* (human life) and *states of belonging* (political life) – are made and unmade and how we might critically engage in this process of making and unmaking (Butler and Spivak 2007). In this chapter I use Bataille's essay as a point of departure with which to develop an account of social abjection that might assist us in thinking about these two states, subjectivity and sovereignty, together. Why abjection? Abjection is a concept that precisely 'hovers on the threshold of body and body politic' (McClintock 1995: 72). As Bataille's account suggests, abjection describes the violent exclusionary forces of sovereign power: those forces that strip people of their human dignity and reproduce them as dehumanized waste, the disposable dregs and refuse of social life (Krauss 1996). However, as a dictionary definition reveals, abjection not only describes the action of casting out or down, but the condition of one cast down – that is, the condition of *being abject*. In this sense abjection allows us to think about forms of violence and social exclusion on multiple scales and from multiple perspectives.

This chapter begins with an account of the politics of disgust; it then offers a summary and critique of Julia Kristeva's account of abjection which aims to clear the ground for a richer understanding of abjection as a mode of governmentality – an abjectionality that might assist in our understandings of changing forms of subjectivization and subjugation.[1] To this end, I draw on feminist and post-colonial theory and in particular the work of Frantz Fanon, Judith Butler and Gayatri Chakravorty Spivak in my account of social abjection. What drives my revision of the conceptual paradigm of abjection is a political concern with thinking about how we might exploit the paradox abjection describes to contest *the state we are in*, the neoliberal states that are effecting new categories of 'wasted humans' (Bauman 2004: 5).

The politics of disgust

Disgust is an urgent, guttural and aversive emotion, associated with sickening feelings of revulsion, loathing or nausea. However, while it is experienced physically, *in the gut*, disgust is 'saturated with socially stigmatizing meanings and values' (Ngai 2005: 11). In his scrupulously researched genealogy, *The Anatomy of Disgust* (1997), William Miller reminds us that '[d]isgust and contempt motivate and sustain the low ranking of things, people, and actions deemed disgusting and contemptible' (ibid.: xiv). As William Cohen argues similarly:

People are denounced filthy when they are felt to be unassailably other, whether because perceived attributes of their identities repulse the onlooker or because physical aspects of their bodies (appearance, odor, decrepitude) do. Actions, behaviors, and ideas are filthy when they partake of the immoral, the inappropriate, the obscene, or the unaccountable – assessments that, whilst often experienced viscerally, are culturally constrained. All of these versions of filth have one thing in common: from the point of view of the one making the judgment, they serve to establish distinctions – 'That is not me.' (Cohen 2005: x)

If disgust was once a neglected topic of intellectual enquiry, over the past twenty years a significant body of scholarship on disgust and other aversive emotions has emerged, much of which is concerned with detailing the social and political function of 'ugly feelings' (Ngai 2005; see also Ahmed 2004; Meagher 2003; Miller 1997; Menninghaus 2003; Nussbaum 2004; Probyn 2000). The first significant study of disgust was made much earlier, in the 1920s, by the Hungarian philosopher and political theorist Aurél Kolnai (1905–73); although his essay 'On Disgust' (1929), was published in an English translation only in 2004 (in Korsmeyer and Smith 2004). Kolnai's Hegel-inspired phenomenology of disgust emphasized the intertwined physiological, emotional and moral qualities of disgust reactions and in so doing prefigured much of the current theoretical preoccupation with aversive emotions. The considerable efforts made by Kolnai to both differentiate between 'natural' (physiological) and 'moral' forms of disgust, and to systematize the differences between disgust and other aversive emotions, such as hatred, fear and contempt, oversimplify what are experienced as tangled emotional and affective responses. Nevertheless, Kolnai makes two important observations. First, he notes that disgust is a 'spatially' aversive emotion. In being disgusted, Kolnai writes, 'we perform a sort of "flight" from the "perceptual neighbourhood" of the revolting thing or person and from possible "intimate contact and union with it"' (in ibid.: 587). If disgust is a reaction to the imagined over-proximity or intrusiveness of the disgusting thing, it creates (or attempts to create) boundaries and generates distance. Secondly, Kolnai introduces the concept of 'moral disgust', which, he suggests, emerges through an associative transference between physically and morally repulsive reactions. That is, in moral disgust, a physical experience of disgust slides into contempt and judgements of value. Yet because disgust is an emotion associated with involuntary bodily reaction, moral disgust is often experienced, or retroactively understood, as a natural response: *anybody would find x as repulsive as I do*. As Korsmeyer and Smith argue, 'So strong is the revulsion of disgust that the emotion itself can appear to justify moral condemnation of its object – inasmuch as the tendency of an object to arouse disgust may seem adequate grounds to revile it' (ibid.: 1).

Disgust consensus

In *Purity and Danger: An Analysis of the Concepts of Pollution and Taboo*, one of the most influential treatises in the recent history of disgust scholarship, the anthropologist Mary Douglas argues that disgust reactions are always anchored to wider social beliefs and structures of taboo (Douglas 1966). In her account, disgust functions to affirm the boundaries of the social body (the body politic) through the (actual or symbolic) expulsion of what are collectively agreed to be polluting objects, practices or persons. Thus, an awareness of dirt – that is, of something or someone being 'dirty' – reveals the social norms and rules in operation in a given social or cultural context. As Michelle Meagher (2003) suggests, what is important about Douglas's argument is that she reveals that there is no 'natural dirt'. Rather, that which is experienced and/or imagined to be filthy (be that faeces on the skin, or a 'foreigner') corresponds with prevailing belief systems, and involves community-wide complicity. In this regard, disgust reactions are always contingent and relational, revealing less about the disgusted individual, or the thing deemed disgusting, than about the culture in which disgust is experienced and performed. As Meagher summarizes:

> disgust is not a condition of an object, but an effect of a beholder's intentional relationship with an object. [...] objects are rendered disgusting or dirty through implicit social agreements. That is to say, rules of dirt and the regulation of bodily contact with dirt are not behaviours that can be reduced to 'personal preoccupations of individuals with their own bodies'. (Ibid.: 32)

I want to emphasize here the social agreements in operation within disgust reactions. There is no disgust without an existing disgust consensus. As Miller notes, an 'avowal of disgust expects concurrence' (Miller 1997: 194). Sianne Ngai similarly describes the ways in which expressions of disgust often seek 'to include or to draw others into [their] exclusion of [their] object, enabling a strange kind of sociability'

(Ngai 2005: 336). In sum, it is through repeated citation, then, that a disgust consensus develops which in turn shapes perceptual fields. It is a disgust consensus that allows disgust to be operationalized in a given social and political context as a form of governance to sustain 'the low ranking of things, people, and actions deemed disgusting and contemptible' (Miller 1997: xiv). When we approach disgust as symptomatic of wider social relations of power, we can begin to ascertain why disgust might be attributed to particular bodies. Disgust is political.

The aesthetics of disgust

In *The Cultural Politics of Emotion* (2004), Ahmed adds a Foucauldian dimension to the scholarship on disgust by emphasizing the performativity of aversive emotions. As she notes:

> when thinking about how bodies become objects of disgust, we can see that disgust is crucial to power relations. [...] The relation between disgust and power is evident when we consider the spatiality of disgust relations. [...] disgust at 'that which is below' functions to maintain the power relations between above and below, *through which 'aboveness' and 'belowness' become properties of particular bodies, objects and spaces.* (Ibid.: 88, emphasis added)

Ahmed describes how the attribution of disgust constitutes the disgusting object in the following way: a subject feels something to be disgusting (a reception that relies on a history previous to the encounter), expels that thing (either literally or metaphorically), and through expelling it finds it to be disgusting. In turn, this disgusted response becomes 'the truth' of the object, thing or person deemed revolting (ibid.: 87). In short, through the act of being disgusted the subject constitutes the disgusting object. Ahmed argues that this process always operates discursively, and that images and signs of disgust become habituated through repetition. Disgust does not come from nowhere, but relies upon 'histories of articulation' which bind signs of disgust to specific objects and bodies (ibid.: 92). As she writes, 'the attribution of quality to substance [...] relies on the *figurability* of disgust' (ibid.: 90, emphasis added).

Throughout this book I consider the figuration and mediation of those deemed abject. For, as Ngai argues, if we want to understand the central role of aversive emotions in, for example, processes of racialization, we need to think 'the aesthetic and the political together' (Ngai 2005: 3). This attention to *revolting aesthetics* resonates with Rancière's argument that the political is always aesthetic, in the sense that regimes of representation and perception delimit 'the visible and invisible' and 'speech and noise' in ways that shape 'the place and the stakes of politics as a form of experience' (Rancière 2004b: 13). If we map the aesthetics of aversive emotions in any given context, we can begin to apprehend the ways in which disgust is provoked, roused and incited in the service of prevailing social and political classificatory practices. Indeed, the ways in which aversive emotions come to shape perceptual fields and the stigmatizing effects of disgust directed towards persons or groups deemed revolting are a central concern of the account of social abjection I develop.

The neoliberalization of disgust

As Martha Nussbaum has argued, disgust has been used throughout history 'as a powerful weapon in social efforts to exclude certain groups and persons' (Nussbaum 2004: 107). All political ideologies – but perhaps particularly those preoccupied with social hygiene, such as racism, xenophobia, eugenics, homophobia and misogyny – are mediated through revolting aesthetics. We might note in this regard what Ngai describes as 'the spectacular appropriation of disgust by the political right throughout history, as a means of reinforcing the boundaries between self and "contaminating" others' (Ngai 2005: 338–9).

In *The Politics of Disgust: The Public Identity of the Welfare Queen* (2004), Anne-Marie Hancock explores incitements of disgust for African-American single-mother welfare recipients in the USA. She details the ways in which an accumulation of longer histories of negative representations of poor black populations coalesce in the figure of the 'Welfare Queen'. Through close analysis of news reports, political speeches, policy documents and interviews with mothers, she suggests that this figure operates as what she terms a 'public identity' that knots together stigmatizing discourses of hyper-fertility, laziness and ethnic difference (ibid.). The figure of the Welfare Queen generates a consensus apparatus that legitimizes negative public sentiments about single mothers in receipt of state support and authorizes punitive economic and social policies. Similarly, Karen Soldatic and Helen Meekosha explore 'the role of disgust in mediating disabled women's experience of workfare in the Australian state' (Soldatic and

Meekosha forthcoming). They argue that neoliberal welfare reform is legitimized through the figuration of disabled women as revolting subjects, 'slothful, lazy and consequently undeserving of public welfare' (ibid.). It is in these ways that longer histories of aversive emotions against minority subjects are instrumentalized as technologies for garnering public consent for the shift from protective liberal forms of welfare to disciplinary workfare regimes (see Chapters 6 and 7).

Within the scholarship on disgust, there is an emphasis on the perspective and experience of the one disgusted, and the ensuing effects of this disgust, in, for example, enabling the constitution of an identity through disidentification with another: the *'that-is-not-me'* function of aversive emotions described by Cohen (Cohen 2005: x). While I will also engage with this perspective I want to develop a more interrelational understanding of aversion and stigma in this book through a focus on those who repeatedly find themselves (made into) the objects or *abjects* of stigma. Disgust is not just enacted by subjects and groups in processes of othering, distinction-making, distancing and boundary formation, but is also experienced and lived by those constituted as disgusting in their experiences of displacement and abandon. As Miller argues, people 'internalise the social judgements made of their stigmatisation as shame, self-loathing, self-disgust, self-contempt and self-hatred' (Miller 1997: 202). This is the process which, Hancock argues, takes place for those interpellated by the figure of the Welfare Queen. Similarly Soldatic and Meekosha describe how heightened stigmatization impacts upon the lives of disabled women within neoliberal states. Reconfigured in the public imaginary from 'victims' to parasitical welfare scroungers, the disabled women they research struggle to find ways to defend themselves against the aversive reactions of others in their everyday interactions with both official state actors and other citizens.

When a person and their bodily appearance are designated as disgusting, they are transformed into a 'magnet of fascination and repulsion', and become subject to forms of dehumanizing violence which are lived and which can be immobilizing in their effects (Kristeva 1995: 118). Indeed, one of the major consequences of the fabrication of national abjects such as 'the welfare scrounger' in public culture is the curtailing of the representational agency of those individuals and groups interpellated by these figures. Symbolic violence is converted into forms of material violence that are embodied and lived. For example, in February 2012, several disability charities in the UK detailed how a governmental rhetoric of welfare fraud was being used to legitimize cuts in disability benefits. This discourse was inflamed by news media stories about 'fake' disability claimants. The consequence of this was an immediate and massive increase in disability hate speech on the streets of Britain. As Peter Walker writes in the *Guardian*:

> charities say they are now regularly contacted by people who have been taunted on the street about supposedly faking their disability and are concerned the climate of suspicion could spill over into violence or other hate crimes. [...] Some disabled people say the climate is so hostile they avoid going out, or avoid using facilities such as designated parking bays if they 'don't look disabled'.
> (Walker 2012)

One man related to Walker how, when he walks the streets on his crutches, he now receives shouts of: "'We're going to report you to the DWP" [Department of Work and Pensions] [...] When there's a bad article in the press, the next day you think, "Do I really need to go out of the house?" We're being forced back into the attic, locked away from society' (cited in ibid.). This story about the impact of negative public figurations of disabled bodies as leech-like bodies within the state illustrates the everyday effects of the deployment of the politics of aversive emotions as a form of neoliberal governmentality.

The psychoanalytics of disgust

In *The Powers of Horror* (1982), Kristeva developed an account of abjection to explore the psychic origins, function and mechanisms of revulsion, aversion and disgust. For Kristeva, the abject is a concept that describes all that is repulsive and fascinating about bodies and, in particular, those aspects of bodily experience that unsettle bodily integrity: death, decay, fluids, orifices, sex, defecation, vomiting, illness, menstruation, pregnancy and childbirth. Abjection also describes experiences of bodily affect, moments of physical revulsion that result in 'a discharge, a convulsion, a crying out' (ibid.: 1). It expresses the subject's response to that stuff which threatens to overwhelm their body border and their attempts to turn away and distance themselves from the 'flow, discharge, haemorrhage' which threatens to engulf them (ibid.: 5). Kristeva suggests that practices and experiences of abjection have a cathartic function for the subject, operating as forms of purging which give expression to a continual need to secure a narcissistic hygienic fantasy of a clean, whole and proper self through the performative enactment of self/other and self/object distinctions. 'At the crossroads of phobia, obsession, and perversion', abjection describes those processes and practices which re-establish subjective integrity in response to a real or imagined transgression (ibid.: 45). As I noted above, in relation to Kolnai's work on disgust, abjection is spatializing, in that the abjecting subject attempts to generate a space, a distinction, a border, between herself and the polluting object, thing or person. Abjection describes the ongoing processes of bordering that make and unmake both the psychological and material boundaries of the subject. As Kristeva notes, abjection is 'the border of my condition as a living being' (ibid.: 3).

Kristeva suggests that through abjection the border 'becomes an object' which the subject can manage (ibid.: 4). However, the matter transformed into an object through abjection always functions as a substitute threat, rather than being a menace in and of itself (Ahmed 2004). That is, the border objects that emerge through abjection enable fear to be named and known, but this naming is always a temporary crystallization (sublimation), of a deeper archaic fear (of death, dissolution). As Kristeva states, 'we may call it a border; abjection is above all ambiguity. Because, while releasing a hold, it does not radically cut off the subject from what threatens it – on the contrary, abjection acknowledges it to be in perpetual danger' (Kristeva 1982: 11). The multiple bad objects constituted through abjection are thus always scapegoats, hence Kristeva's description of the abject as 'a security blanket' (ibid.: 136–7).

Further, while the aversive affects experienced by the subject when faced with a 'revolting thing' appear to emanate from the revolting qualities of the thing that provoked the response, in actuality the subject is always already the source of her own abjection. As Kristeva notes, abjection is 'an extremely strong feeling which is at once somatic and symbolic, and which is above all a revolt of the person against an external menace from which one wants to keep oneself at a distance, but of which one has the impression that it is not only an external menace but that it may menace us from the inside' (cited in Meagher 2003: 33). In her attempt to delineate this strange looping-back temporality of abjection, Kristeva states, 'I expel myself, I spit myself out, I abject myself within the same motion through which

"I" claim to establish myself' (Kristeva 1982: 3). Thus, subjectivity is, in Kristeva's account, always in revolt against itself.

'I feel like vomiting the mother' (ibid.: 47)

Kristeva's theory of abjection was developed out of her earlier work on infant subject formation and the maternal (see Chapter 4). Kristeva argues that the infant, in securing a separate sense of its body-self, becomes estranged from (abjects) its original 'maternal home' and is henceforth always 'out of place', permanently exiled. I will return to the enduring problems with the sexual politics and universal applicability of this psychoanalytic origin story in Chapter 4 (see also Tyler 2009b). Here it is sufficient to note that in Kristeva's narrative, all human desires, insecurities, fears and creativity stem from this primary exile from the m/otherland, which is incorporated within the infant at the moment of its 'birth' as a conscious being, as an internal, unassailable loss of place. In crossing the originary border of the mother's body this exilic subject is henceforth compelled to enact abjection tirelessly, through the classification and demarcation of her/his world. What unfolds from this prehistory is a decidedly negative theory of subjectivity which explains the desires and projects of human beings in terms of a primal, haunting insecurity. In her later work Kristeva proceeds to theorize all acts of bordering – whether at the level of individuals and communities, or at the geopolitical level of nation-building, imperialism and international relations – as symptomatic of the psychic partitioning induced by the abjection of the mother: a matricidal act which makes us always already 'strangers to ourselves' (Kristeva 1991).

The problems with Kristeva's application of this prehistorical theory of abjection to the pressing social and political problems of our own time are made manifest in her account of xenophobia. There has been extensive critical engagement with Kristeva's writing on strangers (see, for example, Barclay 2010; Ahmed 2003; Chanter and Ziarek 2005) and it isn't necessary here to cover this ground in detail, so I will condense the major limitations of her thesis of abjection.

National depression

In *Strangers to Ourselves* (1991) and *Nations without Nationalism* (1993), Kristeva's stated intention is to develop an ethics of 'strangeness' that might counter the rise of xenophobia in contemporary

Europe. In *Strangers to Ourselves* she argues that while citizenship offers a legal framework for belonging to a state, it doesn't address or resolve the deep-seated, 'prickly passions aroused by the intrusion of the "other" in the homogeneity of [...] a group' (Kristeva 1991: 41). This is because, in Kristeva's terms, the foreigner is an uncanny figure who haunts and inhabits not only intersubjective relations but intrasubjective relations: the foreigner is a substitute, a scapegoat, for the abject maternal. In other words, xenophobia is a form of abjection which constitutes the foreigner as a 'border abject' which the citizen-subject, and the community or state, can manage (through aversion). The aversive emotions experienced in xenophobic reactions thus signify for Kristeva 'the psychological difficulty we have of living as an "other" and with others', and 'the limits of nation-states and of the national political conscience' (ibid: 103). Xenophobia thus understood is a psycho-symptomatic response to a perceived threat to both subjective integrity and to the body politic.

Kristeva argues that the solution to the abjectifying effects of xenophobic nationalism is psychoanalysis. Her aim, as Kristeva explains it, is to develop from psychoanalysis an ethics that enables us to 'recognize ourselves as strange in order better to appreciate the foreigners outside us instead of striving to bend them to the norms of our own repression' (Kristeva 1993: 29). In short, Kristeva's argument that psychoanalysis might effect a radically cosmopolitan form of pan-European subjectivity relies on the primacy of an unchanging psychological origin story in which the abjection of the maternal (matricide) is the root of all violence and hatreds. Psychoanalysis is thus imagined as a blueprint for an ethical meta-system, which might be unfolded at the collective level of the state to alleviate the 'defensive hatreds of nationalism' (ibid.: 4) – hatreds which, Kristeva argues, are symptoms of a deeper 'national depression' (see Kristeva 2010).

Kristeva couches her psychoanalytic cure for national depression and the extremist forms of nationalism it effects within a discourse of liberal citizenship. As she notes, the 'recognition of otherness is a right and a duty for everyone' and, again, 'it is reasonable to ask foreigners to recognize and respect the strangeness of those who welcome them' (Kristeva 1993: 31). Politically speaking for Kristeva, the solution to the violence of nationalism involves the forging of more cosmopolitan, liberal and enlightened European citizen-subjects. For this to happen, she suggests, we need to strengthen the citizen's right to privacy. For if we could articulate and come to terms with our aversive emotions within private spaces (analysis, personal relationships, the family), they might not spill out in public domains of social life. It is in this way, she suggests, that psychoanalysis might comprise the means for more tolerant forms of national belonging. However, as the political movements of disenfranchised peoples have taught us, democracy will not be deepened or enriched by shifting or containing historical and current social and political antagonisms in the private realm. Indeed, as many feminists have argued, it is the reproduction of public/private distinctions which is often precisely what needs to be contested in the name of equality (see Chapter 4).

Arguably the strength of Kristeva's thesis resides in her primary claim that 'we are strangers to ourselves': an emancipatory assertion of the fundamental equality of all human beings. However, the promise of this claim is immediately undone as Kristeva proceeds to deploy it as a means of disentangling xenophobic expressions of nationalism (bad nationalism) and liberal ideals of the French Republic (good nationalism). This becomes clear in *Strangers to Ourselves* when she writes that 'the interior impact of immigration [...] often makes it feel as though it had to give up traditional values, including the values of freedom and culture that were obtained at the cost of long and painful struggles' (ibid.: 36). A few pages later she adds, '[i]t is possible that the "abstract" advantages of French universalism may prove to be superior to the "concrete" benefits of a Muslim scarf' (ibid.: 47; Ahmed 2003). Elsewhere she has argued that the wearing of the hijab by French schoolgirls is 'a psychic catastrophe' (Wajid 2006). What Kristeva divulges in these contentious remarks is that *the stranger* is a body that is constituted as foreign (and abject) by the bodies of citizens who compromise the normative body politic of the French state. As Ahmed (2003) suggests, the political promise of Kristeva's radical proposition of the universality of strangeness is negated by her invocation of the fetishized figure of the veiled woman, a post-colonial citizen-subject who is perceived and experienced as a stranger despite her legal entitlement to equality. Kristeva fetishizes this figure and produces her as a national abject who threatens the values of the French Republic, captured in the motto *Liberté, égalité, fraternité*, from within.

In December 2003, Kristeva was one of a group of sixty French female public figures, including feminist activists, intellectuals and celebrities, who were signatories to a petition, published in the French edition of the women's magazine *Elle*, which called for a law against the wearing of the hijab in public places (Winter 2008). In 2010 the proposal to ban the wearing of head- and face-concealing veils by girls and women in public places became law in France. It isn't clear whether Kristeva agrees with the punishments now meted out to those women who flout this ban: a fine and obligatory attendance on a citizenship training course.

Abjection as a memory hole

Kristeva's theory of abjection relies on an absolute opposition between the universality of the (psychoanalytic) subject and the particularity of the body politic in question (here an idealized French Republic). However, this opposition is an unsustainable one, as 'every individual has to be somehow particularised, has to dwell in a particular lifeworld' (Žižek 2008: 120). The imagined universality of the subject is always a fake universality because in actuality the psychic life of the individual is shaped by the particularity of prevailing norms, and existing social divisions, conflicts and relations of power. What is clear is that the Republican *esprit de corps* to which Kristeva appeals is not the radical form of universalism invoked by Alain Badiou, in his maxim 'there is only one world' (2008), but is rather the historically contingent universalism of the neocolonial French state: 'a false ideological universality which masks and legitimises the concrete politics of Western imperialism and domination, military interventions, and neocolonialism' (Žižek 2008: 149). The roots of xenophobia, however unconscious or deeply felt, are not anchored in the prehistory of the subject but are an effect of material histories: in this case France's colonial past, and the psychosocial reworking of this history in the form of the neoliberal racial state. Indeed, it is not psychoanalysis which is required to alleviate the 'defensive hatreds of nationalism', but rather a history lesson (Kristeva 1993: 4). Abjection, I want to suggest, functions within Kristeva's writing as a 'memory hole' that enables the colonial history of the French Republic to be veiled and further supressed.

In Kristeva's writing on nationalism the abject is akin to a 'conceptual colony', an epistemological device through which to enclose, manage and legitimize nationalist political vocabularies of French Republicanism, even while the purported equality of the Republic is struggled over within the contemporary revolts of ethnic minorities against state racism. So while Kristeva's stated aim in her writing on foreigners is to develop an alternative politics of cosmopolitan hospitality, what she actually provides is a psychological alibi for 'hygienic' forms of nationalism. Psychoanalysis, a decidedly Euro-centric theory of subjectivity that emerged in the larger cultural context of colonial expansion and imperial crisis, is put into the service of French nationalism (Fuss 1994). Abjection is, for Kristeva, a theoretical means of 'actively forgetting' the colonial histories which violently resurface in contemporary expressions of xenophobia against both black citizens and newly arrived migrants. Functioning as an alibi, abjection in her account enacts an epistemic violence which is complicit with the Republic's larger 'collective amnesia' about the violence of its imperial past (Stoler 2011: 122).

Ann Laura Stoler (ibid.) describes the process by which the French state disavows colonial violence as 'aphasia', by which she means a form of 'active forgetting' which works to dismember historical memories and lived experiences of racialized violence within the body politic.[2] As she writes, '[l]ike the noun ignorance, which shares its etymology with the verb to ignore, forgetting is not a passive condition. To forget, like to ignore, is an active verb, an act from which one turns away. It is an achieved state' (ibid.: 141). Stoler concludes that:

> [G]overnance in France rests on the logos and pathos of a racial
> state honed in a history of empire. It is a state whose strategies
> of separation and exclusion structure more than state institutions.
> Racial distinctions permeate the unspoken rules and 'choices' of
> residence, the charged debates on secularism, the sensory valua-
> tions that distribute moral disgust, the explanations of sexual vio-
> lence, and, not least, who can walk with ease on what streets and in
> which quarters. But racialized regimes of truth have been refracted
> through a more fundamental and durable epistemic space. They
> shape what issues are positioned at the fulcrum of intellectual
> inquiry and what counts as a recognizable frame of reference in
> scholarly and public debate. (Ibid.: 129)

Extreme Eurocentrism

The publication of the English translation of *Powers of Horror* in 1982 gave rise to a huge number of theoretical and political applications of Kristeva's idiom in the English-speaking world. Many writers and artists claimed abjection as a conceptual category of resistance in their critical and political efforts to destabilize a growing conservative political hegemony in the global North (epitomized in the USA by the Bush presidency). 'The abject America' (Liu 1992) is exemplary of the rise of 'Abject Studies' in US academia: an edited collection of critical essays and visual pieces organized around the theme of 'affirmative abjection'. Anomalously, however, within this collection there is a transcript of an interview with the post-colonial theorist Spivak entitled 'Extreme Eurocentrism'. We are not told when or how this interview took place, whether the interviewer (Edward Ball) and the interviewee met face to face, or to what extent the interview has been subsequently edited. What we can ascertain from what has been transcribed is that the encounter between Spivak and Ball on the topic of abjection is fraught with tension and, on Spivak's part, considerable resistance.

Throughout the interview, Spivak refuses Ball's attempts to produce abjection as an affirmative concept or a transgressive theory. She insists that the concept of abjection was forged within and is fundamentally committed to 'one historical narrative', namely an imperialist, Eurocentric world-view (Spivak 1992: 55). As she notes, 'What are the cultural politics of application of the diagnostic taxonomy of the abject? [...] The diagnostic taxonomy won't do. I might even say, half in jest, that we have no access to the abject' (ibid.: 55). In response Ball asks, 'We? Who is this "we"?' Spivak replies, 'Cultural others. [...] we don't belong in this story-lining of the present' (ibid.: 55). Ball is insistent that abjection has a universal application, pleading with Spivak to 'choose one thing [...] and test whether it fits with the notion of the abject' (Ball, cited in ibid.: 55). Spivak's response is, 'Why should we? That's my question. [...] In what interest do we want to describe it as such? To control it with this diagnosis?' (ibid.: 57). Somewhat defeated, Ball asks, 'Is the abject so culture-bound that it cannot at all be translated?' To which Spivak responds, 'I didn't say the abject was culture-bound. What I said was that the argument about the abject and its usefulness is committed to a single historical narrative, the dominant historical narrative' (ibid.: 59). Spivak's resistance is incisive; she doesn't reject abjection as an explanatory concept, but rather insists on understanding it as a European theory which reproduces the imperial axis of European subjectivity. As she asks, 'why would I want to use as tools for intelligibility a kind of modernist vocabulary of free-form psychoanalysis to give some acceptability [...] to the idea of cultural difference when that itself is a kind of decontextualized alibi?' (ibid.: 56). In Spivak's retort the compulsive fascination with, fear of and hatred for the foreigner which Kristeva describes is folded back out of the memory hole of psychoanalytic origin stories and forced into open confrontation with the violent history of European imperialism which shapes the neocolonial present tense.

What I want to do in what follows is to employ or turn Kristeva's account of abjection against itself. That is, I want to develop a historically grounded account of social abjection which precisely enables a theoretical and empirical focus on those very issues and topics (xenophobia, racism, nationalism) which Kristeva's account seemingly engages with but in actuality mystifies. I am, in other words, twisting and redefining Kristeva's conceptual paradigm for distinctly political and critical purposes. At the same time, what I want to retain from her account is the multiple perspectives which working *with* abjection enables – allowing practices of subject and state formation to be thought together.

Abject normativity

In *Imperial Leather: Race, Gender and Sexuality in the Colonial Contest* (1995), Anne McClintock, like Spivak, argues that abjection (and psychoanalysis more broadly) is a concept forged from imperialist ideologies. However, for McClintock this is precisely why abjection is useful for mapping the mechanisms of imperialist power relations. As she writes:

Under imperialism [...] certain groups are expelled and obliged to inhabit the impossible edges of modernity: the slum, the ghetto, the garret, the brothel, the convent, the colonial Bantustan, and so on. Abject peoples are those whom industrial imperialism rejects but cannot do without: slaves, prostitutes, the colonized, domestic workers, the insane, the unemployed. [...] Certain threshold zones become abject zones and are policed with vigor: the Arab Cashbah [sic], the Jewish ghetto, the Irish Slum, the Victorian garret and kitchen, the squatter camp, the mental asylum, the red light district, and the bedroom. Inhabiting the cusp of domesticity and market, industry and empire, the abject returns to haunt modernity as its constitutive inner repudiation: the repudiated from which one does not part. (Ibid.: 72)

McClintock describes her application of abjection as 'a situated psychoanalysis' which 'refuses a universal and ahistorical account of abjection, in favor of an examination of its distinct, contradictory and interrelated dimensions' in specific locales and historical contexts (ibid.: 72–3). McClintock's account is useful also in drawing attention to the spatial dimensions of abjection as they are made manifest in the abject zones and border spaces of the neoliberal nation-state: such as the council estates and places of migrant detention which I will explore in later chapters of this book.

In a similar vein, if a different scholarly register (philosophy rather than post-colonial history), Butler introduces the category of 'norms' to destabilize the universalistic and ahistorical foundations of psychoanalytic law. As Butler notes, 'a norm is not the same as a rule, and it is not the same as a law' (Butler 2004: 41). For Butler, while psychoanalytic laws might operate as normalizing principles that govern psychic life and 'the social intelligibility of action' (ibid.: 41), they are not immutable or ahistorical facts, but are sedimentations of existing social practices (ibid.: 44). In other words, if we understand psychoanalysis as shaped by material social relations, we can ascertain the performative force of psychoanalytic laws as forms of 'truth' that are in actuality historically contingent norms. Mobilizing the principle of 'the norm' against 'the law' creates a space for the consideration of the specificity of forms of abjection as lived and as contestable. This intervention is pivotal, because understanding abjection as a regulatory norm allows us to examine the ways in which abjection is invoked or employed in the service of other norms and ideals, be they norms of gender, social class, citizenship, national belonging. The effects of a particular form of abjection are dependent upon the ways in which a norm is cultivated, incited, repeated, practised, mediated and performed. For example, as Fanon notes on racial hatred in the USA:

> Hate is not inborn; it has to be constantly cultivated, to be brought into being, in conflict with more or less recognized guilt complexes. Hate demands existence, and he who hates has to show his hate in appropriate actions and behaviour; in a sense, he has to become

hate. That is why the Americans have substituted discrimination for lynching. Each to his own side of the street. (Fanon 2008: 37)

The metropolitan racism described by Fanon here constitutes the subject who hates, but the specificity of the objects of hatred does not originate within the subject but is socially cultivated and ideologically sanctioned.

In her writing on queer marginality, Butler suggests that the political question which emerges from abjection is how 'socially saturated domains of exclusion [can] be recast from their status as "constitutive" to beings who might be said to matter?' (Butler 1993: 189). Matter is the stuff of which a thing is made, its constituent material. Matter is also a synonym for a theme or subject, as in the phrase 'the matter in hand'. To *make something matter* describes an attempt to bring something urgent or pressing to attention. However, as Butler suggests, making something matter can also imply a more violent forcing of matter into an identifiable form or name. As Butler asks: 'How do tacit normative criteria form the matter of bodies? And can we understand such criteria not simply as epistemological impositions on bodies, but as the specific social regulatory ideals by which bodies are trained, shaped and formed?' (ibid.: 54). Butler reminds us here of the violent effects of classification as forms of *mattering*. What I am arguing for here is a contingent account of abjection, in which the force and impact of aversive emotions relate to a subject's particular vulnerability to abuse by power (Butler 1997).

What is emerging here is a social theory of abjection wherein abjection is understood as a mechanism of governance through aversion, which in Butler's terms might be *queered* through alternative citational practices. For example, Butler suggests that queer theory and activism involve 'the politicization of abjection in an effort to rewrite the history of the term, and to force it into a demanding resignification' (Butler 1993: 21). The politicization of abjection which Butler describes involves both the historicization of abjection – which refuses the psychoanalytic account of abjection as a totalizing prehistory of the subject – and the collective demand of those made abject to be heard in the political present tense (ibid.: 21). We need to examine the mechanisms through which *norms of abjection* are fabricated, operationalized and internalized. It is only by critically engaging with abjection as contingent expressions of normativity that we might begin to disarticulate the effects of abjection as lived.[3] That is, to understand how abjection gives rise to resistance, we need to consider the material effects of *being made abject* within specific historical, social and political locales. Only through an empirical focus on the lives of those *constituted as abject* can we consider the forms of political agency available to those at the sharp edge of subjugation within prevailing systems of power.

Hygienic governmentality

Berlant (citing Walter Benjamin) argues that 'hygienic govern-mentality' comprises those modes of state formation which operate through 'asserting that an abject population threatens the common good and must be rigorously governed and monitored by all sectors of society' (Berlant 1997: 175).[4] As she notes, 'especially horrifying to Benjamin are the ways the ruling bloc solicits mass support for such "governing": by using abjected populations as exemplary of all obstacles to national life; by wielding images and narratives of a threatened "good life"' (ibid.: 175). This hygienic governmentality is currently exemplified by the extreme and fetishistic vilification of migrant (and particularly Muslim) populations in Europe, and the accompanying inducement of aversive affects such as revulsion, disgust and fear towards migrant populations. However, this govern-ance through abjection is not restricted to migrant populations, but is operational in a range of forms and practices of social stigmatization and social cleansing. In France in 2005, hygienic governmentality was spectacularly inscribed in the political rhetoric of then minister of the interior Nicolas Sarkozy, who ignited social unrest in Paris when he re-ferred to young citizens in the *banlieues* (the marginal, degraded urban zones at the edges of Paris where many poor migrants and French citizens of North African descent reside) as '*racaille*', which translates as rabble, scum, riff-raff, waste. Yet, as Doug Ireland notes, '"Racaille" is infinitely more pejorative than "scum" to French-speakers – it has the flavour of characterizing an entire group of people as subhuman, inherently evil and criminal, worthless.'[5] Sarkozy promised to cleanse the *racaille* from the streets with a 'Karcher', a high-pressure cleaning system that blasts away the outer skin of encrusted pollution from pavements and buildings (ibid.). (In Chapter 7 I will examine similar forms of symbolic street cleaning in the aftermath of the August 2011 riots in England.)

In his account of nationalism in contemporary France, Badiou argues that the national abjects who are bodied forth in right-wing public rhetoric as 'the agents of a serious moral crisis' are ideological figures designed to uphold and to consolidate nation ideals of selfhood (Badiou 2008: 81). For Badiou this 'fear of foreigners, of workers, of the people, of youngsters from the Banlieue, Muslims, black Africans [...] marks the subjective situation of dominant and privileged people who sense that their privileges are conditional and under threat and that their domination is perhaps only provisional and already shaky' (ibid.: 8–9). In Badiou's account the fear of the foreigner is also, as the theory of abjection suggests, a fear which emanates from within the subject themselves. However, for Badiou, this fear is not a *psychological truth* that has its origins in the prehistory of the subject, but is *incited* by the political elites as a means of securing political power. What this induced fear unleashes is material forms of discriminatory violence, which is to say forms of social abjection operationalized by the state with public consent. For those who are subject to social abjection, particularly young Muslim and black youths in the *banlieues*, the consequences are what Badiou describes as 'daily humiliation' and dehumanization (Badiou 2006: 111).

The politics of the *racaille*

In 2005 a French activist movement, Mouvement des Indigènes de la République[6] (MIR), was founded by activists from the *banlieues*. The MIR offers a distinctly political retort to the aphasia described by Stoler, arguing that the *banlieues* are 'zones without rights, inhabited by an "indigenized" population subject to "colonial mechanisms" of control' (Stoler 2011: 129). As Houria Bouteldja, the spokesperson for the MIR, writes:

> When they refuse to accept us as French citizens, they deny us equality. We need to name this reality: we cannot be French, so we are native. We are second-class citizens; ours is a lumpen-citizenship, just as at the time of the colonies. This imaginary link to colonization and the history of slavery continues to determine how they perceive us, for the body of the indigenous was constructed during the colonial era. As long as this imaginary is alive, we remain native. (Bouteldja, cited in Kipfer 2011: 1158)

This is a situation which Bhabha describes in respect of those

French citizens whose ancestors originated from the former colonies, as the 'anomalous and ambivalent situation of universality-with-racism, and formal citizenship-without-equality' (Bhabha, cited in Fanon 2004: xxiv). MIR's aim is to develop a political vocabulary with which to articulate the 'organized expression of the rage of immigrant populations' (Khiari, cited in ibid.: 12). Inverting the denigration of youth within the *banlieues* with Sarkozy's '*racaille*', the MIR describe their project as the invention of what Tunisian activist and MIR collaborator Sadri Khiari describes as 'a politics of the racaille' (Khiari 2006). In the face of daily social abjection the MIR thus stakes the counter-political claim that France is not a post-colonial but a neocolonial state which calls for novel forms of decolonizing politics. As Bouteldja argues:

> Thirty years of migrant struggle have failed to build a political alternative with which to give a positive meaning to rage and anger of those living with humiliation and discrimination in the ghettos of France. Thirty years have failed to give our legitimate anger political expression [...] [Through a new collective politics] we must protect our children who undergo the extreme violence of the world we live in and, to escape it, find nothing better to do than to repeat it in all its ugliness. (Bouteldja 2012)

This quotation is from an article in which Bouteldja is responding to the events of Monday, 19 March 2012, when, a day before the fiftieth anniversary of the end of the Algerian war of independence from French colonial rule, Mohamed Merah, a twenty-three-year-old French citizen with an Algerian family background, murdered a thirty-year-old man and three small children outside a Jewish school in the French city of Toulouse. In his account of these terrible events, the historian Andrew Hussey insisted that these murders should be read as symptomatic of deepening neocolonial conflicts within the French nation. As he writes:

> Mohamed Merah has been described in the French press and by politicians as 'un loser', a narcissist, a lone wolf, a one-off. *Everybody knows that this is not true.* Indeed, what no one wants to say out loud, politicians or media, is that although he may have been a loser, he is far from being alone. For many young Algerians in the banlieue, Islamist activity is more than a religion; it has

become a badge of cultural revolt, a weapon of war against a world
that they feel hates them and that they hate in return. This is why
they describe their conflict as 'the French intifada'. [...] France
itself is under attack from the angry and dispossessed heirs to the
French colonial project. [...] to be French and Algerian in 2012
is not only to have a ferociously contested identity, but to have an
identity that is denied or hated by one side or the other. (Hussey
2012, emphasis added)

Like the MIR, what Hussey insists is acknowledged is that xenophobic forms of French nationalism, and in particular the scapegoating
of citizens of Algerian descent, are historically shaped. Responses to
the daily humiliations of abjection in the *banlieues*, whether manifested
in riots, in ugly acts of terrorism and murder, religious extremism or
more banal forms of criminality and dispossession, are symptomatic of
the ways in which 'a generation's alienation has erupted into violent
loathing' (ibid.). What the terrible events in Toulouse revealed is that
'memory holes' will always fail to contain the truth, namely that the
violence effected by Muslim youths is an effect of a double denial,
of both colonial history and the neoliberal inequalities of the social
and political present. However difficult the task, we must, as Hussey
insists, do the critical work of understanding the roots of contemporary forms of marginality as symptomatic of ongoing forms of
colonial dehumanization. For, as Stefan Kipfer notes, the 'post-colonial
situation is neither mere historical residue nor simple replication of
colonialism in the metropole. It refers to the selective transformation
and re-inscription of colonial forms' within contemporary modalities
of neoliberal governmentality (Kipfer 2011: 1159). Or, as Badiou puts
it, *we get the riots we deserve* (Badiou 2006: 114).

Being made abject

The MIR makes explicit through activism and within assorted
writings that the politicization of abjection involves 'territorial re-
appropriation' (Kipfer 2011: 1157). If the abject is a spatializing politics
of disgust, which functions to create forms of distance between the
body politic proper and those excluded from the body of the state
(and forced to live in internal border zones such as the *banlieues*), then
the politics of the abject is a counter-spatial politics which attempts
to reclaim the spaces and zones of abjection as radical sites of revolt

and transformation. For the MIR this is a project of *decolonization* which involves material and psychological strategies of counter-control, a psychosocial body-politics: 'France was a colonial state ... France is still a colonial state! ... The treatment of people from the colonies prolongs (but is not reducible to) colonial policy ... *The colonial cancer takes over the mind* ... Decolonizing the Republic is a must!' (MIR, cited in ibid.: 1157–8, emphasis added).

It is *abjection as lived*, as a form of exclusion and humiliation which 'takes over the mind', which was explored by Fanon in *Black Skin, White Masks* (2008) and *The Wretched of the Earth* (2004), his pivotal studies of the psychopathology of colonial oppression and metropolitan racism. Fanon's work offers a unique insight into both what it means to be made abject and, conversely, how subjugated populations might revolt against *abjectionality*.

In *Black Skin, White Masks* Fanon offers an account of the psycho-politics of racialization and the interiorization of inferiority (which he terms 'epidermalization'). His argument is grounded in the insight that the fabrication of race is the central mode of colonial and post-colonial governance. To experience oneself as black is precisely to be made black by a white other, 'who had woven me out of a thousand details, anecdotes, stories' (Fanon 2008: 84): 'a constellation of postulates, a series of propositions that slowly and subtly – with the help of books, newspapers, education, text-books, posters, cinema, radio – work their way into one's mind and shape one's view of the world and of the group to which one belongs' (ibid.: 111).

As Fanon argues, 'not only must the black man be black; *he must be black in relation to the white man*' (ibid.: 83). The implications of this insight are more complex than at first appears. This isn't a simple account of racial alterity, in which power operates through the constitution of the other as an abject. Rather, Fanon's analysis of the psychological consequences of colonialism and post-colonial state racism led him to conclude that 'white power' operates by excluding blacks from the self–other dynamics of subjectivity itself (see Fuss 1994). As he writes, 'The black man has no ontological resistance in the face of the white man [...] I am battered down by tom-toms, cannibalism, intellectual deficiency, fetishism, racial defects, slave ships' (Fanon 2008: 83–5). What Fanon produces, in his extraordinary prose, is an account of colonial and post-colonial power in which subjectivity is the prerogative of the white man alone. As Sylvère Lotringer notes:

People don't just become abject because they are treated like a thing, but because they become a thing to themselves. It is only then, when they are being invaded and exposed to the vertiginous experience of existing apart from the human race, that abjection comes about. (Lotringer 2000)

In *The Wretched of the Earth* Fanon details the debilitating forms of mental illnesses and pathologies which racializing forms of abjection give rise to. As he wryly notes, '[t]he truth is that colonization, in its very essence, already appeared to be a great purveyor of psychiatric hospitals' (Fanon 2004: 181). Fanon offers a series of case studies drawn from the period when he worked as a psychoanalyst in a hospital in Algeria during the war of independence. His intention is to explicate 'the scope and depth of the wounds inflicted upon the colonized' (ibid.: 182). Case no. 3 is that of a nineteen-year-old man, a fighter in the Algerian National Liberation Front who had been committed to the hospital after he murdered a woman. Fanon describes this patient as exhibiting the characteristic signs of 'colonial depersonalisation': deeply depressed, persistent insomnia, suicidal, incoherent thoughts and episodes of auditory hallucination (ibid.: 192). As Fanon writes, 'From time to time, could no longer speak and asked for a pencil. Wrote: "Have lost my voice, my whole life is fading away"' (ibid.: 192). Fanon relates this speechlessness to the patient's recurring hallucination in which his blood is spilled: 'he begged us to stop the haemorrhage and not let them come into the hospital to "suck the lifeblood" out of him' (ibid.: 192). Samira Kawash argues that what is significant about this story is that in his dream the patient does not die but continues to live 'suspended between life and death' in a zombie-like condition, a state or condition which, as we shall see in Chapters 3 and 4, is one frequently described in the accounts of migrant detainees in Britain today (Kawash 1999: 249). What Fanon composes in *The Wretched of the Earth*, by means of this and other case studies, is an account of how colonialism functions by collapsing the ego structures of black men, destroying their self-esteem, desire and purpose: a process of being made abject that he describes as being sealed into a 'crushing objecthood' (Fanon 2008: 82).

What is important about Fanon's contribution to the phenomenology of racialized oppression is that it doesn't stop at documenting the effects of abjection but mobilizes this critical labour to explore the potential within abjection for political agency and resistance. As Fanon systematically argues, colonial power negates the equal humanity of colonized peoples by denying the attributes of humanity. However, 'deep down the colonized subject knows no authority. He is dominated but not domesticated. He is made to feel inferior, but by no means convinced of inferiority' (Fanon 2004: 16). In other words, there is always a disjuncture between the interpellation of the colonized subject (as abject), and their experience of themselves (as human nonetheless). This dissonance between perceptual realities forces the colonized subject to ask, 'Who am I in reality?' (ibid.: 182). As Kawash argues, the question 'who am I?' challenges colonial reality by communicating the disjunction between a reality that demands non-existence and a corporeal presence that nevertheless persists (Kawash 1999: 248). The 'epidermalization of oppression' is always incomplete and this disjuncture allows for a 'reversal into contestation and revolt' (Ziarek 2005: 63). The work of self-reflection and critique leads to forms of action and resistance. Or, as Fanon puts it, 'Having reflected on that, I grasp my narcissism with both hands and I turn my back on the degradation of those who would make man a mere mechanism' (Fanon 2008: 12).

Melancholic states[7]

In an interview with the artist Rainer Ganahl, published in *Revolt, She Said* (2002), Kristeva revealed that she had never read any of Fanon's work and dismissed him as a thinker who 'isn't part of the mainstream of psychoanalytic studies' (ibid.: 110). This extraordinary rebuff is not a minor oversight; Fanon was a central figure in the 1960s left-wing French intellectual scene in which Kristeva's career was fomented (see Brandt, in Chanter and Ziarek 2005). Indeed, it is simply impossible to conceive of the intellectual and political climate of France in the 1960s without a consideration of the influence of Fanon, who inspired and deeply influenced the theory and political praxis of the key intellectual figures of this period: notably Simone de Beauvoir and Jean-Paul Sartre (who published and wrote the preface to *The Wretched of the Earth* in 1961, the year Fanon died). As Homi Bhabha notes, 'on the day of his death, the French police seized copies of *The Wretched of the Earth* from the Paris bookshops' (cited in Fanon 2004: viii). Kristeva's 'whitewashing' of Fanon's influence not only on the May 1968 uprising by students and workers in France, but on many of the most significant subsequent political uprisings of the late twentieth and twenty-first centuries (including the black power movement in the USA, the South African black consciousness movement, the Irish Republican movement, the Iranian revolution and global struggles against the US-led War on Terror), reveals the depth of the theoretical and political 'memory hole' within her writing.

Ranjana Khanna introduces the concept of 'postcolonial melancholia' to theorize the ways in which the post-colonial state – unable to fully acknowledge and hence properly to mourn or memorialize the violent history of empire – ingests colonial history within itself as a kind of swallowed object which cleaves the state from within (Khanna 2006). (Post-colonial melancholia is a much more accurate way of conceptualizing the 'national depression' diagnosed by Kristeva.) The ethical imperative, Khanna suggests, is to work from the sites of ambivalence and dissonance which this melancholia effects. As she writes:

> No map, census, print, or museum can be entirely successful at presenting the nation seamlessly. While the work of mourning may relegate swallowed disposable bodies to the garbage can of modern nationalism, the work of melancholia, critically attesting to the fact of the lie intrinsic to modern notions of sovereignty, is the only hope for the future. (Ibid.)

It is important to note, however, that 'the swallowed disposable bodies' that Khanna describes are often not absent or invisible but are, on the contrary, at the organizational centre of national and political life. As the headscarf ban in France made manifest, colonial aphasia congeals in the public culture of the post-colonial state in the form of figurations of abject others, national abjects, which, in turn, affect new forms of subjectivity and subjugation. National abjects are, in psychoanalytic terms, fetishistic figures. A fetish describes attempts by a subject to defend itself against what it already knows but wishes to forget (Khanna 2011). As Stoler argues:

> histories do not rest in the past. They speak to how new subjects are produced and what they refuse, to the state apparatus that makes people into 'problems,' and to the intimate and social violences that accompany how rights and resources are distributed throughout the world today. (Stoler 2011: 156)

It is in this sense that the account of social abjection that unfolds across *Revolting Subjects* is a psychosocial theory – which speaks to how subjects and states are reconstituted as longer histories of violence and struggle that converge within the bordering practices of the political present. This is the neoliberal present in which imperial conquest continues unabated under the exegesis of global corporate capitalism organized through international asset-stripping institutions such as the IMF and the World Bank, which are remaking 'the nexus of market, state, and citizenship from above' (Wacquant 2010: 213).

Conclusion: social abjection

The state, as the geographer Alison Mountz (2010) reminds us, is not a mysterious, abstract, all-powerful entity that is detached from our daily lives, but is, on the contrary, a constellation of embodied practices. As she writes, '[t]he powerful machinations of the state appear not in the borders drawn on maps and the pages of public policies, but in the fractured fault-lines of daily practice' (ibid.: xii). The state becomes 'knowable through its daily interactions with citizens and others' (ibid.: xxxi–xxxii). Social abjection is an apt interpretive frame through which to examine neoliberal practices of state-making because, as numerous political philosophers have detailed, state power is constituted through exclusion (see, for example, the work of Hannah Arendt, Carl Schmitt and Giorgio Agamben). That is, the state exercises power through exemption – the withdrawal of the law, and the withholding or removal of rights and recognition from people within or at the borders of its territorial space. It is through exercises in abjection that different arms and operations of state are constituted as agencies with power by differentially determining the value of life, adjudicating on who is expendable and who is of worth. What the conceptual frame of abjection reveals is that neither the subject nor the nation-state is a solid or unitary entity, but rather an assemblage of practices. The borders of the subject and the state are continually being made and undone (Butler and Spivak 2007). Indeed, my reason for (re)turning to abjection is because it is a theory of bordering which describes the labour of both subject formation and state formation and as such it allows us to think these different modalities of 'making' together. Further, if state power relies on the production of abject subjects to constitute itself and draw its borders, the state is also that which it abjects.

Bauman (2004) argues that what characterizes globalization is the intensification of human waste production within the state and at its borders by, for example, withholding citizenship from migrants (see Chapters 2, 3 and 4) or enforcing poverty on people through diminishing opportunities for welfare, education or secure forms of work (see Chapters 6 and 7). As I will detail throughout this book, these 'wasted humans' are transformed into national abjects who are employed to legitimize neoliberal forms of governmentality by effecting insecurity within the body politic (ibid.: 5; Wacquant 2010). Social abjection is a theoretical resource which enables us to consider this production of human waste from multiple perspectives, including the perspective of those who are 'obliged to inhabit the impossible edges of modernity', those border zones within the state in which the overwhelming imperative is not transgression, but survival (McClintock 1995: 72). As Bhabha notes, 'the affective experience of social marginality – as it emerges in noncanonical cultural forms – transforms our critical strategies' (Bhabha 1994: 172). The critical task, as Butler describes it, is to consider abjection not as a 'permanent contestation of social norms condemned to the pathos of perpetual failure', but rather as 'a critical resource in the struggle to rearticulate the terms of symbolic legitimacy and intelligibility' (Butler 1993: 3). Or, as Khanna expresses it, 'the challenge is to conceive of forms and categories of political life that will stop the creation of garbage-can populations' (Khanna 2009: 193). The chapters that follow take up this challenge, examining the consequences of 'being made abject' and exploring how abjection is resisted and recuperated in forms of counter-political speech. What I am arguing here is that there can be no real understanding of political agency without working through specific, located, concrete instances of revolt against abjection. Social abjection is a *revolting concept* which names, but also has the capacity to trouble, the symbolic and material forms of violence it describes. It is by employing revolts against abjection as a map or guide that *Revolting Subjects* attempts to 'kick over' the dustbin of history. For it is the insurgencies of those designated as abject which enable us to unravel histories of violence and lay them to waste.

2 | THE ABJECT POLITICS OF BRITISH CITIZENSHIP

> Children and young people born in the UK who have lived
> here all their life may be shocked to discover [...] that they are
> not citizens of the country where they have always lived (ILPA
> 2007)

> [I]f the state is what binds it is also clearly what can and does
> unbind. And if the state binds in the name of the nation, con-
> juring a certain version of the nation forcibly, if not powerfully,
> then it also unbinds, releases, expels and banishes (Butler, in
> Butler and Spivak 2007: 5)

Tracing a route through the recent 'ugly history' (ILPA 2007: 7) of
British citizenship, in this chapter I advance the claim that British
citizenship has been designed to abject specific groups and populations, producing paralysed, dejected and 'deportable' populations of
non-citizens within the internal borders of the nation (Butler, in Butler
and Spivak 2007: 40). Abjection, I will argue, is a design principle
of British citizenship, in the most active and violent sense of the
verb to design: to mark out and disqualify from juridical modes of
belonging populations that are at the same time contained within the
state as an 'interiorized other' (ibid.: 16). This chapter focuses on the
1981 Nationality Act and the violent conflicts between the police and
black communities in Brixton which accompanied the passage of the
Act through the British parliament. Employing Foucault's concept of
'state racism' (2003), I argue that the 1981 Nationality Act (which
came into force on 1 January 1983) marked a pivotal moment in the
design of British citizenship and has operated as the template for a
glut of subsequent nationality legislation which has shaped who can
achieve citizenship. Some of the consequences of the abolition of
birth right citizenship (*Jus soli*) in the 1981 Act and the subsequent
institution of harsh immigration and asylum laws and systems are
then explored through an account of the experiences of a 'failed'
asylum seeker, Sonia, and her children, drawn from interview data

and the campaign materials of anti-deportation activists. Finally, I will explore the neoliberalization of citizenship regimes, a topic I will develop further in later chapters.

The birth of British citizenship

Although a vast theoretical literature on citizenship has been imported into Britain in recent decades, citizenship is still an oddly undeveloped concept within British society and culture. Britain is a constitutional monarchy with a deeply entrenched class system and the British are, historically speaking, accustomed to imagining themselves as subjects of the Crown. While British citizenship has arguably existed in fragmented forms in common law since the medieval period, it was predominantly a legal protection (for landowners) against Crown and/or state power, enabling the wealthy to be free from state interference, rather than offering rights or protections to the majority population (Isin and Turner 2007). It was only after the Second World War, a period of intense post-imperial state-building and significant immigration from former British colonies, that any substantial understanding of citizenship emerged in Britain. As Richard Titmuss argued in 1958, citizenship was in many ways an 'unintended consequence of wartime mobilization and strategies to rebuild post-war Britain in the context of imperial failure' (Titmuss, in ibid.: 7). So Britain became 'a nation of citizens' only comparatively recently as a consequence of a perceived political need to fabricate a new idea of the British state, in the post-imperial and post-war period. The newness of the concept of British citizenship explains the relative absence of historical and/or popular cultural representations of citizenship in Britain (particularly in comparison with France and the USA). When citizenship has been named and represented in the public domain, it has frequently been tainted with negative 'radical' associations: the French Revolution, communism, the rise of National Socialism in Germany, the ridiculing of 'loony left' Labour Party-controlled city councils in the 1980s and, since the 1990s, political struggles around the introduction of pan-European citizenship rights in the European Union[1] (see Dell'Olio 2005 on European citizenship).

The first substantive accounts of British citizenship emerged in the 1940s and 1950s, driven by a trio of influential British economists, social reformers and sociologists, John Maynard Keynes, William Beveridge and Thomas Humphrey Marshall. In *The General Theory of Employment, Interest and Money* (1936), Keynes argued for an inter-ventionist state which, through mechanisms such as taxation, would operate as a check to the free market. For Keynes, writing in the context of the economic depression of the 1930s, full employment was a fundamental tenet of a civil society. Keynes's redistributive economic philosophy inspired Beveridge's pivotal *Social Insurance and Allied Services* (1942), a report that became the blueprint for the creation of the welfare state in Britain. However, it was Marshall's pivotal essay, 'Citizenship and social class' (1950), which placed the concept of citizenship at the centre of debates about the establishment of a new 'civic bargain' between the individual and the state. Marshall is still the most influential theorist of citizenship in Britain and, in a series of essays and books written over three decades, he laid down the principles of a new social citizenship founded in equality and political solidarity across social classes.

Citizen Smith and the 'loony left'

Conversely, however, Gary Day has argued that citizenship was instituted in Britain as a way of breaking up class allegiances through processes of atomization and individualization (Day 2001: 159). As he writes, 'the idea of citizenship was […] largely formulated in opposi-tion to class […] it was based on the age-old distinction between the "deserving" and "undeserving" poor, but women, children, the insane, prisoners and migrant workers were among a number of groups who fell outside this apparently universal category' (ibid.: 159–60; see also Chapter 7). Nira Yuval-Davis similarly describes the ways in which the invention of citizenship in post-war Britain was a measure which, by design, produced a cast of 'moral aliens' at the periphery of the national 'moral community' (Yuval-Davis 1997: 17). Certainly, by the mid-1970s, the toxic combination of global economic recession and rising inflation (stagflation), high unemployment, spiralling taxation and working-class militancy began to test Marshallian notions of social citizenship severely, and a right-wing backlash was initiated against the perceived excesses and failures of rights-based citizenship and the post-war social contract. Margaret Thatcher, then leader of the opposition Conservative Party, was one of the politicians central to the recasting of Marshallian social citizenship as a failed socialist programme of reform. As she stated in a 1977 speech at the University of Zurich:

Socialism promised to raise the provision of education, health, and housing. As is becoming patent to almost everyone, the result has been the opposite. [...] Socialism whetted appetites for more, but has resulted in less being available. People of all backgrounds are casting off socialist illusions in the light of socialist reality. [...] The class struggle is withering away – to adapt a well-known phrase of Marx and Engels. (Thatcher 1977)

It was in this context that the British television sitcom *Citizen Smith* (BBC, 1977–80) provided a rare explicit popular representation of British citizenship. Through the figure of naive, unemployed petty criminal 'Wolfie' Smith (Robert Lindsey), *Citizen Smith* offers us a window into the social and political struggles over the meaning of citizenship which were taking place in Britain during the 1970s, a period of austerity economics and unprecedented strike actions that culminated in the 'Winter of Discontent' (1978/79) and the election of the neoliberal Thatcher government in 1979.

Wolfie, adorned with a beret, a Che Guevara T-shirt and a fake fur coat, was the self-proclaimed leader of an oddball group of friends who called themselves the 'Tooting Popular Front'. The opening title sequence depicts Wolfie walking out of Tooting tube station in London to a rousing rendition of the internationalist socialist anthem 'The Red Flag' and culminates in his cry, with a raised fist, 'Power to the people'. The comedy of *Citizen Smith* hinges on age-old distinctions between the authentic/sham and deserving/undeserving working class (see Chapters 6 and 7). This is dramatized in the programme through skirmishes between the welfare-dependent, feminized masculinity of Wolfie and the 'authentic' working-class masculinity embodied by the father of Wolfie's girlfriend, Shirley, ex-miner Charles (Peter Vaughan, Tony Steedman). In Episode 13, Series 1, after arranging a failed 'right-to-work' protest, Wolfie is forced by the local labour exchange (jobcentre) to take a position as a security officer at a local factory, where, it transpires, he will be working directly under Charles. By the end of his first day at work, and much to Charles's horror, Wolfie has formed a union, initiated a strike and resigned. Wolfie's comic and drag-like performances of 'political citizenship without a cause' revealed the precariousness of the post-war contract. For while *Citizen Smith* was affectionate in its depiction of Wolfie, this comic infantilizing depiction of class struggle, unionism and left-wing militancy is a precursor to the popular stereotype of the 'loony left' that emerged in tabloid newspapers in the 1980s and communicated a growing middle-class intolerance of the perceived economic burden of the welfare state and the feckless, workless youth and parasitical dependants it was imagined to have created.

During the 'Winter of Discontent' Thatcher's Conservative Party election campaign incited and capitalized on the fears of the populace that the state was disintegrating. In an election broadcast in January 1979, Thatcher spoke of the 'industrial action directed straight at the public to make you suffer – directed even at the sick and disabled. [...] picketing that threatens to bring the country to its knees – emptying our shops, endangering our farms, closing our factories, taking our jobs' (Conservative Party 1979a). She ended her address proclaiming, 'We have to learn again to be one nation, or one day we shall be no nation. If we have learnt that lesson from these first dark days of 1979, then we have learnt something of value' (ibid.). What learning to be a nation again meant for Thatcher was eradicating the failed project of social citizenship by diminishing 'the big state'. This entailed creating the conditions in which the state and state borders could be most thoroughly penetrated by 'the free market'. As she argued, 'the post-war settlement has failed [...] the tide is beginning to turn against collectivism, socialism, statism, dirigism, [...] and this turn is rooted in a revulsion against the sour fruit of socialist experience' (Thatcher 1977). The Conservative Party finessed their message in an election broadcast in April (Conservative Party 1979b), produced by the advertising firm Saatchi & Saatchi, which opened with apocalyptic news footage of mountains of uncollected rubbish piled in the streets, empty shelves in supermarkets, stationary lorries, grounded aeroplanes, closed cemeteries and picketed hospitals, overlaid with an increasingly hysterical voice-over declaiming 'Crisis? What crisis?', a phrase that had been misattributed to the then Labour prime minister James Callaghan by the *Sun* newspaper.

With the election of the right-wing Thatcher government in May 1979, the post-war consensus was at an end and citizenship was not only thoroughly dislocated from any Marshallian redistributive ideals, but also from any positive political project. Wacquant describes this shift as a period of state 'remasculinization' provoked by 'the institutionalization of social rights [workers' rights and the rights of women and other minorities] antinomic to commodification' (Wacquant 2010: 201). As he writes:

> The new priority given to duties over rights, sanction over support, the stern rhetoric of the 'obligations of citizenship,' and the martial reaffirmation of the capacity of the state to lock the trouble-making poor (welfare recipients and criminals) 'in a subordinate relation of dependence and obedience' toward state managers portrayed as virile protectors of the society against its wayward members [...]: all these policy planks pronounce and promote the transition from the kindly 'nanny state' of the Fordist-Keynesian era to the strict 'daddy state' of neoliberalism. (Ibid.: 201)

This new neoliberal 'daddy state' was personified in Britain by Thatcher's public persona as the 'Iron Lady', a public image that was caricatured in a notorious sketch from the popular satirical puppet show, *Spitting Image* (ITV, 1984–96) that depicted Thatcher wearing a man's suit and pissing at a urinal alongside male cabinet ministers. The constellation of the welfare state, social rights and class equality which inaugurated the birth of British citizenship was hijacked by penal definitions of citizenship concerned with borders, immigration and security and the punishment of the poor. As the 1981 Nationality Act makes manifest, citizenship was redesigned as an abjectifying technology, a mode of neoliberal governmentality which in turn produced and continues to produce new abject classes of failed and stateless citizens within the British state.

The 1981 Nationality Act

First mooted in the 1979 Conservative Party manifesto, the 1981 Nationality Act was not concerned with the constitutional rights of citizens, nor with delineating the relationship between citizen and state. Rather, it was an immigration Act designed to define, limit and remove the entitlements to citizenship from British nationals in the Commonwealth (the former colonies), thereby restricting immigration to the territorial space of the British Isles and creating 'aliens' within and at the borders of a newly circumscribed nation-state. This Act instituted a 'citizenship gap' within the British state, and between the 'motherland' and the former British colonies, as large numbers of British nationals found they had been abjected from the rights of citizenship (Brysk and Shafir 2004).

Political geographer Brad Blitz argues that 'the revocation of the rights to citizenship and residency' often takes place 'during periods of state building' (Blitz 2006: 453). Indeed, the 1981 Act was passed by the conservative Thatcher government (1979–90) during a period of intense institutional reorganization that was to transform Britain into a neoliberal nation-state, a transformation more significant than the social and infrastructural reforms that took place in the post-war period. The 1981 Nationality Act scaled citizenship by creating several categories of nationality and citizenship, including a category of 'Commonwealth citizenship', removing from British nationals in the Commonwealth and Hong Kong their historic rights to residency in the United Kingdom. As the *Sunday Times* reported in 1981, the Act 'for the first time seeks to define British Citizenship and those who "belong to Britain" [and] to abolish the historic right of common British Citizenship enjoyed by the colonial peoples' (Baucom 1999: 195). Thatcher, on a visit to India in 1981, was forced to address directly the concerns of Indian politicians that the Act was intended to rescind the rights to immigration by Indian British nationals to the British Isles. She defended the Act in a speech to the Indian parliament, arguing that 'Britain is perhaps the only country in the world without a clear definition of its own citizenship' (Thatcher 1981). However, while race and ethnicity were never directly named in the wording of the Act, it redesigned British citizenship so as to exclude black and Asian populations in the Commonwealth while leaving 'routes home' for white nationals born within the territorial boundaries of the British Empire. As post-colonial theorist Ian Baucom notes, 'to be British, [the Act] mandated, one had to trace a line of descent to an ancestor born on the island. In effect, the law thus drew the lines of the nation [...] around the boundaries of race' (Baucom 1999: 195). The passage of this Act through Parliament was thus a significant event in the history of British race relations, a moment when, through citizenship, racism was implicitly incorporated within the judicial body of the state, becoming an active component part of its operational system of 'legal justice'. Indeed, the lawyer David Dixon described the Act as 'constitutionalising racism' (Dixon 1981).

The Brixton riots

The Nationality Act provoked a public debate about the meaning of Britishness and the relationship between the United Kingdom and the existing and former colonies of the Commonwealth. While the Act was making its passage through Parliament, riots broke out in Brixton, a borough of London with a significant black population. The riots coincided with Thatcher's trip to India, and she made a reference to the riots in her speech to the Indian parliament, stating that 'The government, like its predecessors, is committed to creating a racially just and harmonious society. [...] Whatever the difficulties – and the last few days (just before my visit) have shown that they are very real – we shall stick to that commitment' (Thatcher 1981). In fact the Brixton riots marked the beginning of a significant period of civil unrest sparking three months of intensive rioting by black, Asian and white youths across England.

In Brixton, public anger was directed towards the Metropolitan police force, and the uprising was triggered by a police operation called Operation Swamp 81. The operation's name was widely interpreted as a reference to a notorious comment by Margaret Thatcher in a 1978 television interview in which she implied that the white indigenous population feared being swamped by 'people of a different culture' (Thatcher 1978). Operation Swamp 81 was purportedly part of a citywide operation to reduce street crime in London. In actuality it focused on Brixton, employing ancient vagrancy legislation, the infamous 'sus laws', to stop and search young black people. In the first six days of the operation, 120 plainclothes officers stopped and searched 943 people in Brixton, arresting 118 predominantly black male youths.

Lord Scarman's influential report into the causes of the Brixton riots, *The Scarman Report: The Brixton Disorders 10–12 April 1981* (Lord Scarman 1982), argued that the black population in Brixton had been subject to 'disproportionate and indiscriminate' policing. The sus laws were abolished on the recommendation of his report (although, as we shall see in Chapter 7, police 'stop and search' powers have since incrementally increased). Scarman also acknowledged that social deprivation and racial prejudice had contributed to the riots, a claim that Thatcher refused to accept. Yet Scarman refuted assertions of institutional racism within the police force or indeed other parts of the state apparatus. The report argued that institutional racism referred to a society 'which knowingly and as a matter of policy discriminated against Black people', and denied that this was the case in Britain (ibid.: 28). Nevertheless, others have insisted that the Brixton riots should be read, in part, as a response to the 1981 Nationality Act (see, for example, Rushdie 1982). The creation of a 'second-class' Commonwealth citizenship and news coverage of the Act created palpable anxiety and rage within black communities across Britain. These communities rightly perceived that a new form of post-imperial racism was driving the citizenship agenda. As an anonymous commentary in the journal *Race and Class* argued in 1981, the Nationality Act transformed immigration law into an instrument of domestic social control and formed 'the administrative basis for what is tantamount to a pass law society. [This Act has] brought immigration law within doors' (Anon. 1981: 242).

At the same time, it is important to note that the framing of the 1981 summer riots as 'race riots' within the news media and political rhetoric diminished the central role of youth unemployment in the riots, and the involvement of disenfranchised and unemployed white poor within the rioting and looting as riots spread across Britain. In Toxteth, Liverpool, scenes of some of the most intensive battles with the police in the summer of 1981, reports suggested that the majority of the rioters and looters were white (Harman 1981). While the Conservatives had swept to power during a period of high unemployment – approximately one million in 1979 – and on the back of an advertising campaign that claimed punningly 'Labour isn't working', by 1982 unemployment had risen to a historic high of 3 million. In Toxteth, in 1981, it was estimated that 60 per cent of the black population were unemployed, in an area in which levels of unemployment stood at around an incredible 45 per cent (ibid.). These were the riots of many young people who felt disenfranchised by Thatcher's Britain.

State racism

The 1981 Nationality Act illustrates what Foucault termed 'state racism': a means of classifying, distinguishing and dividing a population on the basis of appeals to essentialist categories of origin: 'the administrative prose of a State that defends itself in the name of a social heritage that has to be kept pure' (Foucault 2003: 83). In *Society Must Be Defended* (ibid.), Foucault argued that the political form and structure of contemporary societies were determined by the invention of race (and associated notions of 'native' entitlement). The 'war against race' is, he suggests, what constitutes the nation-state and is the source of conflict from which sovereignty generates legitimacy. This is a new formation of racism in which 'a disdain or hate of some races for others' is harnessed as a technology of power 'that permits biopower to exercise itself' (Stoler 1995: 86). Racism, Foucault argued, 'is tied to the functioning of a State that is compelled to use race [...] to exercise sovereignty' (ibid.: 86). Foucault suggests that neoliberal forms of class struggle need to be understood from the perspective of 'race war', arguing that racism is a means of 'eliminating class enemies as though they were racial enemies' (Foucault 2003: 83). What Foucault attempts to delineate, by thinking race and class together, is the common (Enlightenment) roots of colonialism, fascism and capitalism. This in turn allows us to focus on the commonalities of the often fractured forms of struggles against the neoliberal state which are shaped by the intertwined histories of class and racialized violence and oppression.

It is this same insistence that we need to think class struggle and post-colonial struggle together which characterized much of Stuart Hall's early foundational work in British cultural studies in the late 1970s (Hall et al. 1978). Hall suggests that the emergence of Thatcher's 'racist state' was an integral component of the epochal shift from industrial to neoliberal capitalism, and from colonial to neoliberal forms of population control. As he writes:

> political restrictions on blacks, the growth of racist ideology and of explicitly anti-Immigrant organisations, the toughening of social discipline in the areas of black residence, the general 'unsettling' of the black population cannot be attributed solely to 'discriminatory attitudes' on the part of particular individuals or employers. [...] the conditions of economic recession are being used to drive through a major recomposition of black labour by capital itself. [...] What we are dealing with here is a structural feature of modern capital, and the pivotal role which black labour now plays in the metropoles of capital in a major phase of its recomposition. (Ibid.: 344)[2]

In the context of Britain in the 1980s, a post-imperial class struggle over the resources of a diminished empire was under way. The 1981 Act produced 'ethnic hierarchies' in Britain which, combined with existing and deepening class divisions, led to civil unrest among both black and white urban poor. This in turn enabled disenfranchised populations to be constituted 'as a threat to the social body' and directly targeted through policing and penal reform.

Home rule

The claim that the Act was ushering in a new period of 'home rule' through state racism was central to Salman Rushdie's polemical 1982 essay 'The new empire within Britain'. Rushdie argued that, as the British Empire contracted, the borders of the empire were being reproduced at home through newly legitimized practices of state racism, which in turn explained hostility towards the police as agents of state power. As Rushdie wrote, 'For the citizens of the new, imported Empire, for the colonized Asians and blacks of Britain, the police force represents that colonizing army, those regiments of occupation and control' (Rushdie 1982). The 1981 Nationality Act, and the nostalgia for a British homeland implicit within it, exposes the manufacturing of a fear by and among the ruling elites that Britain was losing its sense of national identity as it lost its hold on the empire. Right-wing MP Enoch Powell, who was in many ways the political figure behind this Act, declared, on hearing that it had passed through Parliament, 'from the humiliation of having no nation to which we distinctively belong, the people of the United Kingdom are now setting themselves free' (cited in Dixon 1983: 1975). The Nationality Act, Powell stated, marked 'the end of our brief imperial episode ... and the laying of that ghost, the Common-wealth' (ibid.: 175). The associative link established in the 1981 Act between post-imperial national identity, democratic freedom and immigration controls has since been cemented into a form of common sense within British government policies. It drove the New Labour citizenship agenda and continues to inform the rhetoric and the policies of the current coalition government. As Prime Minster Gordon Brown stated in a 2008 speech on citizenship:

> there is a real danger that while other countries gain from having a clear definition of their destiny in a fast changing global economy, we may lose out if we prove slow to express and live up to the British values that can move us to act together. [...] being more explicit about what it means to be a British citizen we can not only manage immigration in a way that is good for Britain – for our citizens, our way of life, our society, and our economy – but at

the same time move forward as a more confident Britain. (Brown 2008)

State racism is legitimized predominantly through the need for border security and the idea that non-citizens threaten to overwhelm the diminishing resources of the welfare state and are stealing the resources which rightfully belong to citizens. Perversely, appeals to Marshallian rights-based notions of citizenship, rooted in welfare and distributive justice, are thus used to legitimize the abjection of 'illegal' populations from the protections of citizenship and the enforcement of brutal and inhumane immigration controls. As Nicholas de Genova notes, the securitization of migration 'is inextricable from a concomitant securitization of citizenship itself' (De Genova 2007: 440).

Home front

In the last decade, 'security' has emerged as a central preoccupation of European and North American governments. Increasingly, the idea of security is framed less in relation to external threats than in terms of securing the state from the hidden threats of 'dangerous classes' within the 'nation home'. In the USA this is perhaps best encapsulated by the establishment of the office of Homeland Security in 2001, a title that echoes the now defunct British government office, the Ministry of Home Security, established during the Second World War to manage civil defence in anticipation of foreign invasion. In this context, the nation-state is implicitly or explicitly redesignated as a 'home front', a battle line behind which the civilian populace is mobilized as a supporting arm of the military. It implies the imperative of effective militarization of a society during wartime. This shift legitimizes the militarization of everyday life and presumes a popular consensus in favour of forgoing democratic freedoms in the face of external and internal threats to the body politic.

Michael Hardt and Antonio Negri describe the shift from 'defence' to 'security' as a movement from 'a reactive and conservative' to an 'active and constructive' mode of government (Hardt and Negri 2005: 20). For Hardt and Negri this shift is framed by a simultaneous movement to a 'perpetual state of war' in which war is an active and indeed integral component of state governance, 'justifying constant martial activity in the homeland and abroad' (ibid.: 21). Britain, understood as 'a nation at war', is thus able to implement endless 'security measures', including the use of 'terror laws' to suspend indefinitely the liberties and rights promised by citizenship. Indeed, changes to the Terrorism Act in 2006 criminalized 'anti-governmental' activities in ways unprecedented since the Second World War. There have also been calls for Britain to develop its own Homeland Security Office; a development which many predict will be a key recommendation of the Government's Commission on National Security in the 21st Century. The first publication to result from this commission, entitled 'The new front line: security in a changing world', states that 'old notions of the security front line no longer work and some front lines now exist overseas in places like Afghanistan, while some also exist at the local community level here at home' (Kearns and Gude 2008: 7).

William Walters terms this reconfiguration of the relations between citizen, state and territory 'domopolitics': 'a fateful conjunction of home, land and security' that 'rationalizes a series of security measures in the name of a particular conception of home' (Walters 2004: 241). As he writes:

> [Homeland] has powerful affinities with family, intimacy, place: the home as hearth, a refuge or a sanctuary in a heartless world; the home as our place, where we belong naturally, and where, by definition, others do not; international order as a space of home [...]. Domopolitics embodies a tactic which juxtaposes the 'warm words' of community, trust, and citizenship, with the danger words of a chaotic outside – illegals, traffickers, terrorists; a game which configures things as 'Us vs. Them'. (Ibid.: 241)

'Domopolitics' is a performative politics which employs the rhetoric of home as a means of sanctioning exceptional measures, including the violent abjection of non-citizens. Citizenship, a legal sign of belonging to the nation home, is integral to this refiguration of the nation and, indeed, of the international order as a space of territorial homes. Furthermore, domopolitics is perfomative because the mechanisms through which the militarization of everyday life is ushered in are not clandestine but take place in full view with public sanction. From police brutality in Brixton to the current policies of constituting populations within the state as 'illegal' and 'stateless', and the creation of the apparatus (border police, detention centres) to process, capture and deport hundreds of thousands of non-citizens, British citizens demand it. As Didier Bigo suggests, the militarization of the nation is figured as part of a necessary 'security continuum' that 'stretches from terrorism to regulation of asylum rights, including drugs, action against crime, clandestine immigration, and migratory flows' (cited in ibid.: 240). Citizenship plays a central role within this securitized state, enabling specific groups and populations to be legitimately targeted and criminalized as non-citizens, or failing citizens. Central to this home rule is a 'transfer of illegitimacy' in which previously 'protected' populations, such as regular migrants and asylum seekers, and their British-born children, find themselves subjected to diverse bio-political and carceral technologies (ibid.: 240).

Stateless within the state

The 1981 Nationality Act has formed the basis for some of the most discriminatory and dehumanizing state practices to take place on British soil in the modern era. It designated who could be a citizen and who could be legally deprived of citizenship. For example, Section 40 of the Act granted powers to the Secretary of State to deprive a British citizen of their citizenship status if s/he 'is satisfied that to do so is conducive to the public good' (Lord Goldsmith 2008). Being without citizenship in a world of states is often devastating. As political scientist Matthew Gibney argues: 'In an international system where sovereign states each claimed the right to fashion their entry and citizenship policies according to their own national or ethnic criteria, refugees were outcasts. They were, in Arendt's words, "the scum of the earth"' (Gibney 2004: 3).

While international protections, such as the Convention Relating to the Status of Refugees (1951) and the Convention Relating to the Status of Stateless Persons (1954), were put in place by the international community ostensibly to enable non-citizens to have access to the protection of states, since the 1980s individual states and regional governments have increasingly flouted international law. Since the mid-1990s, Britain has witnessed one of the largest imprisonments of people on the basis of their dubious citizenship since the internment of German nationals during the Second World War, with the deportation of hundreds of thousands of failed asylum seekers and irregular migrants and the enforced destitution of at least 250,000 men, women and children who have failed to secure citizenship, and have no access to the provisions of the welfare state, but are unable or unwilling to return to often war-torn countries of origin. This final group, by far the largest, is de facto stateless; they have no civil or political rights, no legal right to work, no access to any social security, housing or healthcare (except in life-or-death situations), and they are consequently vulnerable and subject to exploitation (Blitz 2006).

I have argued that from the perspective of the 1981 Act the proliferation of categories of abject people variously marginalized by or excluded from citizenship (and the rights that flow from this status) is not an unintentional 'design flaw' but is an integral component of British citizenship design. If British citizenship has been designed to fail, it has been thus designed in order to govern populations within the state by producing some subjects as successful citizens and others as variously precarious or failed. These failed citizens, who have been legally abjected from the state, whether 'incarcerated, enslaved, or residing or labouring illegally', are paradoxically stateless within the state, contained and sometimes detained 'within the polis as its interiorized other' (Butler, in Butler and Spivak 2007: 16). They are in the strange position of being outside the legal protections of citizenship, but nevertheless subject to the full force of state power. As Butler describes it, they are 'both expelled and contained [...] saturated with power at the moment in which [they are] deprived of citizenship' (Butler, in ibid.: 40). In the next part of this chapter, I will introduce the story of one family of 'failed citizens' to examine the ways in which, since the 1981 Act, citizenship has been constituted through abjection.

Sonia and Mary

In 2006 a heavily pregnant West African teenager, 'Sonia', was apprehended trying to leave Britain with a false passport. Sonia, escaping sexual violence and an arranged marriage, had made a claim for political asylum which had been rejected. Despite her young age and her condition, the Crown Court, employing new legislative guidance, deemed it appropriate to punish this offence with a six-month jail sentence in an adult prison. The court also recommended that Sonia be deported immediately after serving her sentence. For a decade now, Britain has been engaged in a significant deportation programme. According to the British government, 63,140 non-citizens were deported in 2008, amounting to 'one person every eight minutes' (Byrne 2007). The brutal treatment of unwanted migrants at the borders of European states and at the land and coastal borders of the European Union became routinized during the 1980s and 1990s. Within the securitized imaginary that currently predominates in Britain, the mass imprisonment and deportation of failed asylum seekers and other unwanted or suspect foreigners are widely perceived as the only logical solution to the threats posed by immigration (Tyler 2006). Sonia's case is thus not exceptional, but it nevertheless enables us to focus on some of the micro-practices that are a consequence of the constellation of citizenship, borders and abjection that I have been describing. One of the few notable things about Sonia's case is that it was reported, albeit very briefly and factually, in a national newspaper. In one sense, this news story simply reinforces the perception that Britain is 'tough on illegals'. These kinds of news stories are deployed as a 'deterrent' to unwanted migrants. From another perspective it is an extraordinary story since Sonia's 'crime' involved an attempt to *leave* Britain, a country in which she had been deemed to be illegally residing and from which she now wanted to escape.

When I interviewed Sonia, she explained that when she was arrested at the border she was desperate to migrate from Britain. She had been evicted from the temporary accommodation she had been allowed while her family's asylum claim was being determined, and was now destitute. She explained that when she arrived in Britain her husband claimed asylum and she was considered his dependant. His claim was rejected and so was his subsequent appeal. She feared what would become of her and her unborn child on the streets of Britain, as she had no rights of access to medical care or welfare assistance, but she feared equally what might become of her if she was forcibly deported to her country of origin as she felt her life was under threat there. Now, her asylum claim failed, she faced limited choices. Without a passport, as this had been taken from her by border officials when her husband made his asylum claim, she hatched a plan to obtain a forged passport and travel alone to another African state where she had some friends and contacts.

Asylum seekers convicted of crimes, however minor, rescind their rights to political asylum in Britain. For the purposes of this chapter, the legitimacy of Sonia's claim for refugee protection under international law is less significant than her disproportionate treatment by the British state. A teenage girl, heavily pregnant in a foreign country, she was imprisoned for six months and detained for over a year for using a fake passport. Sonia is totally traumatized and deeply ashamed at being treated 'like a criminal … I just really … really … I didn't think it was true … I just couldn't believe it … I worried very much [about] what would people [at home] think of me if they found out' (interview with Tyler, 2009). Sonia served the full six-month custodial sentence at Holloway Prison, where she gave birth to her daughter, 'Mary'. She recalled being taken in handcuffs to antenatal appointments and had to endure the presence of prison officers throughout her labour and childbirth. A convicted criminal, Sonia's ability to make a fresh claim for asylum on her own behalf had been severely compromised, and she has exhausted her right to make any more legal appeals for leave to remain.

After serving her prison sentence, Sonia and Mary were transferred directly to Yarl's Wood Immigration Detention Centre, then the largest immigrant prison for women and children in Europe, to await their deportation to West Africa. The detention of people subject to migration control in Britain was first codified under the 1920 Aliens Order and elaborated in the 1971 Immigration Act. Britain now has more wide-ranging powers than any other European nation to imprison foreign nationals. However, before 1988 non-citizens were rarely detained, or, indeed, deported. There were on average between 200 and 300 people in detention at any given time. By 2003, that had 'escalated to over 2260 people detained, including children and pregnant women' (Welch and Schuster 2005: 402). Mary, who had been imprisoned since her birth, was, like most children in detention, failing to thrive in conditions which the British government's own prison inspectors and the government's Children's Commissioner for England have repeatedly described as totally inappropriate for pregnant women, nursing mothers and children (see, for example, Aynsley-Green 2010).

Every child matters?

Despite the fact she was born in Britain, the government was able to imprison Sonia's daughter, Mary, indefinitely from birth because under the Nationality Act of 1981 children born in Britain to non-citizen mothers are not entitled to British citizenship. As the UK Border Agency states on its website:

> Even if you were born in the United Kingdom, you will not be a British citizen if neither of your parents was a British citizen or

legally settled here at the time of your birth. This means you are not a British citizen if, at the time of your birth, your parents were in the country temporarily, had stayed on without permission, or had entered the country illegally and had not been given permission to stay here indefinitely. (UK Border Agency 2008)

Mary's birth certificate, like that of all de facto stateless children born in Britain, was confiscated by the immigration authorities. Had Mary been born before 1983, she would automatically have been granted citizenship, and as a citizen her indefinite detention as a British citizen could have been legally challenged. As it stands, Mary, like thousands of other children born in Britain each year, is in the extraordinary position of having entered Britain illegally at birth. With the cut of the umbilical cord and her first breath she became subject to the full force of Britain's border controls, including indefinite detention within a rapidly expanding, privately owned, 'for-profit' immigration prison estate.

In 2004 the British government committed itself to a comprehensive system of reforms under the Every Child Matters (ECM) policy framework. Under this agreement, the government stated that every child in Britain has a right to access the support they need in order to 'Be healthy', 'Stay safe', 'Enjoy and achieve', 'Make a positive contribution' and 'Achieve economic well-being' (HM Government 2004: 9). While the government stated that ECM applied equally to every child in Britain under the age of eighteen whatever their background or their circumstances, in practice the children of parents who are subject to immigration controls are excluded from the ECM agreement. This is despite the fact that it was the brutal torture and murder of a migrant child from the Ivory Coast, Victoria Adjo Climbié, by her guardians in London which galvanized the policy changes which led to the development of the ECM programme.

ECM was to be supported legislatively by the creation of the position of Children's Commissioner for England. The first commissioner was Sir Al Aynsley-Green. When he held this post (2005–10) Green argued consistently that 'the way the British immigration system treats children is "positively cruel" and "inhuman"' (O'Keeffe 2008). He called on the government to 'live up to its rhetoric by making sure that every child really does matter' (cited in ibid.). Yet children like Mary, born in Britain but subject to UK immigration control, are routinely excluded from the ECM framework of protection. Indeed, perversely, the government started routinely to detain children at the same time as the ECM programme was being developed. The Immigration Law Practitioners' Association report, 'Child first, migrant second: ensuring that every child matters', exposes the routine failure of the government to protect non-citizen children (Crawley 2006). As this report details, Her Majesty's Chief Inspector of Prisons, an independent inspectorate which reports to the government on the conditions for and treatment of those in prison, young offender institutions and immigration detention facilities, has repeatedly raised concerns about the detention of children for the purpose of immigration controls. In repeated visits to immigration detention centres in Britain, HMIP expressed grave concerns about the conditions and length of time children were being detained (HMIP 2005; Crawley 2006) – report after report after report, inspection after inspection after inspection. Yet the detention of the children continues. Today, children are no longer detained at Yarl's Wood but at a specially redesigned site called Cedars at Pease Pottage near Gatwick Airport, which activists describe as an 'internment camp for refugee families with children' run by the global securities giant G4S (see Chapter 3) and the children's charity Barnardo's (NoBorders 2011).

Sonia

Sonia's homeless and destitute husband 'Jonah' was prevented from visiting his wife and daughter in detention. Sonia's body shakes as she recounts to me what happened to Jonah: 'he was shouting and screaming at them [the guards] … they just said we can't tell you if she is here or not because you don't have a [visiting] pass … they [the guards] told me later that he went crazy right there … ripping at his clothes … crying … finally they brought a doctor [and] took him away' (interview with Tyler, 2009). Jonah was later sectioned under the Mental Health Act (1983). As far as Sonia is concerned he had literally been driven to insanity by the British state. Months later, with the support of anti-deportation activists, Sonia managed to obtain a lawyer and, with the help of a friend, was eventually granted bail out of detention. Mary had spent the first six months of her life in prison.

When I interviewed Sonia in 2009, she was living in social housing in a city in the North of England with Mary, now a toddler, and a new baby, 'Sam'. She tells me Jonah doesn't live with her and his children but that he visits them regularly. She suggests, indirectly, that he is struggling with mental health problems and is still homeless. Like all asylum seekers and failed asylum seekers, Sonia cannot legally work. She receives absolutely minimal benefits, significantly below those deemed necessary to support a dignified life for British citizens, and she has no legal access to health or social care. She is dependent on charity for basics such as clothing and furniture and receives social housing because she has children (otherwise, as a 'failed asylum seeker', she would be made forcibly homeless, as she was when she was pregnant). Sonia and her children are like many thousands of irregular migrant families living in absolutely abject conditions of crushing poverty and deprivation. When I ask her how she managed to survive, she reassures me that things 'aren't that bad now' and describes as a counterpoint a period immediately after she had been bailed from immigration detention but before she was in receipt of any state benefits: 'I was so hungry, I thought I was going to die – the terrible pains in my stomach,' she said, grasping herself as she spoke. My field notes read:

> There is little very furniture, or stuff in the house, apart from a television, which is playing an African movie very loudly, and a sofa. Everything is clean but I am shocked by the condition of the children, Mary seems tiny for her age and they are both covered in eczema and rashes, and they are dressed in dirty clothes. Sonia is also dishevelled; it occurs to me that she is frightened of me. Outside in the garden I see a washing line with all the family's clean clothes blowing dry in the wind. I feel ashamed that I am passing judgement on her, as though I could possibly know what it means to be living her life. (Tyler, field notes, 2009)

Having exhausted all legal appeals for leave to remain in Britain, Sonia nevertheless remains under 'bail conditions', subject to detention and deportation at any time. Sonia detailed her daily routines, explaining how she has to register at the local immigration office each week; ironically, this is in case she absconds. Many migrants without legal status are taken back into detention when they register, and Sonia describes how she always leaves her children with a friend when she registers at the immigration centre, as she thinks that the border officials will be less likely to detain her without them. Registering with the immigration and border control can take many hours if it is busy. She explains that 'this is much better than before because when they first moved me here I had to register every day and it was a long way from my house, two buses'. Throughout my interview with her, Sonia is extremely agitated and wary. She is literally on the edge of her seat. She relaxes only at the end of the interview when I turn off the recorder. I represent the state that has treated her 'worse than a dog', or perhaps one of 'those activists' who she worries will draw unwanted attention to her. At her last and final asylum appeal the immigration judge had made it clear that the involvement of anti-deportation activists in support of her case, and the publicity this had generated, had informed his decision to reject her appeal to the court to remain on humanitarian grounds. What Sonia wants now is to become invisible: 'The longer nobody comes [to deport her and the children], I keep thinking, it is possible they have forgotten about me, and that I can stay and have [a] normal life, then the door knocks ... I think, *No!* ... because I cannot describe it [the prison and the detention centre] ... I cannot go back ... anything is better than that' (interview with Tyler, 2009).

Migrant abjection

Abjection, as De Genova writes, 'is an especially apt interpretive frame through which to appreciate the complexities of the migrant condition, [...] because migrants are always-already within the space of the state and can never really be entirely expelled' (De Genova 2010: 104; see also Hyndman 2000). Sonia's story illustrates the paradox of abjection made manifest on the scale of both the individual body and the body politic. Sonia has been constituted as 'illegal', somebody with no right to reside or remain in Britain. She cannot escape Britain, she tried and failed, but she is also deprived of access to the resources which human beings require to make a liveable life within the state. Sonia is excluded from British citizenship, its rights and protections, but, paradoxically, remains under the direct and suffocating control of the state; her everyday life is saturated with state power. Indeed, her attempts both to leave and to remain have been mobilized by state actors, immigration judges and the news media, as a deterrent to others. She has been made 'an example', first when she attempted to leave Britain, and secondly when she attempted to politicize her struggle to stay by enlisting the support of activists and humanitarian campaigners. With no rights of residency and no rights of citizenship, she now exists in an unliveable mode of statelessness with her stateless children. Butler writes that:

> The abject designates [...] those unliveable and uninhabitable zones of social life which are nevertheless densely populated by those who do not enjoy the status of subjects, but whose living under the sign of the 'unliveable' is required to circumscribe the domain of subject. (Butler 1993: 3)

When we apply this account of abjection to the nation-state, we can see how, as a 'national abject', the abject 'other' of citizenship, Sonia has come, despite her best efforts and many years of struggle, to embody the inner constitutive boundary of Britain. If we are, as Kristeva suggested, our own abjects, then Sonia is also, paradoxically, as British as it is possible to be. Sonia embodies British citizenship.

Sociologist Saskia Sassen (2003) argues that the criminalization of migration is slowly poisoning European civic societies. In particular she suggests that the growing numbers of (predominantly African) migrant deaths at European borders 'represent a failing policy, but also a gradual corrosion of the sense of citizenship, responsibility, and ultimately humanity itself' (ibid.). Sassen's intervention is important, but the risk of this argument about 'moral bankruptcy' is that it fails to acknowledge the ways in which citizenship itself has become a central abjectifying technology of border control. As I have argued, the 1981 Act instituted a mass classification of types of citizens and non-citizens, a scaling of citizenship that was designed to exclude specific post-colonial populations and manage 'migrant' populations within the nation home. The abjection of migrants like Sonia and her British-born children, who came to Britain from a former European colony, is a direct effect of the racist design of British citizenship, and in particular the abolition of birthright citizenship and removal of residency rights from people of the former colonies.

Sonia's story also reveals how the management of borders is a highly gendered practice. As Martha Escobar argues, '[i]deal migrant labor is frequently defined as sojourner and exploitable, meaning that they migrate, labor for a while, and return to their home countries. The presence of migrant women disrupts this ideal since they represent reproduction and settlement' (Escobar 2006; see also Escobar 2009). We know that there are many thousands of people like Sonia and Mary who are living 'unliveable lives' at the borders of the British state. Since the abolition of birthright citizenship, maternity wards across Britain have become 'border zones' through which 'aliens' enter Britain (see Chapter 4). In migration studies, borders have tended to be understood as places; however, the concept of abjection reveals borders to be unstable, dynamic and embodied practices which need to be continually remade and reaffirmed. For non-citizen mothers the everyday activities of parenting, attending toddlers' groups, accessing health services and making the 'school run' can become routines fraught with risk as they make themselves and their children visible and vulnerable to immigration control. As Nyers argues, 'For people without status, everyday activities (working, driving, and going to school) are at risk of being transformed into criminal and illicit acts with dire consequences' (Nyers 2008: 166–7). The anxiety expressed by irregular migrants like Sonia, about the dangers of visibility in everyday situations, is not misplaced. As Liz Fekete has noted, the British Home Office issued border and immigration officials with a manual advising on 'the rounding up of children from schools to be detained with their families' (Fekete 2005: 75). For pregnant women and mothers the possibility of 'flying below the radar' to avoid triggering the bureaucratic machinery of detention and deportation is almost impossible.

However, as I will explore further in Chapter 4, if migrant mothers are soft targets for border controls, they are also sites of migrant resistance. For, while their status as mothers often constitutes their vulnerability and otherness, as maternal figures who represent 'life itself', they carry moral and ethical weight that exceeds or troubles the abject logic of citizenship, which is why mothers and children feature so prominently in anti-deportation campaigns. This is a political visibility that in Sonia's case seriously undermined her attempts to appeal for leave to remain on humanitarian grounds.

Neoliberal black worlds

Detention centres in the UK are generally screened from public view and, as one humanitarian report on conditions inside detention centres notes, 'The voices of the people affected by detention are seldom heard in the debate about immigration detention [...] Detainees are forcibly physically separated from the outside world. As a result, their rage, bewilderment and shock at what is happening to them [remain] largely hidden' (Cutler and Ceneda 2004: 12). If they are released, detainees are often afraid to speak out about their experiences, fearing backlash and targeting from immigration authorities. Hence there are few accounts of detention and few representations of British detention sites in mainstream circulation.[3] Few images exist of the physical structures themselves and little documentary evidence of what takes place within the regimes of detention is available. Places of detention are internal borders, abject zones, and in some respects they constitute what artist and activist geographer Trevor Paglen terms 'black worlds', spaces of cartographic silence (Paglen 2009). Paradoxically, however, detention centres are banal and ordinary places of work, and the existence of detention centres is a matter of public fact, a fact that is routinely capitalized on in governmental rhetoric as a means of demonstrating Britain's 'toughness'. Conversely, however, these institutions are also often used to support claims that Britain isn't 'tough enough' (see Chapter 3). As one newspaper headline put it, 'Luxury for migrants in new centre':

> The full extent of the five-star facilities at a controversial new centre for asylum seekers can be revealed today. Set in lush grounds, it will have state-of-the-art housing and facilities including a crèche, library, information technology and email connection plus a minibus for jaunts into nearby towns. No expense will be spared in building the centre at Piddington, near Bicester – the first of five planned sites – to make the 750 asylum seekers to be housed there feel at home. (Knowsley 2003)

While the newspaper report cited here expresses outrage and incites envy for 'the five-star facilities' which immigrant detainees enjoy, they are also imagined as just sites of punishment. For example, McNevin argues that the mushrooming for-profit immigrant prisons operate as 'performances of political closure designed to assuage those made vulnerable by [a] neoliberal economic trajectory' (McNevin 2007: 611). In this way, the tough border controls that immigrant prisons represent function performatively to placate and appease those citizens whose own dreams of 'the good life' have become increasingly precarious in the face of the neoliberal erosion of social democracy and welfare provision (Berlant 2011; Plant 2010). Detention centres are mediated as spatializing devices, symbolically marking the segregation of the deserving and the non-deserving. In multiple, contradictory ways these immigrant prisons play a central symbolic role in assertions of nationality and belonging in neoliberal Britain. As abject zones, they establish the borders of Britain as a modern racist nation-state.

In Australia, Europe and the United States multinational corporations bid for lucrative government contracts to build detention centres and lock up irregular migrants, with global banks, investment bankers and airlines lining up for a slice of the action. Detention policies and practices in the UK are driven by corporate interests and the continuing expansion of the detention estate is motivated by business interests, as corporations compete to win and maintain government contracts. Since I began to research global detention companies in 2000, profit margins have massively increased. Profits are in line with an increase in 'turnover' of migrant captives. The detention of Sonia and Mary in 2006 cost British taxpayers at least £2,000 a week. A six-month detention would have cost the British taxpayer around £50,000. This extraordinary sum was paid to Global Solutions Limited (GSL), the multinational company that managed the Yarl's Wood immigration detention centre during this period.

The British immigration industry is booming. Immigration detention is a global multibillion-dollar business, one profitable part of a massive immigration detention and prisons complex. GSL is now an arm of the multinational security company G4S, which describes itself as 'the largest security services provider globally with operations in more than 120 countries on 6 continents' (G4S 2012). In 2008 the group had a turnover of £5.9 billion, and with over 700,000 employees is the largest employer listed on the London stock exchange (ibid.). I will return to the abject economics of asylum in Chapter 3. For now I want to note that if Marshall (1950) believed that capitalist enterprise could, if regulated, contribute to the deepening of citizenship in Britain, where citizenship was understood as an element of a large redistributive project of social justice, today citizenship itself has been thoroughly capitalized as companies like G4S trade in and profit from the abject politics of contemporary British citizenship regimes.

Conclusion

In Chapter 1, I outlined Bataille's argument that abjection is the imperative force of sovereignty, a founding exclusion that constitutes a part of the population as outcasts: 'represented from the outside with disgust as the dregs of the people, populace and gutter' (Bataille 1993 [1934]: 9). In this chapter I have detailed some of the ways in which British citizenship was redesigned as a technology to abjectify undesirable migrants from the former colonies. Today, British citizenship is a legal, political and social field of intelligibility which abjects some people outside of the realm of citizenship altogether, constituting them as illegal but, paradoxically, as Sonia's case made manifest, fixing, capturing and paralysing them within the borders of the state. Being made abject in the context of citizenship regimes might mean not being in possession of the right kind of paperwork, being unable to produce the right kind of evidence, or economic capital, to secure leave to remain, or it might, as in Mary's case, mean being unfortunate enough to be born in Britain to an 'illegal' mother. As Rushdie argued, the abolition of birthright citizenship in the 1981 Nationality Act was an act of state racism, which transformed citizenship into *a gift of government*, the implications of which would impact on all the people of Britain, stripping away fundamental freedoms. As he wrote:

> For nine centuries any child born on British soil was British. Automatically. By right. Not by permission of the State. The Nationality Act abolished the jus soli. From now on citizenship is the gift of government. You were blind, because you believed the Act was aimed at the blacks; and so you sat back and did nothing as Mrs. Thatcher stole the birthright of every one of us, black and white, and of our children and grandchildren for ever. (Rushdie 1982)

Understanding citizenship through the lens of abjection allows us to perceive some of the mechanisms through which populations found 'wanting' vis-à-vis citizenship are included through their exclusion. As De Genova argues, citizenship has become 'the premier instrumentality' for the subjection 'of those whom states "contain" within their juridical and spatial confines' (De Genova 2007: 440).

The central point I want to make in this chapter is that the growing number of failed, illegal and stateless people within Britain is not an accident of flawed design, but constitutes the very borders of Britain as a neocolonial, neoliberal nation-state. Materially and/or symbolically present in the form of objects of disgust (abjects), migrant illegality operates as a figurative prop in support of the wider theatre of neoliberal governance. As citizenship has become the means through which territory is established through the assertion of nationalism, 'belonging to Britain' is increasingly circumscribed by and dependent upon the reproduction of waste populations within the state.

Any account of British citizenship will be provisional because citizenship describes a heterogeneous field of modes of legal status, identity and modes of belonging which are continually re-created through complex legal, political, social and pedagogical practices. Different kinds of citizens emerge at the intersections of formal and informal practices and relations. I do not wish to devalue the diverse, rich and important history of citizenship in global democratic struggles, or claim that citizenship can never again be a positive force for social change. I also acknowledge, as Giorgio Agamben puts it, that citizenship has always been 'two-faced', 'the bearer both of subjection to sovereign power and of individual liberties' (Agamben 1998: 125). However, for many national minorities the lived realities of these neoliberal regimes of citizenship stand in stark contradistinction to contemporary governmental accounts of citizenship, which stress community cohesion, political participation, social responsibility, rights and pride in shared national belonging. As I will detail in Chapters 6 and 7, this neoliberal refashioning of citizenship has impacted not only on migrants, but upon all citizens, and has intensified class divisions and conflicts within the state. We must acknowledge the abjectifying consequences of neoliberal citizenship, the vast monstrous bureaucracy from which flow categories of destitute peoples marginalized by, excluded or disqualified from citizenship. If citizenship has been designed for purposes of abjection, disenfranchisement and political dispossession, in what sense can it be said to retain any radical promise for social justice? In Chapters 3 and 4 I will explore the ways in which protests by immigrants in Britain respond to and expose the abject politics of citizenship, often by *harnessing abjection as a form of politics*, and in so doing offer us routes for thinking of political agency in ways which both fracture and exceed the frame of neoliberal citizenship.

3 | THE ASYLUM INVASION COMPLEX

Illegal immigrants, asylum seekers, bootleggers and the scum of
the earth – drug smugglers – have targeted our beloved coastline
for some unwanted attention. We are left with the backdraft of
a nation's human sewage and NO CASH to wash it down the
drain. (Nick Hudson, editor of the *Dover Express*, 1999)

Why not develop a certain degree of rage against the history
that has written such an abject script for you that you are
silenced? (Spivak 1990: 62)

Introduction

What would Britain look like if we mapped it not by its geological
features – mountains, hills, rivers and lakes – or its conurbations –
cities, towns and villages – but by its places and practices of immigration detention, dispersal and deportation? What economic picture of
Britain would be produced if we mapped its booming immigration
and securities industries? At the heart of Britain's rapidly expanding
asylum and immigration industry and estate is a transnational traffic in bodies. This is an industry fuelled by the import and export
of human misery. If we understand the injury, violence, rage and
desperation in which this industry trades and profits as a distinctly
neoliberal form of state-crafting, what kind of psycho-social map of
contemporary Britain would this produce? The picture of the state
which emerges is, as I will detail, a deeply melancholic map of Britain.
This melancholia is inevitable as the abjects the asylum industry trades
in are largely invisible and nameless (and are thus unmournable).
However, if melancholia is a trauma or loss that is not sanctioned
through public mourning, it is incorporated all the more integrally in
the body of the nation, in the form of internalized scars and wounds.
Moreover, while this highly secretive market, and the buildings, locations, processes where its transactions take place, are largely hidden
from public view, this dirty trade occasionally oozes to the surface
of national consciousness, infecting the state from the inside out. In
these rare moments of rupture, the plaints of abject migrants can be

discerned, through acts of immigrant protest, the riots and hunger strikes in detention centres, medical reports which detail the tortured psyches and bodies of migrants, humanitarian campaigns that resist the deportation of specific individuals or categories of people such as children, undercover journalism, guerrilla media, whistleblowing accounts by workers in the immigration detention industry, politically engaged literature and artworks, and community activism. However, these minor revolts offer the abjectified migrant little in the way of recognition. The recognition of suffering and injustice has limited transformatory political potential in a context where the deliberate conflation of migrants into a singular national abject – the bogus asylum seeker – has overwhelmed public culture. Nevertheless, the *melancholic states* that critical processes of counter-mapping make visible are important critical responses to the ontological obliteration of personhood that is central to Britain's neoliberal immigration industry. This mapping can produce alternative ways of looking, however partial, depressed, reactive and liminal the ensuing knowledge may be. By mapping Britain's asylum invasion complex, this chapter attests to ways in which the relentless dehumanization of others is central to neoliberal governmentality. The aim is to puncture the narcissistic justifications of the state and its corporate sponsors within the global media and securities industries.

Abas Amini

In May 2003, Abas Amini, a Kurdish-Iranian asylum seeker, stitched up his mouth, ears and eyes in protest against a decision by the British government to deport him (Figure 3.1). Thirty-year-old Amini had been repeatedly detained for his political activism in Iran, spending a cumulative total of six years of his life in prison. A poet, atheist and member of an underground communist organization, he had been involved in a Kurdish resistance movement from the age of twelve, but in later years his primary act of protest was the writing of poetry critical of the Islamic Republic, which he distributed at social and political gatherings. Amini was well known in Iran for his dissenting verse about figures in the regime such as Sadegh Khalkhali, 'the hanging judge' (Ayatollah Sadeq Givi).[1] During periods of imprisonment in Iran, Amini suffered long spells in solitary confinement, beatings (often on the soles of his feet) and mock executions, during which he was suspended off the ground, on some occasions for more than two days.

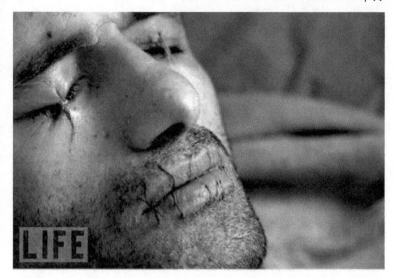

3.1 Iranian refugee sews his face in protest

Amini escaped from prison and a twenty-two-year prison sentence in June 2001, after friends bribed a guard to release him. Leaving his wife, children and siblings behind in Iranian Kurdistan, he escaped across the border to Turkey and then crossed over to Greece, where he stayed for several months. 'He then hid on a boat going to Italy and took a train to France, locking himself in the toilets for most of the journey north. He reached England by strapping himself to the bottom of a truck going through the Channel Tunnel' (Hodge 2004).

Despite the stopovers en route to Britain, Amini's lawyers felt his claim for political asylum in Britain would be straightforward. Not only was Amini known to be a vocal opponent of the regime in Iran, he had medical evidence of the torture he had endured in prison.[2] He waited for two years to hear whether his application for political asylum was successful, during which time his case was adjourned five times. In the spring of 2003, he was finally granted leave to remain, but a few weeks later he received a letter informing him that the Home Office had launched an appeal against the decision of the immigration court. As his solicitor Suzanne Gardner noted, 'Abas [...] was in sight of the finishing line and then the Home Office [...] appeal [...] tipped him over the brink' (cited in Branigan 2003). Destitute and facing deportation, Amini, in his words, 'couldn't take

3.2 'Abas Amini is our friend'

any more [...] the pressure on me was so huge that I got to the point where I thought there was no hope' (cited in ibid.). Amini made the decision to die in Britain rather than be returned to detention and torture in an Iranian prison: 'I would rather die like this gradually, a thousand times, than face the injustices, the oppression, the lack of any human rights or any humanity I was facing in Iran' (cited in Lyall 2003). So he found himself, standing before a mirror in his Nottingham home, needle and thread in his hand, determined to communicate and protest against his abject constitution as 'living dead' (Kawash 1999: 247).

If Amini's protest began as a singular act of revolt, it rapidly garnered wider support as up to two hundred people gathered in solidarity in the street in front of the modest terrace house in which he lived with other destitute migrants. His home was transformed into a shrine for anti-deportation activism, adorned with printed and handwritten posters and banners, declaring 'Abas Amini is our friend', 'FREEDOM', 'EQUALITY', 'HUMANITY has NO BORDERS' (see Figure 3.2). The Federation of Iranian Refugees, together with other migrants, asylum advocacy groups and human rights activists, briefly transformed this small part of Nottingham into a place of resistance to protest against the incremental erosion of the rights to asylum within the British state. This protest was a response also to the figure of the 'bogus asylum seeker', a national abject which had saturated news media and political rhetoric for a decade and which was responsible for inciting public consent for the implementation of a punishing legislative and bureaucratic framework to manage 'the refugee crisis' in Britain (see below).

Since Britain began to institute its inhumane asylum system in the 1990s, lip-sewing, hunger strikes, self-harm and suicides have become ordinary features of national life for those caught in the 'abject diaspora', the 'deportspora' at the borders of the British state (Nyers 2003: 1070).[3] Indeed, there was nothing exceptional about Amini's case or his protest, except for the extraordinary media attention it garnered. For his protest not only gathered local support but attracted significant national and international news coverage, and it continues almost a decade later to have a considerable documentary afterlife in activist publications, newspaper stories, photographs, theatrical plays (Lyddaird 2005; Harrison 2008), artworks and exhibitions (Collins 2003), in academic writing on migrancy and citizenship (Edkins and Pin-Fat 2004, 2005; Walters 2006; Soguk 2006; Isin and Rygiel 2007; Rygiel 2010), and in scholarly work on abject aesthetics and body protest (Walker 2004; Mirzoeff 2005; Richards 2005; Kear 2008; Jones 2009; Skartveit and Goodnow 2010; Jeffers 2012). In short, through this protest, Amini became 'an international cause célèbre' for those who oppose the British government's systematic erosion of the rights to asylum (Branigan 2003).

In this chapter, and with his permission, I employ Amini's protest and its documentary afterlife as a political parable through which to begin my examination of the constellation of historical, political and economic forces which gave rise to the fabrication and institution of an 'asylum invasion complex'[4] within the British state. The mapping of the asylum invasion complex I will undertake in this chapter will focus on the public stigmatization of asylum seekers as revolting subjects during the period of New Labour government (1997–2010), and the abject zones within which migrants are captured at the borders of the state.

The invasion complex

One of the most powerful British national myths is that this state has an ancient and proud history of granting asylum to foreign nationals fleeing religious or political persecution. Despite the continued repetition of this myth, those welcomed to Britain, and those banished from its territorial space, have long been classified and hierarchized along class and racial lines according to the prevailing ideological climate of the time. It was in the Victorian era that the myth of the 'ancient right of asylum' became embedded in national life, as part of Britain's self-fashioned imperial identity as a paternalistic, liberal and civilizing force in the world (see Porter 1979). In the face of international pressure to deport a number of high-profile political asylum seekers in 1853, a *Times* editorial pronounced:

> Every civilized people on the face of the earth must be fully aware
> that this country is *the asylum of nations*, and that it will defend
> the asylum to the last ounce of its treasure, and the last drop of
> its blood. There is no point whatsoever on which we are prouder
> and more resolute [...] We are a nation of refugees. [...] all Europe
> knows and respects the asylum of these isles. (Cited in ibid.: 7)

Karl Marx, then a German political refugee who later died stateless in London in 1883, is retrospectively celebrated as one of those dangerous political agitators whom foreign governments called on Britain to expel. In a letter published in the *Spectator*, the *Sun* and the *Northern Star* in 1850 in response to a proposed revision of the 1798 Alien Bill which would allow the British government to deport undesirable foreign nationals, Marx (along with Friedrich Engels and August Willich) described 'the long-established reputation of England as [the] safest asylum for refugees of all parties and of all countries' (Marx et al. 1850).

A campaigner for the rights of refugees, Marx was highly critical of what he perceived as the erosion of rights to asylum in Britain. In particular, he was concerned with the double standards around the promotion of a liberal rhetoric of asylum, and the British government's imperialist policies, which were producing increasing numbers of political and economic migrants. Given his politics, Marx was most concerned about the impact of internal migration from the wider British Isles to English industrial towns and cities, which he perceived to be creating ethnic divisions and hatreds within the proletariat population. Hence, he focused his critical attention on migrations effected by the pauperization of rural peasants in England and the Scottish highlands, and on the mass evictions, religious and political persecution of Irish peasants (Ireland was then under English rule). As Marx notes in an 1853 *New York Daily Tribune* article entitled 'Forced emigration': 'Begin with pauperising the inhabitants of a country, and when there is no more profit to be ground out of them, when they have grown a burden to the revenue, drive them away, and sum up your Net Revenue!' (Marx 1853).

As Marx argued, while up to two thousand upper- and middle-class political refugees (like him) lived relatively freely in London during the nineteenth century, largely tolerated by the government and frequently mobilized in boastful political rhetoric as evidence of British liberalism, the vast majority of migrants were treated with suspicion and ruthlessly exploited by industrial capitalists. Migrants from Ireland were undoubtedly the most widely despised, criminalized and stigmatized group in this period. As a *Times* editorial on Irish immigration to the English mainland put it:

> Ireland is pouring into the cities, and even the villages of this island, a fetid torrent of famine, nakedness, dirt and fever. Liverpool, whose proximity to Ireland has already procured for it the unhappy distinction of being the most unhealthy town in this island, seems destined to become one mass of disease. The ports of Wales are deliberately invaded by floating pest-houses despatched against them by Irish authorities with the help of English alms. The metropolis itself is menaced with the same danger. Who knows how soon every suburb, and even every court and lane of this city, may exhibit, or rather conceal, within narrower limits, and in more frightful accumulation, the horrors of Sligo, Bantry, Scull, and Skibbereen? (Times 1847: 4)

This Victorian invasion complex imagined Irish migrants as a catastrophic natural disaster, a fetid torrent of diseased bodies over-whelming the borders of the national body. In fact, Marx and Engels were also guilty of reproducing essentialist pejorative and stigmat-izing stereotypes about Irish migrants in their writing (Engels 1887). However, they were also pivotal in exposing the gaps between politi-cal rhetoric, policy and practice around asylum and migrant labour in the nineteenth century. As Engels argued, the English Industrial Revolution was dependent upon 'the numerous and impoverished population of Ireland, a reserve at command' (ibid.). As we shall see, this argument prefigures contemporary debates about the dependency of neoliberal economics on the availability of cheap migrant labour, and the ways in which migrant labourers are (better) exploited through their stigmatization and criminalization (Mezzadra 2004; De Genova 2011). Marx and Engels also highlighted the central role of the news media in inciting ethnic hatreds and antagonisms towards migrants. As Marx wrote:

> Every industrial and commercial centre in England now possesses a working class divided into two hostile camps, English proletarians and Irish proletarians. The ordinary English worker hates the Irish worker as a competitor who lowers his standard of life. [...] He cherishes religious, social, and national prejudices against the Irish worker. His attitude towards him is much the same as that of the 'poor whites' to the Negroes in the former slave states of the U.S.A. [...] This antagonism is artificially kept alive and intensified by the press, the pulpit, the comic papers, in short, by all the means at the disposal of the ruling classes. This antagonism is the secret of the impotence of the English working class, despite its organisation. It is the secret by which the capitalist class maintains its power. And the latter is quite aware of this. (Marx 1870)

What Marx identifies here are the ways in which ill-feeling towards migrant workers was deliberately incited and inflamed in media discourses and by community leaders (in the Church), as a way of both assuaging class-based political grievances against factory owners *and* more thoroughly capitalizing native and migrant labour.

This Irish invasion discourse portended a major shift in British immigration policy at the turn of the twentieth century, when a considerable political and popular backlash gathered steam against both impoverished migrants (primarily Jewish immigrants from the Pale of Settlement) and the sheltering of political asylum seekers. The Aliens Act of 1905 introduced new immigration controls into British law, bestowing the state with powers to register, refuse entry to and deport undesirable migrants. The day after the Act was passed an effusive editorial in the *Manchester Evening Chronicle* entitled 'The unwanted, the unfed, and the unemployed' stated that 'the dirty, destitute, diseased, verminous and criminal foreigner who dumps himself on our soil and rates simultaneously, shall be forbidden to land' (1905: 2). As we shall see, this same politics of disgust still shapes contemporary media discourses about diseased and criminalized bodies of 'illegal' migrants pressing at the borders and 'swamping' schools, hospitals and communities. To take one example from Britain's best-selling newspaper, the *Sun*, in 2003, a few months before Amini's protest: 'BOGUS asylum seekers are bringing HIV, TB and hepatitis B to our shores' (Sun 2003). What is notable here, however, is the extent to which, from the mid-1990s, it was the refugee who became the focus of political and media expressions of xenophobia. Over the course of a decade the figure of 'the asylum seeker' was systematically reconfigured from a mythic figure of state hospitality and benevolence into an exemplary national abject, a synonym for migrant illegality. As Agamben suggests, 'the paradox here is that precisely the figure that should have incarnated the rights of man par excellence, the refugee, constitutes instead the radical crisis [of the concept of rights]' (Agamben 1995). How and why did this happen?

The fabrication of the asylum seeker

The United Kingdom is a signatory to the 1951 United Nations Convention Relating to the Status of Refugees. The Convention was initially conceived as a protection for European refugees displaced by the Second World War, but a 1967 Protocol radically expanded its global scope (see UNHCR 2012). According to Article 1 of this Convention, a refugee is a person who:

> Owing to a well-founded fear of being persecuted for reasons of race, religion, nationality, membership of a particular social group or political opinion, is outside the country of his nationality and is unable or, owing to such fear, is unwilling to avail himself of the protection of that country. (Ibid.)

While the term 'refugee' has a specific international legal genealogy, the term 'asylum seeker' began to gain significant political, legal and popular currency in the UK only in the 1990s. In contrast to the term refugee, which names a (legal) status, the concept of the asylum seeker invokes the non-status of a person who has not been recognized as a refugee. Asylum seekers are thus people paradoxically classified as awaiting recognition as a class. It was by inscribing the category of asylum seeker in British law, through the enactment of a series of punitive asylum laws and policies, and through the simultaneous constitution of the figure of the bogus asylum seeker in public culture, that Britain has been able to manoeuvre around the rights of the refugee and its international obligations as a signatory to the 1951 Convention.[5]

According to national statistics, asylum applications in the UK rose dramatically from 4,256 in 1987 to a peak of 84,130 in 2002 (Gibney 2011). This considerable rise was a consequence of a series of conflicts: in 2001, for example, people fleeing from conflicts in Iraq, Iran, the Federal Republic of Yugoslavia, Sri Lanka, Somalia and Afghanistan made up nearly half of the total of applications (Kate Allen, Amnesty International, 2001). All of these conflicts were, to differing degrees, ones in which British military interventions, British foreign policies and British arms manufacturers had played a part. The issue of asylum came to dominate the political agenda of the New Labour government (1997–2010) as asylum figures began to rise as a share of net migration (Spencer, cited in Gibney 2011).[6] During this period the government was trying to redesign immigration policies in ways which would attract more migrant workers to Britain in order to sustain Britain's economic competitiveness in the global marketplace. Attempts to implement 'managed migration' policies which would open Britain's borders to temporary migrant workers were politically unpopular, with claims made from the political left and right that neoliberal economic policies were pulling too many economic migrants to Britain, driving down wages (as intended), creating unemployment, putting a strain on welfare and education systems, and deepening ethnic and racial tensions. The 'refugee crisis' presented a political opportunity to steer the immigration debate away from the issue of migrant labour, towards refugees, a class of migrants who, through processes of legal (re)classification and the institution of draconian policies that would exclude them from state welfare systems, and bar them from paid work, among other effects, would be construed as the major 'immigration problem' of the time.

The New Labour government introduced six major pieces of asylum legislation variously aimed at accelerating the asylum process, expanding detention capacity, increasing deportations (through fast-tracking), and enforcing destitution on failed asylum seekers ostensibly in order to encourage them to return to countries of origin (Gibney 2004, 2011). Not only was there little mainstream political opposition to the incremental introduction of the new asylum regime, but, on the contrary, the Conservative opposition appealed throughout this period for even harsher measures to be implemented, including the adoption of the Australian policy of detaining all asylum seekers on arrival. In its early years, the New Labour government rebutted right-wing calls for mass detention, but this was subsequently adopted as its primary asylum strategy following the US terrorist attacks in September 2001: 'Detain all asylum-seekers,' screamed a *Sun* newspaper headline in January 2003, amid claims that 'Ministers were urged [by the US government] to lock up all asylum seekers after September 11 to prevent other terror strikes' (Cecil 2003).[7]

In the Nationality, Immigration and Asylum Bill (2002) the government committed itself to the massive expansion of its immigration detention capacity. In what Home Secretary David Blunkett described in Parliament as an 'end to end system' it was proposed that all asylum seekers arriving in the UK should be imprisoned in 'induction centres'; once processed they would be moved either to 'accommodation centres' or 'removal centres' from which they would be deported. Within this regime of continual imprisonment, it was hoped that most asylum seekers would never set foot on British soil proper. *Asylum City: An independent review of the government's proposed accommodation centres for asylum seekers* (Asylum Coalition 2004)[8] vividly detailed how the new regime would operate through the construction of extraterritorial mini-towns within the state. In July 2007, the immigration minister, Liam Byrne, presented a paper entitled 'Border security and immigration: our deal for delivery in 2008', in which he announced that one failed asylum seeker was deported every eight minutes. He promised to improve vastly on this 'performance target' through further massive expansion of Britain's detention estate. These policies, Byrne argued, were necessary to keep 'Britain safe in an era of global movement' (Byrne 2007).

During their administration, the New Labour government was also at the vanguard of EU attempts to 'offshore detention', through the creation of 'regional protection zones'. Indeed, Prime Minister Tony Blair was a key architect of what critics termed 'Fortress Europe' policies, which saw the emergence of novel transnational partnerships and regional confederacies to manage irregular migration from the global South through the lifting of arms embargoes and the development of new trade deals with (primarily North African) states bordering Europe.[9]

As a consequence of the asylum laws introduced under New Labour, if you arrive in the UK today to claim refugee status under the 1951 Convention, you enter an extremely complex bureaucratic system. The first and most critical moment in this process is being identified as an asylum seeker. During the period while you are waiting for your application to be processed, you are given 'temporary admission' to the UK, which means that, while your physical presence is lawful, you are 'legally considered not to have entered the country' (Sawyer and Turpin, cited in Gibney 2011). This paradoxical status not only enables border officials to speed up removal in the event of a failed claim, but conversely makes your status in terms of the rights and protections of the state radically uncertain. As Mountz describes it, migrants are 'treated as though they are walking through the long tunnels of an international airport' (2010: xiv); they are *not yet landed*. This ambiguous classification was made possible through the institution of the asylum seeker as a legal category and is conferred upon migrants through a series of surveillance and control technologies: you are issued with an asylum seeker's identity card ('smart cards' that carry fingerprints and photographs); you have to register at regional border and immigration offices, sometimes more than once a week; you are subject to detention, dispersal and electronic tagging; you are barred from access to paid work, 'confirming public stereotypes that asylum seekers are simply a drain on the public purse and do not contribute to society' (Gibney 2011). You have limited access to healthcare, social housing and economic support and, unless you are a child, have no access to state education. As Mountz suggests, in these ways asylum seekers are locked within interstitial processing zones, struggling through a process which they hope might end with them actually legally disembarking on sovereign territory (2010: xiv–xv). Deprived of recognition and rights, asylum seekers find themselves in a state of suspension outside of 'the constituting condition of the rule of law' (Butler 2006: 67). However, while the state increasingly refuses to recognize asylum seekers as refugees, this is not the same thing as saying that 'they' are not recognized at all. On the contrary, in being identified as asylum seekers, they are recognized as 'not-refugees', bogus, illegals, the unwelcome.

Through the implementation of a series of legal strategies and policy manipulations, the ability of an asylum seeker to mount a successful case or appeal for leave to remain has also become increasingly precarious. As Gibney summarizes:

[In] recent years, many refugee advocates, legal experts and academics have criticized what they see as the poor quality of decision making in asylum judgements, claiming that a 'culture of disbelief' operates in the Home Office. This culture is seen as evinced in a presumption by officials that applicants are attempting to abuse the system. [...] Concerns have also been expressed about the ability of governments to manipulate the chances of asylum seekers making successful claims through changes to procedural rights and entitlements [such as] legislative and policy changes that have withdrawn in-country appeal rights for certain categories of applicant [...] and [...] the fast-tracking of asylum claims deemed unlikely to succeed. (Gibney 2011)

While the possibility remains that some asylum seekers will be granted initial leave to remain (25 per cent in 2010), the possibility of being granted full 'refugee status' has been significantly eroded. Since 2005, even if an initial asylum application is granted, it applies for only five years, after which the case will be reviewed, with the ever-present threat that '[t]his may lead to your status being revoked and removal from the UK' (Home Office 2012). If your asylum claim is refused, your situation becomes rapidly dire. All benefits and housing are automatically removed after twenty-one days (unless you have children). As a consequence there are 'hundreds of thousands of people currently living in the UK' who are unwilling or unable to return to their countries of origin but have no access to state welfare and no means of legally securing a livelihood through paid work (Crawley et al. 2011). The public was told by government that this legislation, while harsh, was necessary and was driven by a deterrence agenda which sought to diminish asylum 'pull factors' to the UK. A decline in asylum applications, to 17,916 in 2010, is often cited as evidence of the positive impact of these deterrence principles (Gibney 2011).

Soft-touch Britain

Bigo argues that 'the securitisation of immigration' is legitimized by a consensus that the nation-state is a vulnerable, precarious body 'over whose boundaries control is sought' (Bigo 2002: 65). The legislation which reconstituted the refugee as a national abject was made possible by the manufacturing of an asylum invasion complex within the public sphere. This invasion complex hinged on the accumulation of political and media representations of Britain as a 'soft touch'. Until its enlistment as a metaphor for the emasculated nation-state (see Mountz 2010: xvi), 'soft touch' was a term ordinarily used to describe a person who is naive, gullible and easily imposed upon, somebody who might be swindled or taken advantage of. From the early 1990s onwards, the repeated citation of images and metaphors of national softness invoked an image of Britain as a feminized and disabled body. The three main beliefs condensed in this idea were that Britain's borders were too porous, that sovereign self-determination had been disabled by 'insane' liberal human rights laws, and that citizens were too easily affected by the (bogus) suffering of others. As the idea of 'soft-touch Britain' circulated with increasing frequency and strength, it incited and sanctioned public fear, anxiety and disgust against refugees which would, in the space of a decade, completely transform the very meaning of asylum.

It is easy to track this amplification through citations of 'soft-touch Britain' within British newspapers and political commentary. For example, in October 2000, the BBC drew upon the results of a MORI poll which presented evidence that 'Eight out of 10 believe that refugees come to Britain because they regard it as "a soft touch"', and that 'Too much is done to help immigrants and asylum seekers' (BBC News 2000). In February 2001, a headline in the *Sun* stated that Britain is 'a soft touch for every scrounger on the planet' (Travis 2000), and a *Daily Mail* headline claimed that 'Britain is seen as the softest of soft touches' (Daily Mail 2000). This rhetoric of softness was voiced and embodied by powerful political actors and public figures within the state as they jostled to be seen as the 'toughest' through repeated accusations regarding the 'softness' of their opponents. In April 2000, for instance, leader of the opposition Conservative Party William Hague declared that the Labour government had turned Britain into 'the biggest soft touch in the world' and promised to expand massively the detention estate and imprison all asylum applicants on their arrival at the borders (cited in Barkham 2000; and see Hague 2001).

In 2004, the Information Centre about Asylum and Refugees published a report entitled 'Media image, community impact: assessing the impact of media and political images of refugees and asylum seekers on community relations in London' (ICAR 2004). This report drew on detailed media analysis and focus groups to give a 'snapshot' of the ways in which a politics of disgust was shaping British news media coverage of asylum. The report details the words repeatedly employed in newspaper stories about asylum; these include:

> crime, dirty, thieves, fraud, deception, bogus, false, failed, rejected, cheat, illegal, burden, drugs, wave, flood, influx, scrounger, sponger, fraudster, tide, swap, flood mob, horde, riot, rampage, disorder, race war, fight, brawl, battle, fighting machine, deadly, orgy of violence, fury, ruthless, monsters, destruction, ruin. (Abridged from ibid.)

The scale of the rhetoric of disgust directed against asylum seekers was extraordinary. On 1 October 1998 the local newspaper in the southern English port town of Dover, the *Dover Express*, began a crusade against asylum seekers, running with editorial headlines such as 'We want to wash dross down drain'. As the group Campaign Against Racism and Fascism (CARF) detailed at the time, asylum seekers faced a sharp rise in racist violence as a consequence. 'Families of refugees had lighted rags and fireworks pushed through their letter boxes and bottles thrown through their windows. The words "we will burn you out" were painted on one house' (CARF 1999). The addresses of the migrant families who were attacked had been printed by the national newspaper the *Daily Mail*. Further, it transpired that the local council had purchased 'cheap quilted jackets in bulk, for distribution to asylum seekers. As the jackets were identical and bore a manufacturer's logo, those wearing them were instantly identifiable as asylum seekers' (Commission for Racial Equality 1999). When wearing these jackets, asylum seekers became the subject of racial harassment on the streets.

In terms of national tabloid print journalism, a 2006 report by the United Nations High Commissioner for Refugees detailed that the *Sun*, the *Daily Mail*, the *Daily Express* and the *Daily Star* (and their three Sunday editions) had together produced 8,163 scare stories about asylum seekers in the five years from 1 January 2000 to 1 January 2006 (Guterres 2006). In this metaphorical context, it is not surprising that rape figures largely in xenophobic media coverage of migrants, with the widely disproportionate reporting of rape charges brought against asylum seekers in tabloid newspapers (and on right-wing websites) giving rise to far-right claims of a 'rape epidemic' effected by asylum-seeking men (MRCF 2011: 4). The figure of the asylum-

3.3 Steve Bell cartoon from 2003 depicting the tabloid media hysteria around the 'refugee crisis'

rapist exaggerated fears that 'the motherland' was being penetrated by criminal foreign bodies. As intended, the hardening public consensus that Britain's borders were too soft prompted 'calls for severe and exceptional remedies' to crack down on the 'asylum invasion' (ICAR 2004: 9).

Media theatrics

The negative coverage of asylum seekers peaked in around 2003, a year in which the *Daily Express* ran twenty-two front-page asylum-scare stories in one thirty-one-day period (MRCF 2011; see Figure 3.3). In the same year the *Sun* began a campaign to 'Stop the Asylum Madness', which instructed readers to cut or print out and sign a petition to the government to stop 'the asylum meltdown'.

> THOUSANDS of angry Sun readers yesterday rushed to join our campaign to save Britain from asylum madness. Our office was flooded with emails, faxes and petition coupons demanding the Government acts now to stop the country from being a soft touch

for illegal immigrants. In our Read This And Get Mad article we told how 1,500 illegal immigrants get into Britain every WEEK. [...] Gerald McTaggart said: 'When is Blair and Blunkett going to stop these parasites from entering our country. The only reason they are coming here is to get as many free handouts as possible.' [...] TORY leader Iain Duncan Smith warned last night that many refugees have terror links. Visiting a West London school, he said: 'People are coming out of the asylum system who have terrorist backgrounds. It's a real concern for us all.' Print this page and fill in petition. (Thompson 2003)

The confusion of categories of migrants in this extract is telling. The torrent of anti-refugee publicity over this decade produced the new figure of the 'bogus asylum seeker': refugees, 'illegal immigrants' and terrorists were are rolled together into one revolting parasitical figure. According to Hansard, the edited verbatim report of proceedings of both the House of Commons and the House of Lords, there were approximately 512 references to bogus asylum seekers in the Houses of Commons and Lords between 1991 and 2005. While some MPs and lords were contesting the use of this phrase, and expressing concerns about the racial tensions it was creating in communities, the vast majority employed the term in a pejorative way. By way of contrast in the 1980s, there were only eight mentions of 'bogus asylum seeker' recorded in Hansard. Indeed, the consensus between the two main political parties on the issue of asylum was striking. For example, on 1 January 2001, the MP (now Lord) Michael Heseltine wrote an 'exclusive' article for the *Mail* in which he stated that:

As Deputy Prime Minister [in 1995–97] [...] I came to three stark conclusions. The first is that a very large number of those seeking asylum are *cheats*, quite deliberately making *bogus* claims and *false* allegations in order to get into this country. [...] The second was that the demands on scarce housing and medical care made by *dishonest* 'economic migrants' [were] likely to stretch the patience of voters and I could well understand why. The third was that the problem of phoney asylum-seekers was likely to grow as the impression spread that this country was a soft touch. Above all, I could see no reason why my most vulnerable constituents – honest and hard-working people who had paid their taxes all their lives – should be pushed to the back of the queue for housing and hospital treatment by dubious asylum-seekers. (Cited in Geddes 2005: 331–2)

Bogus, phoney, dishonest, cheats: it is not simply that the asylum seeker became a scapegoat for public grievances, but that fear-inducing speech constituted the figure of the bogus asylum seeker. It was this inflammatory but authoritative language which legitimized the consensus that *society was under siege*.

In a submission to the Leveson Inquiry in 2011 into the culture, practices and ethics of the press, the Migrant and Refugee Communities Forum (MRCF) details how a million 'asylum madness' petitions from *Sun* readers 'were periodically taken in a large number of sacks, with *Sun* photographers in tow, and dumped at the Home Office' (MRCF 2011). The Home Office wouldn't have been surprised to receive these sacks of petitions; it is an open secret that Downing Street press officers not only knew about the *Sun*'s anti-asylum campaign before *Sun* readers did, but that the government was working in concert with the tabloid press (Dean 2012). Together, figures at the highest level of government joined forces with corporate news media organizations to ratchet up public fears about an imminent asylum catastrophe. Asylum fear stories sold newspapers and were a means of authorizing what Eiko Thielemann describes as a 'competitive downgrading of refugee protection standards' (Thielemann 2004: 47).

In 2001, the Association of Chief Police Officers expressed concerns that 'Racist expressions towards asylum seekers appear to have become common currency' (Travis 2000; MRCF 2011). The figure of the bogus asylum seeker transformed public perceptions of refugees and came to be inscribed on migrant bodies in everyday spaces as they were increasingly perceived as suspect foreign bodies (Mountz 2010: 116). As the *Media Image, Community Impact* project detailed, xenophobic depictions of bogus asylum seekers 'breaching' the national body were not only met politically with tough border controls, but these border controls were acted out within the body of the community, through acts of racist violence (ICAR 2004). Documented incidences of violence against asylum seekers included acts of hate speech, vandalism of property and physical violence, as the racism incited through media and political rhetoric travelled in everyday spaces. Migrants found themselves 'immobilized' by the threat of violence and deterred from becoming members of the community.

The neoliberal economics of illegality

Erik Swyngedouw uses the term 'governance innovation' to describe the way in which expanding purportedly democratic forms, such as citizenship, operate as mechanisms of neoliberal ideologies; freedoms are retracted from individuals and communities, and wealth and power become concentrated in the hands of social and political elites and global corporations (Swyngedouw 2006: 1991; Tyler 2010). As I argued in Chapter 2, a 'reality gap' has opened up between normative political rhetorics of 'deepening democracy' through citizenship, and the abjection of 'illegal' populations from the rights and protections of citizenship through the enforcement of often brutal and inhumane immigration controls. This 'liberal paradox' is further complicated by the incongruity between the opening up of international borders to flows of capital and the simultaneous 'damming' of states and regions against 'undesirable' migrants from the global South: a migratory pull which is paradoxically fuelled by market demands for cheap unregulated migrant labour in the global North (De Haas 2007).

Neoliberal economic policies such as privatization, deregulation, unrestricted foreign investment and the contracting out of state-run services are dependent upon the porosity of borders to flows of capital, including the availability of precarious migrant labour. Thus there is a major discrepancy between policies aimed at curbing immigration and the sustained demand for cheap (often irregular) migrant labour. It is in the context of this 'double agenda' of state formation and economic management, securing the borders and opening the borders, that refugees became scapegoats. The manufacture of 'the asylum problem' (criminalizing asylum seekers in the news media, withdrawing their rights to welfare and work and the introduction of an extraordinary series of border-control and security measures) was an attempt to manage and assuage public opinion. The reclassification of the asylum seeker as a national abject, in concert with the institution of concrete policies of destitution, detention and exclusion directed towards this population, has been capitalized upon, politically and economically, in three central ways.

First, the punitive treatment of asylum seekers and other unwelcome classes of irregular migrants has been employed rhetorically to symbolize territorial sovereignty and strengthen the affective ties of national belonging in the face of the erosion of the welfare state. As I argued in Chapter 2, the securitization of state borders is most visibly evident in the mushrooming of for-profit immigrant prisons which operate as 'performances of political closure designed to assuage those made vulnerable by [a] neoliberal economic trajectory' (McNevin 2007: 611). That is, the abject figure of the bogus asylum seeker (often conflated since 2001 with the figure of the Muslim terrorist) became increasingly constitutive of public articulations of national belonging.

Secondly, the implementation of asylum laws has proved enormously costly, labour intensive and *profitable*. The securitizing of asylum has opened up significant 'asylum markets' enabling global securities conglomerates (in particular G4S and Serco) to penetrate further into the economic and social fabric of the nation-state (Grayson 2012b).[10] In his important research into the economics of asylum in Britain, activist John Grayson has detailed the ways in which 'Private security firms have come to dominate detention, transport and escort services for asylum seekers, displacing politically accountable public provision' (Grayson 2012a). Despite many hundreds of complaints and official reports about the degrading and inhumane treatment of migrants within private for-profit detention centres, and alarming numbers of incidents of self-harm, suicides, riots, fires and hunger strikes, the tenders granted to these companies by the government have continued to mushroom. While the political rhetoric of austerity economics justifies this outsourcing in terms of cost–benefit considerations (those employed by private companies are paid lower wages than public sector workers), in actuality detaining asylum seekers costs significantly more than detaining citizens in state-run prisons. It is estimated that the private security business in the UK is now worth £3.97 billion per annum (ibid.; Krahmann 2009).

The marketization of asylum created a precedent for the further outsourcing of previously state-run and state-accountable services and industries. G4S, for example, is now involved in the running of education services, prisons, police services, forensic crime services and hospitals, and was awarded a £100 million contract to provide security for the 2012 London Olympics. At the time of writing, it had been involved in controversial trials to reassess claimants for Disability Living Allowance and was bidding for seven-year regional contracts to assess a further 3.2 million people for disability benefits. It has also been involved in the delivery of workfare programmes to assist unemployed young people in finding employment (Grayson 2012b; Boycott Welfare 2012). In short, asylum seekers were not only political scapegoats but also experimental subjects in a programme of neoliberal economic reform which has marked the decisive end of the post-war social contract in Britain.

Thirdly, despite the huge amounts of taxpayers' money handed to multinationals to manage the borders, most failed asylum seekers and irregular migrants determined to be illegal are not deported but remain in limbo 'under excruciatingly vulnerable socio-political conditions' (De Genova 2011). The gap between labour demands and the tightening of citizenship regimes, and border and immigration controls, has led to a substantial increase in irregular migration to Europe. As De Haas argues, 'policies to "fight illegal migration" are bound to fail because they are among the very causes of the phenomenon they pretend to combat' (De Haas 2008: 16). This analysis recalls Marx and Engels's account of the dual political and economic function of the vilification in the nineteenth century of Irish migrants, who, through incessant stigmatization, became a political scapegoat for 'native' workers' rage against their own exploitation, held responsible for driving down wages while constituting a highly exploitable labour force for industrial capitalists. De Genova makes a similar argument about the dual political and economic function of illegality:

> the more the anti-immigrant frenzy of right-wing politics howls and shrieks for 'exclusion,' and the more the border is militarized, the more the inclusion of these 'illegal' workers [...] terrorized by the state's immigration law enforcement tactics [...] continues – inclusion as labor subordination. (De Genova 2011)

While there is little substantive empirical research on illegal working in the UK, in the case of asylum seekers, De Genova's claims are supported by research with destitute asylum seekers, who survive by working 'illegally' on the black market and in the sex industry. As Crawley et al. note in their research, 'Wages were mostly reported as being between £1 and £3 per hour, and in some cases were even lower. Most examples of illegal work involved low-skilled jobs, with low pay, long hours, poor working conditions, and a constant fear of being raided by immigration officials' (Crawley et al. 2011: 6). Perhaps most perversely, migrants detained in immigration detention centres are now regularly employed by the corporate managers of the centres to undertake cleaning and other menial tasks in return for phone cards and 'pocket money'.

In short, the fabrication of the category of the asylum seeker was the source of considerable political capital as it enabled the government to be able to claim that they were 'tough on immigration'. At the same time, the asylum legislation was designed in ways which would enable the abjection of asylum seekers to be economically capitalized upon by allowing a new global market in asylum determination, detention and deportation to open up within the state. Mezzadra argues that 'European policies on migration, despite their rhetoric, do not aim to hermetically seal European borders. Their objective and their effect is the establishment of a system of dams and eventually the production of an active process of inclusion of migrant labor by means of its criminalization' (Mezzadra 2004). If we understand this process through the concept of abjection, we can perceive the ways in which the abjection of migrants through citizenship is deployed not only to constitute the borders of the nation-state through the production of illegality, but as part of a global neoliberal economic project in which the border, and border abjects, are transformed into human capital, either as a labour force or, in the case of workless asylum seekers, as *objects of labour*, which the state can manage and exploit.

The dilemmas of migrant and refugee activism

The last decade has witnessed an explosion of immigrant protests and political mobilizations by irregular migrants and pro-migrant activists. Indicative examples include: the rise of the Sans-Papiers movement in France (McNevin 2006), the spectacular protests of millions of undocumented Latin American workers in the USA in spring 2006, under the banner 'A Day Without Immigrants' (De Genova 2009, 2010; Marciniak forthcoming), events which in turn inspired the 'A Day Without Us' marches and strikes in Italy, Greece, Spain and France in 2011. In Britain, refugee and migrant activism has been an important critical, political and social field in countering myths of soft-touch Britain and challenging stigmatizing perceptions of asylum seekers. Refugee activists have engaged coalitions of citizens and non-citizens in various forms of direct action, advocacy and political lobbying around the enforced destitution of asylum-seeking populations and the 'lucrative political economy of border policing and immigrant detention' (De Genova 2011). Often driven by immediate humanitarian considerations, a diverse range of local and national, voluntary, semi-professional and professional advocacy organizations and support networks have sprung up to assist destitute asylum seekers in a variety of ways, such as 'visiting asylum seekers in detention, helping to prepare their legal cases, providing creative, artistic, spiritual, health-related, political and practical support, advocating on their behalf with authorities and policy makers' and raising the profile of asylum seekers in news media and other public forums (Gill et al. 2012). However, one of the findings of Making Asylum Seekers Legible and Visible (2011/12), an ESRC-funded research project with which I was involved, was that asylum advocacy organizations are increasingly co-opted within 'the asylum market'. This 'thirdification' has created tensions within the asylum and migrant advocacy and support sector (ibid.). This is particularly the case when organizations and charities have entered into direct partnerships with the government and with subcontracted global securities companies to work as service providers for the destitute populations that the state produces. As a consequence of the ties (and perceived ties) between refugee support organizations and the state, asylum seekers are often suspicious of the organizations from which they might seek support, perceiving them to be arms of the state and fearful that any information they share might be passed on to border officials (Crawley et al. 2011).

In terms of challenging the wider public perceptions of asylum, the organizations surveyed and interviewed for the Making Asylum Seekers Legible and Visible project stated that they understand a large part of their work, which involves visiting schools, youth groups and church groups, as repairing the damage that pejorative depictions of asylum seekers has wrought. This involves the collection and mobilization of first-person accounts of experiences of seeking asylum and deployment of moving personal testimonies of hardship. 'The strategy of giving a "human face" to the asylum seeking population is widely understood as the best way to reach the "undecided middle who have not firmly established opinions about migrants"' (Gill et al. 2012). Through these 'technologies of the close-up' (Tyler 2006), organizations incite positive identifications through appeals to common humanity and compassion. Partly as a consequence of this humanitarian media activism and partly as a consequence of waning asylum applications since a 2002 peak, negative political rhetoric and stigmatizing media coverage of asylum issues have diminished. However, media scholars suggest that the stigmatization of asylum seekers is now so thoroughly entrenched in the public imaginary that while '"[n]egative" words are much less in evidence [...] there appears to be no need any longer to use negative words because the [...] simple mention of the word asylum now seems to be enough to connote [an] entire [negative] conceptual field' (Gross et al. 2007: 6, 9). Nevertheless, the political and media organizations that fabricated an asylum invasion complex in the public imaginary have begun to distance themselves from anti-refugee discourse.

By 2007, the weight of evidence that stigmatizing media coverage was impacting directly upon migrants' lives led the government's Joint Committee on Human Rights (JCHR) to conduct a hearing on the treatment of asylum seekers and refugees by the press. Around the same time some senior political figures, notably Liberal Democrat leader Nick Clegg and Conservative politician Iain Duncan Smith, began to reinvigorate the myth of Britain as 'the asylum of nations', reclaiming the figure of the refugee and the language of hospitality.[11] However, as yet, the revival and valorization of humanitarian discourses of refugeehood within the public sphere have not effected any substantive policy changes. The profits of the asylum market are, after all, dependent upon the creation of migrant illegality. Furthermore, humanitarian discourses often remain wedded to governmental distinctions between 'genuine' and 'bogus' asylum seekers, which are in turn coupled to the public consensus determined by the asylum invasion complex and shaped by the prevailing socio-political and economic forces I have described.

The autonomy of migration

As Joe Rigby and Raphael Schlembach argue, protest on what they term 'humanitarian realist' grounds 'reduces protest to a contest over "the possible" which can only ever mean, at a fundamental level, a conservative acceptance of the existing framework for grasping problems and their solutions' (Rigby and Schlembach forthcoming). Rather, they argue, we need to think of protest not as 'the art of the possible', but as 'the art of the impossible', 'that which seeks to transform the very parameters of what is considered "possible" in the existing constellation' (ibid.; Žižek 1999: 199). In these terms, if it was the creation of the category of the asylum seeker which enabled the capture and violent subjugation of so many irregular migrants within the state, then it is this classification which has to be contested. The securitization of migration, the proliferation of legislation to limit, hierarchize and scale citizenship, the criminalization of 'undesirable' migrants, the emergence of a global business in immigrant prisons and the normalization of detention and deportation as instruments of governance are, in this sense, a *class conflict* that has to be radically resisted through 'declassificatory politics' (see Chapters 6 and 7).

In the face of the incremental militarization of national and regional borders and the emergence of a global market in asylum seekers, immigrant protests constitute critical counter-political voices, highlighting and protesting against deteriorating conditions for irregular migrants and refugees 'on the ground', exposing the violence engendered by border controls, and challenging the abstract and fetishized political rhetoric of 'illegal immigration'. For example, the Sans-Papiers movement began as a struggle by undocumented workers in France demanding residency papers and regularization, but it became a movement which more radically questioned the neocolonial function of citizenship itself. As Ababacar Diop, a spokesperson for the Sans-Papiers of St Bernard in Paris, notes, 'The struggle of the Sans-Papiers has to go beyond obtaining our papers and must address the underlying questions [...] What is the purpose of migration policies? Should frontiers be open?' (Diop 1997). The Sans-Papiers movement has inspired important forms of migrant activism, notably the European NoBorders movement, which calls for an end to all border controls, and a body of theoretical work, the 'autonomy of migration' scholarship, which examines 'migratory movements and conflicts in terms that prioritize the subjective practices, the desires, the expectations, and the behaviours of migrants themselves' (Mezzadra 2011: 121). Within the 'autonomy of migration' scholarship terms such as asylum seekers and illegals are rejected as state-centric categories of political belonging even while an alternative vocabulary 'with which to articulate the ambiguous status of many irregular migrants and residents' remains elusive (McNevin 2007: 655).

Conclusion: fearless speech

The confiscation of speech is the beginning of exploitation. The end of exploitation demands that speech be given back to the exploited. [...] to learn about domination and emancipation, the intellectual will have to be taught by those who suffer and rebel. (Deranty 2003: 140)

I began this chapter with Abas Amini, whose protest, in 2003 at the height of the asylum invasion complex, provocatively staged the violent political economy of asylum which had transformed failed asylum seekers into 'human sewage' (Hudson, cited in CARF 1999). Some refugee organizations express disquiet about forms of protest which spectacularize state violence in this way, suggesting that 'the more outlandish the trauma' the harder it is to get 'the public' to relate to asylum seekers as human like them (interviewee cited in Gill et al. 2012: 28). From this perspective, a focus on trauma and violence and the divisive debates generated by radical actions such as Amini's are perceived as a hindrance to the work of migrant and refugee advocacy and activism. In one respect these criticisms are correct in that Amini generated exactly the kind of *deterrent publicity* which the New Labour government sought. For example, writing in the *Sunday Mirror*, columnist Carole Malone described Amini's protest as a 'stitch-up':

> In one of the sickest stunts ever to be witnessed in this country, Abas Amini stitched up his eyes and his mouth in his fight to stay in Britain. Well I'm sorry, no human being in this country has ever stitched his eyes and his mouth up in protest at anything. And why not? Because quite simply it's barbaric and in Britain we don't 'do' barbaric. Which is precisely why Mr Amini and thousands of others like him are allowed to stay here every year. We aren't a cruel or barbaric people and we hate other people's suffering – and it's precisely because of that we've become the mugs of Europe. That kind of barbarism isn't part of our national identity and I don't want to see that changed by Kurdish refugees or anyone else. And we don't want patently sick people [...] being given the freedom to roam our streets at will because if he can do that to himself what the hell could he do to other people? (Malone 2003)

Malone interprets Amini's protest as evidence of his 'barbarism' and confirmation of his inhumanity. Speaking as though *the voice of the nation*, she argues that Britain needs to be protected against Amini and 'thousands of others like him' (ibid.). She suggests that asylum seekers who protest in this way are dangerous and violent and pose a risk to the lives of citizens (ibid.). Her views were echoed by far-right white nationalists who used online blogs to communicate their revulsion about Amini's protest:

That photo is disgusting! What's the matter with some people? Hijacking, self-mutilation ... apparently there's no limit to what you can get away with to obtain something you've no right to. [...] I just find it revolting.

I say let him die and make an example of him which should be sent out to the world ... put him in the big brother house so we can watch him die in agony.

What that guy did is absolutely sick, basically animalistic in nature, and should be prevented from being used as an example in the future to sway the authorities. (Comments extracted from *Stormfront Britain*)

These xenophobic responses to migrant protests are precisely what concern some refugee organizations when they talk about the need to despectacularize asylum issues in order to better enable them to get on with the work of political lobbying and humanitarian assistance (Gill et al. 2012: 28). Certainly, in a context where the very act of seeking asylum has become a premier site of capture, control and subjugation, the price of making visibility is that it enables you to be recast as of no account: 'I say let him die'. However, I want to argue that the political instrumentalization of abjection in migrant protests such as Amini's opens up a 'third space'[12] which can move us beyond the deadlock of normativity and abjection and can cut through the traffic between same and other, similar and inalienably different.

Amini refused to be the abject other of the British state, or a (passive) object of humanitarian protection. Rather, by acting out his abjection, he challenges us to confront him as a political actor, a migrant activist. Through 'grotesque mimicry' Amini wanted to make the everyday violence of xenophobic discourses and practices visible in another register (Bhabha 1983: 27). His intention was to communicate the juridified state of dispossession he found himself in by transforming his abjection into a form of political speech (see Rygiel 2010). As one newspaper headline put it, 'He found his voice by stitching up his lips' (Branigan 2003). This protest was an expression of being made abject *and* a refusal of its mummifying effects. At the height of asylum invasion hysteria, Amini insisted that his face was a true face of Britain.

After eleven days of protest, and after the British government withdrew its appeal, Amini allowed the stitches to be cut open, stating to a journalist that 'getting rid of the stitches to open my mouth is not a sign of surrender. I want to stay alive to continue the struggle' (BBC News 2003). An astute and seasoned activist, Amini was intent on capitalizing on the publicity his protest had generated. He wrote a poem to mark the occasion, which was spoken on his behalf to the friends, supporters and journalists who gathered outside his home.

> He sewed up his lips so he could speak out.
> He sewed up his eyes to make others see.
> He sewed up his ears to make others hear.
> You whose eyes, ears and mouth are free can hear and speak out.
> (Hodge 2004)

The third-person grammar of Amini's poem reflects the fact that it was intended to be read out by somebody else. Amini could barely speak after eleven days with limited fluids and no food. However, the use of 'he' also meant that his poem could be spoken by the many hundreds of thousands of others living in unbearable and prolonged states of radical uncertainty as they await the outcome of claims for refugee status or languish in destitution in the hidden enclaves and internal borders of the state. Further, as is clear from the final sentence of the poem asking the reader/listener to 'speak out', the poem is intended to move others to action.

Rancière argues that 'nothing is political in itself', but anything may become political if it gives rise to a meeting of two logics, namely the logic of the state and the logic of equality (Rancière 1999: 32). In his account the political is located not within the official workings of government or the hegemonic aesthetics of mass media which I have explored in this chapter, nor in the 'event' of protests like Amini's, but rather in the 'dissensus' – or the third space – such protests can open up in the public sphere. Rancière suggests that what matters is the *interruption* which 'fearless speech' like Amini's gives rise to, and the disputes which unfold from fighting words. Such disputes, Rancière argues, can produce new inscriptions of equality 'and a fresh sphere of visibility for further demonstrations' (ibid.: 40).

What we might understand by this is that the possibilities of resistance to migrant abjection lie not in singular acts of resistance but in the building of wider communities of struggle that question the inclusive/exclusive logic of citizenship, the economics of illegality and the global marketization of migration. It was not Amini's protest but the publicity it generated which transformed him into a counter-political figure of resistance for those activists and academics, including myself, who seek to learn about and to teach others about the injustice of Britain's asylum laws and policies. As Amelia Jones argues, 'political knowledge about and empathetic reactions towards such actions are thus provoked largely through their documentary residues' (Jones 2009: 47). Jones relates the case of Israfil Shiri, a destitute Iranian refugee who was refused asylum and immolated himself in the offices of Refugee Action in Manchester. Shiri was a former member of an elite state paramilitary organization, but he was also gay and had fled when he discovered the state intended to prosecute him for his sexuality. In Britain, he was unable to find a lawyer willing to represent him and was unable to produce 'expert evidence' on the persecution of gay people in Iran (Tatchell 2004).[13] As Jones notes, it was only the documentary afterlife of Shiri's death, including the play produced by the In Place of War research group at the University of Manchester, *I've Got Something to Show You* (2005), which gave his protest a public voice (Jones 2009).

The incredible afterlife of Amini's protest is testament to the ways in which the 'theatricalization of political rage' (Butler 1993: 232) can trouble prevailing forms of common sense about the meaning of democracy and rights. While Amini was immobilized at the borders of Britain, his protest crossed borders and freely travelled the globe. The artist Phil Collins's photograph of Amini, *abbas amini 2003*, was displayed in galleries across the world, for example (Kear 2008), his story was retold in Alan Lyddiard's 2005 travelling theatrical production *1001 Nights Now*, and he appeared in Tony Harrison's play *Fram* (Harrison 2008). *Fram* appropriately explores the ability of art and poetry to communicate horror and injustice and effect social change.[14] In *Fram*, Harrison restages Amini's protest, depicting him as a tragic figure of mythic proportions, a messenger who haunts and exposes the failure of refugee politics, singing through sewn lips as he ascends to the afterworld of poets.

So, while protests like Amini's might register as little more than minor disturbances within the public sphere, the restaging and repetition of these acts form part of a critical practice of counter-mapping which creates an unravellable fabric of political resistance within the state and beyond its borders. It is the accumulation of 'small acts' which strains against the invisibility and inaudibility of abject lives within the borders of the British state.

4 | NAKED PROTEST: MATERNAL POLITICS AND THE FEMINIST COMMONS

> We'll go naked. We will do our naked because you people want us to suffer. We're not taking that. Fear will come. (Lucky Ogodo, community activist, Niger Delta, 2005)

> I took my clothes off because they treat us like animals. We are claiming asylum, we're not animals. (Mercy Guobadia, protester, Yarl's Wood Immigration Removal Centre, England, 2008)

> Expose BP. Expose that Drill, Baby, Drill means Spill, Baby, Spill. After all, what's at stake is nothing less than our planet. And that's the naked truth. (Diane Wilson, CodePink co-founder and Texas Gulf shrimper, 2010)

Crane Wing, Yarl's Wood Immigration Removal Centre, England, April 2008

On 10 April 2008, detention officers at Yarl's Wood Immigration Removal Centre moved to deport two detainees, a Burundian mother and her British-born baby. The mother, a refused asylum seeker, took temporary refuge with her baby in a chapel inside the detention centre. In solidarity, a group of fellow African detainees within the removal centre's family unit, which is called Crane Wing, confronted the officers, arguing that the young mother and her baby had not had access to adequate legal representation. During the ensuing altercation a pregnant detainee was forcibly restrained, separated from her six-year-old son and placed in solitary confinement. The following day the Yarl's Wood mothers staged a second protest in a corridor outside a staff office demanding to know what had happened to the women who had been removed. During this gathering several of the mothers proceeded to remove their clothes, some baring their breasts and others stripping to expose their genitals. One of the protesters, Mercy Guobadia, stated in a phone call to an anti-deportation campaigner that this naked protest was a direct response to the inhumane treatment of their children and themselves by the British state: 'I took my clothes off because they treat us like animals. We are claiming asylum, we're not animals' (cited in Dugan 2008). The mothers followed their naked protest with a hunger strike, and released an open letter to the British government, documenting their concerns about the impact of prolonged and indeterminate imprisonment on the health of their children.

As I noted in Chapter 3, there is nothing exceptional about these kinds of migrant protests. Like Abas Amini's protest, this naked protest by fifteen mothers at Yarl's Wood was remarkable only because it became public. It leaked out from inside what Liz Fekete has described as 'the European deportation machine' and was reported in activist and mainstream national and international news media (Fekete 2005). As Mercy Guobadia stated, she and the other mothers took off their clothes as a deliberate (media-oriented) tactic to draw attention to the conditions in which they and their children were being detained. In the context of a Western media gaze, public images of naked and sexualized female bodies are, of course, routine to the point of banality. However, the idea of a group of protesting naked maternal bodies is provocative in the context of long-standing (if now shattered) taboos around the visual representation of pregnant bodies (Tyler 2011b). Even in the absence of actual images of the protest, the sensationalism of the idea of a group of pregnant women and mothers stripped naked before the detention centre guards transformed this small and unexceptional event into a 'newsworthy' story.

Naked protest, long used as a means of generating public dissent through political spectacle, 'went global' in the last decade. As Isaac Souweine argues:

> From anarchists and activists to soccer moms and sex workers, nudity has become a familiar term within the broadly progressive political vocabulary. In sheer numbers, the re-emergence of naked protest is dominated by Western women, many of them protesting US militarism in Iraq by spelling out anti-war slogans with their naked bodies. Taken as a whole [...] naked protest crosses race, nationality and gender and includes protestors of almost every stripe. They include anti-globalisation activists of all colours: British men and women protesting fox hunting, South African women protesting slum clearance and Indian women resisting police and army brutality. [...] In an era where modes of public dissent have

experienced a surge in popularity and innovation, naked protest is undoubtedly ascendant. (Souweine 2005: 536)

In the case of the Yarl's Wood naked protest the consequences of their brief moment of media visibility were swingeing for the women involved. Mercy Guobadia, the Nigerian mother who was instrumental in communicating the events unfolding in Yarl's Wood to activists and journalists outside the detention centre, was moved to another detention centre and shortly after deported with her two young children (South Wales Evening Post 2008). At the same time the significance of the protest was diminished in official statements. Serco Limited, the global securities corporation that is contracted by the British government to manage Yarl's Wood, reported that: 'discussions had taken place between residents and staff, but "no significant protest" had occurred' (Dugan 2008). However, the 'failure' of this protest does not diminish its significance as a political parable for our time.

Introduction

This chapter will mobilize the Yarl's Wood protest and a naked protest by mothers in the Niger Delta as a means to think about the significance of maternal protests as acts which trouble the conceptual and theoretical frames through which we apprehend the political agency of disenfranchised populations. Weaving together activist materials, news reports, interviews, documentaries and historical data, I will explore the transnational connections between these protests and the common forms of 'maternal politics' which are mobilized by women in different geopolitical spaces in their resistance to the gendered architectures of expropriation effected by neoliberalism.

This chapter contributes to a growing body of feminist scholarship on gender, migration and citizenship and the critical focus in this literature on the role of native mothers in securing 'the reproduction of the nation' and the identification of migrant mothers as a target of border-control mechanisms (Yuval-Davis and Anthias 1989; Yuval-Davis 1996, 1997; Lentin 2004; Luibhéid 2006). Developing this work in dialogue with feminist political writing on the commons (Federici 2011), I will make two central claims. First, that the rich, transnational seam of maternal politics illustrated through these protests challenges the 'catastrophic functionalism' of both Kristevan accounts of the maternal abject and Agamben-inspired accounts of 'bare life' and offers an alternative lens through which to perceive the political claims of disenfranchised women (Papadopoulos et al. 2008). Secondly, that through their invocation of 'natality' these mothers introduce a vital 'tension about value and most particularly the value of life itself' (Khanna 2009: 195) that destabilizes Eurocentric and masculinist understandings of sovereignty and is redolent of what I will term a 'maternal commons' (Tyler and Baraitser forthcoming).

The securitization of reproduction

In *Means without End: Notes on Politics* (2000), Agamben argues that the modern nation-state was until recently a state that imagined nativity or birth as the foundation of its sovereignty. Within this natural understanding of the relationship between birthplace and citizenship 'the natives' of any given place are understood by virtue of their birth to be rightful natural citizens of a territory. This idea of sovereignty is grounded in a myth that 'generations reproducing within an almost unchanging territory in almost stable relationships for centuries have passed on an unchanging essence' (Buckel and Wissel 2010: 33). In the early twentieth century this myth began to erode as nation-states sought to manage and control their populations more rigorously and intimately (bio-politically) and began passing laws which sought to denaturalize specific populations within the state through the scaling of citizenship (Tyler 2010). Agamben argues that the erosion of the rights of citizenship – 'and the mass statelessness resulting' from this – marks 'a decisive turn in the life of the modern nation-state as well as its definitive emancipation from the naive notions of the citizen and a people' (Agamben 1995).

Famously, he also argues that '[t]he fundamental categorical pair of Western politics is not that of friend/enemy but that of bare life/ political existence, *zoē/bios*, exclusion/inclusion' (Agamben 1998: 12). Bare lives are lives stripped of agency – rightless lives – lives severed from the political community proper. It is the figure of bare or naked life, exemplified by the stateless refugee, who, Agamben states, reveals the true horror of purportedly democratic politics in the global North; hence his argument that totalitarianism is not the opposite of democracy, but rather its other face (ibid.: 13). As I detailed in Chapter 2, children born in Britain to non-citizen mothers are not entitled to British citizenship. These children are the quintessential illustration of the break between nativity and nationality, for they are an indigenous population denied the rights of citizenship. In this respect we could argue that the Yarl's Wood mothers are precisely protesting against the constitution of their stateless children as 'bare lives'.

The trinities of state–nation–territory and citizen–nation–biological kinship which underpin mythic conceptions of sovereignty are central to right-wing political rhetoric about migrant invasions. Migrant women represent a specific threat to nativist ideologies. The figure of the 'reproductive migrant' who threatens to populate 'our country' with 'foreign children' incites nativism, and proliferates fears about both a loss of ancestry and the future of the nation-state itself. As Priscilla Huang argues (writing from the perspective of the USA), 'immigrant women are particularly prone to ideological attacks, as well as punitive welfare and immigration policies, because of their capacity for child-bearing [...] immigrant women's bodies have become the economic, demographic, and political battleground for America's future' (Huang 2008: 398). The bodies of non-citizen pregnant women and mothers have become 'particularly powerful loci through which the state both extends and legitimizes its exclusionary immigration practices' (Luibhéid 2006: 74). Indeed, the specific forms of subjugation experienced by migrant mothers reveal how the bodies of pregnant women, mothers and children have been transformed into corporeal border zones. It is also remarkable that while 'birth' is central to the 'crises of sovereignty' which Agamben and many other political theorists have described, surprisingly little work has engaged critically with the sexual politics of the 'state of exception'. In particular, there is a lack of theoretical engagement with the relationship between the securitization of migration and the securitization of reproduction, which makes Lentin's work in this area all the more important (Lentin 2011; see also Russell 2011). I will return to the theoretical implications of this failure shortly. First I want to offer some examples of the securitization of reproduction of migrants' lives within and at the borders of the British state.

Policy

In 2007, the British government's Border Agency published *Enforcing the Rules: A strategy to ensure and enforce compliance with our immigration laws*, a report which identified a series of 'new threats' to Britain's borders and issued guidance to border officials on safeguarding against these threats (Home Office 2007). One of these threats was named as 'the health tourist', a figure that hadn't previously appeared in immigration policy documents and a reference, it was revealed, mainly to 'heavily pregnant women'. As the report notes:

> There is evidence of small-scale but very deliberate abuse of the NHS. For example, a sampling exercise last year at one airport suggested that health tourists were being detected at the rate of about 15 per month. This primarily involved heavily pregnant women arriving in the UK with an intention of using NHS maternity services. (Ibid.: 14)

In 2008, in a series of questions filed under the British Freedom of Information Act (2000), the Home Office was asked for clarification of these 'facts' and was forced to admit they had no evidence for these claims. It even admitted that there had been no 'sampling exercise' at an airport. This evidence had nevertheless shaped the new policies for how foreign women should be vetted for entry to the UK.

> In the case of a female passenger where the Immigration Officer has suspicions from her appearance, that she may be pregnant, the passenger will be asked if she is expecting a child and what her plans are for the birth. If the passenger claims not to be pregnant then the Immigration Officer may refer her to the port medical inspector, who will then examine the passenger and determine the approximate gestation of the pregnancy, if any. If the gestation of the pregnancy suggests that the passenger will be giving birth within the previously claimed period of stay [...] then she may be refused leave to enter. (Home Office 2008)

These extraordinary 'handling guidelines' reveal that suspected pregnancy is managed in much the same way as drugs or weapon smuggling. Women are subjected to body searches to ascertain whether or not they are attempting to 'smuggle' unborn foreign nationals into Britain.

Media stigmatization

From Singapore to New Zealand, this imagined explosion of 'birth tourism' has become a central feature of the mediation of an immigration invasion complex, as politicians have sought to stoke popular opposition to *jus soli* provisions, seeking legitimacy for abjectifying policies, and attempting to convince citizen-publics to stomach the destitution, detention and deportation of migrant women and their children. Luibhéid has detailed the ways in which the Irish government incited support for the abolition of the *jus soli* principle (see the Irish Nationality and Citizenship Act 2004) through a concerted press campaign in which migrant women where depicted as 'childbearing against the state' (Luibhéid 2004). In Britain, news media 'hysteria' about birth tourism generates acute fears about the erosion of the welfare state. A 2006 *Daily Mail* article entitled 'NHS health tourism is rife but I can't turn sick patients away' draws on the 'evidence' of leading gynaecologist and media personality Professor Lesley Regan:

> Professor Lesley Regan told how heavily pregnant women are coming to the UK on 'shopping trips' then giving birth here. Many end up at her London hospital, she said, and she simply cannot turn them away. [...] She said: 'Someone will be 38 weeks pregnant and come here on a "shopping trip" – ooh look, suddenly she's in labour'. By the time the registrar has worked out whether or not they should be paying for the service they have gone. 'It makes me angry because if I went to Ghana or somewhere I wouldn't even be given a free cup of coffee.' (Wheldon 2006)

'Maternity tourism', 'citizenship tourism', 'anchor babies', 'passport babies': this hysteria of naming intensifies beliefs about the 'uncontrollable and debilitating "invasion" of migrants' (De Genova 2007: 434) and congeals in the figure of *the conniving reproductive migrant* intent on perverting citizenship and nationality norms (Lentin 2004: 301). It is difficult to imagine a more naked borderline state than the act of giving birth. Yet increasingly birth is associated not only with the breaching of bodily borders but with the invasion of territorial borders. Migrant mothers pose a terroristic threat, as illustrated by an Irish newspaper headline, 'State alert as pregnant asylum seekers aim for Ireland' (cited in Luibhéid 2004: 339).

Experience

The explosion of public discourses about health tourism and news headlines about soaring birth rates among migrant women has had a devastating impact on irregular and undocumented migrant mothers 'on the ground', whose rights of access to medical and welfare assistance have been severely curtailed since the mid-1990s. In 2010, in a report entitled *The Mothers in Exile Project: Women asylum seekers' and refugees' experiences of pregnancy and childbirth in Leeds*, Megan Waugh presents a vivid picture of the lives of mothers caught in the asylum process, focusing on how for 'refused asylum seekers who are destitute [...] access to healthcare is reduced as their vulnerability and need for healthcare increases' (Waugh 2010: 8).[1] Irregular migrant mothers are reluctant to approach health service providers for fear they might be captured by border control officials and/or separated from their children. The majority of women had been dispersed from other parts of the country. Many spent their pregnancy living in hostels, emergency or shared accommodation and would be moved at short notice either when their status changed or when their housing provider lost a contract with the Home Office. Waugh gives examples of a woman evicted from her home while she was in hospital giving birth and another who described being pressurized into sex by a housing support officer in return for preferential treatment. All of the women she interviewed described experiences of appalling living conditions and some shared experiences of bringing newborn babies back to cramped bedsits, filthy unheated rooms crawling with cockroaches, mice and rats (ibid.: 19). One interviewee described how she had been forced to live on the streets for a month with a ten-year-old child while she was six months pregnant: 'You just have to sit in the street – there are a lot of women like this. Who have no support, some who are pregnant, some with children – who have nothing' (ibid.: 19). Other women described being taken into detention with their babies after dawn raids, and spending several months imprisoned.

Against abjection

It is possible to interpret the securitization of reproduction I have detailed so far in this chapter as a gendered effect of the crisis which Agamben describes: a crisis in which the 'species life' of the 'native' nation-state is imagined as under threat from the reproductive force of foreigners and as a consequence migrant women become the target of specific technologies of surveillance and border control. What it is more difficult to theorize is how the particular 'states of exception' in which these migrant mothers are caught relate to long-standing feminist understandings of the maternal as abject. It is tempting to say that these women are 'doubly abject' as maternal bodies and as bare life. I think, however, there is something else to be learnt here about the interrelationship between sexual politics, sovereignty and capitalism.

In 'Against abjection' (Tyler 2009a) I questioned the limits of Kristeva's conceptualization of the maternal as abject and warned against the celebration of this account in Anglo-American feminist theoretical work. I will briefly summarize my argument here. Within Kristeva's writing the maternal has an oblique status as the submerged matrix of symbolic and social life. The maternal is conceived as the border which guarantees all other borders, such as those between social and psychic life, private and public life (see Tyler 2000, 2001; Baraitser 2009). In this psychoanalytic 'origin story' matricide is the unconditional condition of life itself: 'For man and for woman the loss of the mother is a biological and psychic necessity, the first step on the way to autonomy. Matricide is our vital necessity, the sine qua non condition of our individuation' (Kristeva 1989: 38).

Kristeva's psychoanalytic account of the subject's disavowal (abjection) of maternal origin relies upon her crafting of a deeply ambiguous conceptual status for the maternal which is founded in a distinction between the maternal as abstract thing and the maternal as lived and embodied modes of being. However, the maternal abject (and the matricide it assumes) is not a prehistoric, unchangeable fact but is a disciplinary norm that has been established through processes of reiteration and has taken on the appearance of a universal truth. As Young notes, 'the association between groups and abject matter is socially constructed; once the link is made, however, the theory of abjection describes how these associations lock into the subject's identities and anxieties' (Young 1990: 145).The appearance of the maternal as abject shapes the perception of maternal bodies and the experience of maternal subjects in the social world: it abjectifies women (Tyler 2009a). Indeed, the break Kristeva posits between the maternal and maternal subjectivities enacts a classificatory violence which is lived (by all women) and is one which feminist politics must refuse by taking theory at its word.

Federici's work on the prehistory of capitalism offers us another route through which to examine why maternal bodies have historically been constituted as abject (Federici 2004). Federici draws our attention to Foucault's theory of bio-power, which is grounded in the idea that a break occurred in Europe (in the seventeenth to eighteenth centuries) between forms of governance which centred on the right of sovereign power to kill, and forms of governance that focused on 'the administration and promotion of life-forces such as population growth' (ibid.: 16). As Federici suggests, while Foucault offers ample evidence for this shift, he fails to account for why it occurred. She argues that 'If we place this shift in the context of the rise of capitalism [...] the promotion of life-forces turns out to be nothing more than the result of a new concern with the accumulation and reproduction of labor-power' (ibid.: 16). This was a historical context in which 'an almost fanatical desire to increase populations prevailed' and a new concept of human beings as 'raw materials' for industrial capitalism emerged (Heckscher, cited in ibid.: 88). If industrial capitalism needed to manage and control the supply of labour, then women's social role as the producers and reproducers of labour power (people) made them (along with the colonized peoples of the empire) the specific targets for the institution of the bio-political regimes of control that Foucault describes.

The shift to bio-political forms of governance required by capitalism inaugurated the mass securitization of reproduction: a process that Federici describes as 'primitive accumulation'. As she writes, 'in a system where life is subordinated to the production of profit, the accumulation of labor-power can only be achieved with maximum violence' (ibid.: 16). In her account of this process, Federici details the war that was waged against women which 'aimed at breaking the control they had exercised over their bodies and reproduction' (ibid.: 88). This war was effected by campaigns of fear and terror (epitomized by the European witch-hunts) and the legal imposition of penalties against contraception, abortion and infanticide (which became a capital crime). Extraordinary surveillance measures were put in place to monitor and control reproductive practices. Unmarried mothers became subject to extreme forms of stigmatization and had destitution forced upon them. In France (from 1556) women were required to register every pregnancy, and if the death of an infant resulted from a concealed pregnancy the mother would be killed (ibid.: 88). Indeed, more women were executed for infanticide in sixteenth- and seventeenth-century Europe than for any other offence (ibid.: 88).[2] As Federici concludes, 'while in the middle ages women had been able to use various forms of contraceptives, and had exercised an undisputed control over the birthing process, from now on their wombs became public territory, controlled by men and the state, and procreation was directly placed at the service of capitalist accumulation' (ibid.: 89). Industrial capitalism developed a statist institutional apparatus (the patriarchal family, the medicalization of childbirth, the redrawing of public/private spheres) through which the reproduction of labour power could be more effectively managed and controlled.

Federici highlights the ways in which the transition to industrial capitalism in Europe was dependent upon the statist patriarchal control of women's bodies and the colonial marketization of labour power in the Atlantic slave trade. What her analysis suggests is that Kristeva's 'abject maternal' describes a specific bio-political shift in the European history of women's relationship to reproduction which was effected by capitalism. Read from this perspective, one of the many and considerable problems with Kristeva's theoretical horror story is that it mystifies the historical, economic and political forces that required the alienation of women from reproductive labour as a means of more effectively managing population control.

We can draw a useful parallel here between the maternal abject and Agamben's (1998) account of bare life. Agamben draws on Bataille to argue that the contemporary juridical-political order has 'the structure of an inclusion of what is simultaneously pushed outside' (ibid.: 18). Sovereignty is effected by the interiorization and confinement of those whom it abjects as waste populations: 'There is politics because man is the living being who, in language, separates and opposes himself to his own bare life and, at the same time, maintains himself in relation to that bare life in an inclusive exclusion' (ibid.: 8).

Similarly for Kristeva the authority of symbolic law is derived from the disavowal of maternal origins and the assumption by 'the father' of power over life and death. Both bare life and the abject maternal thus describe 'the hidden foundation on which the entire political system' rests (ibid.: 12). This 'hidden foundation' operates simultaneously at the level of the subject and the state, securing individual and national identity but in doing so makes us 'strangers to ourselves'. For both Kristeva and Agamben this inclusive exclusion effects a 'constant need to redefine the threshold in life that distinguishes and separates what is inside from what is outside [...] a line that must be constantly redrawn' (ibid.: 77). What is clear is that in spite of the seemingly very different theoretical terrain in which they work, the same Bataillean logic underpins their writing. Namely that sovereignty is constituted through an abjection which returns to haunt us in the form of the stranger within oneself and within the nation-state.

While Kristeva concerns herself with abject mothers and foreigners,

Agamben suggests that it is the refugee who is the figure of bare life par excellence in our time. Radically excluded, the stateless refugee exposes 'the very codes of political power', revealing the fascistic heart of the liberal democratic state (Agamben 1995: 5). However, the theoretical solutions both of these thinkers offer to the horrors of modern nationalism is fundamentally the same, that we must acknowledge our own alterity. As Agamben writes, it is only when 'the citizen will have learned to acknowledge the refugee that he himself is, that man's political survival today is imaginable' (ibid.). What are omitted through this gesture are the attempts by those who are disqualified from being (political) subjects to represent themselves from the perspective of their own experience. Abject bare life becomes a figurative mirror for the sovereign subject's own disavowed exclusion/displacement.

Naked but alive

Legal scholar Stephanie Silverman argues that an 'understanding of refugees as apolitical actors' devoid of agency predominates within legal, charitable and academic discourses about asylum and immigration (Silverman 2008: 1). When we read reports such as Waugh's, it is easy to see why and how the representational frames of victimhood predominate within sympathetic counter-political representations of refugees. There are enormous pressures on asylum advocacy organizations to produce testimonial accounts which will 'shock' the system into policy change. Furthermore, destitute migrant mothers do undoubtedly experience their situation as abject. However, while the emergence of asylum as an abjectifying technology of governance has constituted populations without formal rights and protections, it would be a mistake 'to assume that all we are left with is a wasteland of abject subjectivities, discarded and jettisoned from political life' (Nyers 2004: 207). On the contrary, 'with each act of desubjectification comes another attempt of resubjectification by both the state and political subjects themselves' (ibid.: 207). In this regard, through sharing their stories with Waugh, the mothers in Leeds are not only allowing their plight to be known, but are working with Waugh to protest their degradation. Similarly, through their naked protest the Yarl's Wood mothers communicated to their children, family, friends, activist allies, the detention centre guards, the British public, the British government and the international news media the fact that they were *naked but alive*.

Drawing on interviews with Australian immigration detainees, Richard Bailey (2009) details how for the Australian immigration detainees he interviewed, protest was a central means of drawing themselves out of the long depressive periods during which they sank into a state that one detainee described as 'walking death'. Similarly, one of the Yarl's Wood protesters, 'Jane', described to me how participation in the naked protest had brought her 'back to life':

> I was nothing ... dead inside. Then [when the protest began] I went a bit crazy [laughs] ... I was shaking all over [demonstrates this shaking by holding her hands out to me], and I was really crying for my kids and for the others [in detention] ... some women pulled their shirts up and some even their skirts ... that African curse ... do you know it? I was even shouting, maybe my English was not very good but I was so angry [laughs] it is funny. (Interview with Tyler, 2009)

Jane's account of being 'living dead' is a common theme of interviews with detainees in a range of national and border contexts. It also recalls what Fanon describes as the depersonalization of colonized subjects, consigned to 'a zone of non-being' (Fanon 2008: 2). It is significant that protests are recalled by immigration detainees as moments when they feel themselves come alive. In my interview with her, Jane not only describes but enacts her reanimation in the protest, recalling her shaking body, showing me how she shook, and impersonating in the interview the sound of her own 'protest voice' crying and shouting.

Jenny Edkins and Véronique Pin-Fat argue that the use of the body in protests by asylum seekers can be interpreted as 'the assumption of bare life, that is, the taking up of one of the very forms of life that sovereign power seeks to impose' (Edkins and Pin-Fat 2005: 3; Darling 2009). Edkins goes farther in claiming that 'The ultimate protest against sovereign power's production of its subjects as "bare life" is the unconditional acceptance of that designation. Protests as "bare life" are the effective contestation of sovereign power' (Edkins 2001). Within this interpretative frame, stripping before the detention centre guards might be understood as 'an occupation' by the mothers of their bestowed status as speechless bare life.

However, the mothers in Yarl's Wood organized their protest autonomously, phoning activists and journalists and releasing a public letter and statements to the press. They were engaged in *doing* politics and, in so doing, transformed the abject zone of the detention centre into a highly charged space of resistance. The mothers in Yarl's Wood are not the speechless emissaries of a private and incommunicable dehumanization but come together as a community they call 'Family Unite from Crane' in order to stake a claim for their status, and for their children, as *political prisoners*. The Yarl's Wood protesters stripped naked in a deliberate impersonation of their dehumanization in order to refute it. Impersonation is a knowing performance: 'I took my clothes off because they treat us like animals. We are claiming asylum, we're not animals' (cited in Dugan 2008). Through this performance they reveal the fabricated and contingent structure of bare life itself, a status which is a consequence not of any essential quality of being, or indeed of any act or crime, but is a consequence of the statist classification of them and their children as 'illegal' life (see Chapter 3). Through their impersonation of bare life the Yarl's Wood protesters signal their refusal of their (and their children's) designation as disposable human waste, engendering a defiant agentic maternal subjectivity against bare life.

Infinitely clothed

In order to understand better the decolonizing sexual politics of this naked drag act, it is useful to consider writer and activist Mahasveta Devi's celebrated short story 'Draupadi' (in Spivak 1981), about a Santal tribal woman who is captured and punished by the Indian army for her role in peasant uprisings in Bengal. The immediate historical context for this story is the insurgencies and subsequent violent subjugation of landless peasants in West Bengal in 1972 by the Indian army, but its meaning is also shaped by the infamous Santal Rebellion against British colonization in the mid-nineteenth century. In the ancient myth of Draupadi, a celebrated heroine of the Indian epic *Mahabharata*, an enemy king attempts to defrock and shame Draupadi in front of his court. She diligently prays to Krishna and when he pulls at her sari it unravels, but further and further layers are extended since 'Draupadi is infinitely clothed and cannot be publicly stripped' (ibid.: 387). Devi reworks this epic scene into a political parable with which to document the central role of indigenous women in the fight against the enclosure and appropriation of their land. There is no divine intervention in Devi's restaging of the tale. Rather she reverses the story; Draupadi is captured, stripped naked and raped repeatedly by Indian soldiers at the behest of the army officer and state terrorism expert Senanayak. After the rape, she is brought before Senanayak but refuses to put on her clothes, stating, 'You can strip me, but how can you clothe me again? Are you a man? [...] There isn't a man here that I should be ashamed. I will not let you put my cloth on me. What more can you do? Come on, counter me – come on, counter me?' (Devi in ibid.: 402). Drawing on Spivak's interpretation of this story, Deepti Misri writes:

> By refusing the disciplining power of shame scripted into the act of rape, Draupadi becomes [...] a 'terrifying superobject' [...].
> At the end of the story it is Senanayak, the army officer who has sanctioned her rape, who stands before the naked Draupadi – 'an unarmed target' – in a state of terrified paralysis usually associated with the victim. (Misri 2011: 603)

As Spivak argues, Devi's Draupadi remains 'publicly naked at her own insistence [...] the story insists that this is the place where male leadership stops' (Spivak 1981: 388). The detained mothers in Yarl's Wood stage their naked maternal bodies as a political response to their constitution as abject (as reproductive subjects and as refugees). Like Devi's Draupadi, the Yarl's Wood mothers are naked at their own insistence: 'You can strip me, but how can you clothe me again? [...] What more can you do? Come on, counter me – come on, counter me?' (in ibid.: 402).

Sitting on a man

While naked protests have 'gone global', I want to further explore the colonial and maternal genealogy of 'the naked curse'. As anthropologist and political activist Terisa Turner details, in an African context the threat of the exposure of the naked mother's body carries an ancient, powerful symbolism.

> [T]he [naked] curse is invoked only under the most extreme of circumstances. Before it is even threatened, women usually take a formal vow to honour the enormity of its symbolism. We all come into the world through the vagina. By exposing the vagina, the women are saying: 'We are hereby taking back the life we gave you' [...] It'[s] about bringing forth life and denying life through social ostracism, which is a kind of social execution. Men who are exposed are viewed as dead (cited in Ekine 2008)

This form of protest, also known as 'sitting on a man', also includes public ridicule of powerful men through collective acts of singing and dancing, as well as the feared act of naked protest. The baring of the naked maternal body is a shaming act, a staged incivility. Turner suggests that 'sitting on a man' is often one of few routes available to African mothers to wrest back agency and a collective political voice in situations of extreme subjugation (cited in Ekine 2009). If the naked protest of mothers incarcerated at Yarl's Wood was imagined through the frame of Western news media as a sensational and/or sexualized act of protest, through this African perceptual frame the naked protest invokes the more terrifying power of Devi's Draupadi, a specifically maternal power which threatens to render that objectifying (male) gaze impotent.

In a study of Igbo women in the Delta region, anthropologist Judith van Allan (1972) argues that we need to be attentive to the ways in which received understandings of the boundaries between public and private spheres are always already an effect of historical, colonial, economic and sexual relations of power. British colonialism ushered in forms of gender politics which undermined much of Igbo women's traditional power and autonomy. Imperialism impacted on women's access to high-status social roles in public life, and, perhaps more significantly, eroded the Igbo maternal public sphere, a sphere composed of women's autonomous political institutions and spaces (women-only meetings, the marketplace and kinship networks), women's economic independence, and the rights of women, as a group, 'to use strikes, boycotts and force' to affect decision-making (ibid.: 165). When the African mothers in Yarl's Wood Immigration Removal Centre protest against the statist and corporate forms of power which constituted them as human waste they invoke this longer African history of maternal politics and resistance.

It was a chance remark in my interview with Jane (see above), one of the Yarl's Wood protesters, that led me to trace the historical roots of naked protest to West Africa. In what follows I want to examine the connections between the naked protest in Yarl's Wood and a naked protest by indigenous mothers against global corporate oil companies in the Niger Delta in 2003. I don't intend this as a comparative account. Rather, by taking 'naked protest' as a trope, and by restaging these protests together in the space of this chapter, my aim is to make tangible the existing relationship between these geopolitical sites: the common neocolonial economic logic which underpins them. This logic, albeit in different ways, constitutes these two populations of African mothers as disposable, a 'disposability' which their respective naked protests refuse (Khanna 2009). The citationality of the naked curse reminds us that neoliberal struggles over citizenship are reconfigurations of what Federici describes in her account of 'primitive accumulation': colonial, capitalist and patriarchal modes of expropriation and enclosure. The environmental degradation, confiscation of land and wealth, and forced migration of the colonial period continue unabated, with siphoned wealth and disenfranchised peoples following the same centuries-old routes to the imperial centres of capital (Ifekwunigwe 2004).

July 2002, Escravos Oil Facility, Niger Delta

On 8 July 2002, hundreds of unarmed mothers and grandmothers descended, singing and dancing, on the largest oil-producing facility in the Niger Delta, Escravos Oil Facility, owned by Chevron. This highly organized group of women took control of the facility by threatening to strip naked in front of the male workers. Helen Odeworitse, a representative for the protesters during the ten-day siege, stated that 'our weapon is our nakedness' (cited in BBC News 2002). Mobilizing the threat of the naked curse, the women held the international workforce of 700 men in a state of lockdown, halting the production of half a million tons of oil a day. As Sokari Ekine, the International Coordinator of the Niger Delta Women, notes:

> The stripping off of clothes particularly by married and elderly women is a way of shaming men – some of whom believe that if they see the naked bodies they will go mad or suffer some great harm. The curse extends not just to local men but also to any foreigner who it is believed would become impotent at the sight of 'the naked mother'. (Ekine 2008)

Naked protest is not undertaken lightly. As one of the managers of the Escravos oil depot explained, 'it is a taboo in our land for mothers to say that they will go naked. It means every [other] means of protest has failed' (cited in Schermerhorn 2010).

The Niger Delta has long been an area of intensive and long-standing 'colonial resource extraction'. Indeed, Escravos is a Portuguese word for slave. In the nineteenth century, when a number of

European states and corporations juggled for control of the region, it was nicknamed 'the Oil Rivers' owing to its economic importance in the production of palm oil. This was the oil that lubricated the machines and engines of the Industrial Revolution in the global North. In 1884 the British government granted the British National Africa Company (an amalgam of British commercial interests which was latterly renamed the Royal Niger Company) monopoly control over trading in the area. In the early twentieth century the British government instigated more direct forms of imperial government in the region, violently subjugating indigenous populations and imposing the ideological and geopolitical structures which laid the ground for what would become the nation-state of Nigeria. In the 1950s massive reserves of crude oil and natural gas were discovered in the Delta, and an international scramble for control of 'the black gold' began (Watts 2008). While Nigeria formally gained independence from Britain in 1960, the earlier mechanisms of imperial governance instigated through the chartering of European companies to control resource extraction in the Delta region were ostensibly reconfigured in the form of a collaboration between the Nigerian government and global oil conglomerates. This relationship took institutional form as the deeply corrupt state-owned company Nigerian National Petroleum Corporation (NNPC), which was established in 1977 in partnership with European and North American-owned oil companies. Its main corporate partners to date have been Royal Dutch Shell, Chevron, ExxonMobil, Agip, Total SA and the various predecessors and successors of these super-major energy companies. For many decades, these companies have systematically polluted the land and water in the region.

Protests by indigenous groups have been brutally suppressed by the Nigerian state with ongoing programmes of mass beatings, executions and rapes in the region by the Nigerian army and state-funded paramilitary groups (Ekine 2000).[3] While the indigenous peoples in this area are legally and formally citizens of Nigeria, any substantive rights of citizenship have been eroded by global oil corporations working in cooperation with the Nigerian state, which have militarized the region to maximize the extraction and flow of crude oil. In 2010, for example, WikiLeaks published cables in which Shell officials boast to the US government that they have infiltrated every department of the Nigerian government and have influence over state decision-making

The Naked Option: a last resort

We'll go naked.

You Tube

4.1 Still from *The Naked Option: A Last Resort* (dir. Candace Schermerhorn)

in the Delta region (Smith 2010). In was in the face of this appalling history of colonial, state and corporate violence and corruption that indigenous woman protesters deployed the naked curse en masse, demanding compensation, clean water, electricity, jobs and social investment. Anino Olowu, a protester who led a negotiating team on behalf of the naked protesters at Escravos, insisted that meetings with Chevron management took place in a village in the shadow of the oil facility, so that the company representatives were forced to confront the enormity of the environmental conditions facing local people. As Olowu noted in a newspaper interview at the time, 'I don't know how [Chevron] can allow other human beings to live like this. Why do they treat us like animals?' (cited in Doran 2002). Over the following months, thousands of women employed the threat of the naked curse to occupy eight oil facilities in the Delta region. As protester Lucky Ogodo expressed it, 'We'll go naked. We will do our naked because you people want us to suffer. We're not taking that. Fear will come' (Figure 4.1).

Common roots

We are all born. Working against a long philosophical tradition that has given primacy to the shared horizon of death, in 1958 Arendt stated that 'Natality and not mortality may be the central category of political thought' (Arendt 1958: 9). Arendt's insistence on positing natality as the basis for politics is radical in the context of a European tradition so overwhelmingly preoccupied with death, loss, terror and mourning. However, for Arendt, natal politics bears no relation to childbirth and the reproductive sphere. The labours of women (social reproduction) are for Arendt hidden within the private realm of the household, while of course being absolutely foundational to and sustaining the public sphere. As for Kristeva, so for Arendt – birth is imagined as an experience 'beyond speech', which is 'antipolitical by definition' (ibid.: 63). For both these European thinkers the public sphere depends on the fact that 'man does not know where he comes from' (ibid.: 63).[4] If we read against Kristeva and Arendt and literalize natality we can see why a revolting maternal body politic has a particular capacity to unveil the deadly logic and radical inequalities of sovereignty. As Joanna Long (2006) argues, the pregnant woman or mother is a figure who fundamentally troubles Agamben's thesis of bare life (ibid.).[5]

Through the baring of their naked maternal bodies the mothers at Yarl's Wood and in the Niger Delta insist that maternal origin is acknowledged and in so doing refuse their constitution as wasted humans. These protests also recall other maternal fronts: the struggles of indigenous mothers in north-east India, and the protests of mothers for 'the disappeared' across South America in the 1970s and 1980s (see Das 2008). As Samir Kumar Das writes: 'the politics that secretes out of the metaphor of motherhood turns pure motherhood, as it were, on its head. It disentangles motherhood from any given mother–child relationship and thereby decontextualizes itself. Every woman is a mother – potential or real – and there is a mother in every woman' (ibid.: 63).

These mothers enact political solidarity beyond the bonds of citizenship or statist politics, forms of solidarity that are grounded in what Ifi Amadiume describes as 'umunne or the spirit of shared motherhood' (Amadiume 1987: 56). Amadiume argues that this 'matrifocality' poses a fundamental challenge, an epistemic challenge, to Eurocentric theoretical accounts of sovereignty (ibid.; Amadiume 2000). From this post-colonial perspective we might understand the birth of networks of women activists in the Delta and beyond as the emergence of new forms of maternal publics. By contrast, a maternal commons that is read through a Eurocentric epistemological frame would be unimaginable.

Conclusion: 'expose the naked truth'

During 2002, in the lead-up to the invasion of Iraq by US and British forces, a new feminist network emerged in the USA. Naming themselves CodePink as a response to the US government's colour-coding of security levels, their aim was to 'wage peace': 'to end U.S. funded wars and occupations, to challenge militarism globally, and to redirect our resources into health care, education, green jobs and other life-affirming activities' (CodePink 2002). They call for women to 'wage peace' against the 'war on terror':

> We call on women around the world to rise up and oppose the war in Iraq. We call on mothers, grandmothers, sisters and daughters, on workers, students, teachers, healers, artists, writers, singers, poets, and every ordinary outraged woman willing to be outrageous for peace. Women have been the guardians of life – not because we are better or purer or more innately nurturing than men, but because the men have busied themselves making war. (Ibid.)

On 24 May 2010, after the massive oil spill in the gulf, Code-Pink undertook a naked protest against the global oil conglomerate BP. Calling their action 'expose the naked truth', sixty-one-year-old grandmother and CodePink co-founder Diane Wilson stated, 'If the Nigerian women could use their bodies on the Niger Delta, why can't we do it in downtown Houston?' CodePink has since blossomed into an organization with more than eighty chapters throughout North America and was a central force in the US Occupy movement in 2011.

In 2011 Federici called for a 'feminist commons' to respond to the democratic deficits, staggering economic inequalities and laissez-faire violence which are central to the operation of neoliberal globalism (Federici 2011). By making or threatening to make their birthing bodies naked in public, the women behind the protests I have restaged in this chapter stake a common claim for a life-centred political economy against neoliberalism, an ideology Berlant has described as 'the capitalist destruction of life in the project of making value' (Berlant 2007: 282). Indeed, we might understand these political acts as forms of 'commoning'. They are political parables with which to imagine different kinds of transnational politics: a 'maternal commons' (Tyler and Baraitser forthcoming).

5 | THE BIG SOCIETY: EVICTION AND OCCUPATION

Tinky tinky Tinker whar was you born?
In among the tatties wi' your breeks all torn.
Tinker, oh tinker, cover your face,
You're no' a paid-up member of the human race

Cited in MacColl and Seeger (1964)

Today is the start of a deep and serious reform agenda to take power away from politicians and give it to people. That's because we know instinctively that the state is often too inhuman, monolithic and clumsy to tackle our deepest social problems. We know that the best ideas come from the ground up, not the top down. We know that when you give people and communities more power over their lives, more power to come together and work together to make life better – great things happen. (Cameron 2010)

It doesn't matter how quiet, clean or law-abiding you are, if you live in a caravan you are scum in the eyes of most of the British population [...] the memories of countless evictions from my childhood are etched in my mind. (Freeman 2011)

19 October 2011, Dale Farm, Essex, England

As I detailed in the introduction to this book, on 19 October 2011 riot police converged on the largest Gypsy and Traveller site in Europe, Dale Farm in Essex, England, to enable Basildon Borough Council and the notorious private bailiff company Constant and Co. Ltd to carry out the biggest forced eviction of British citizens from their land and homes in living memory (Figure 5.1).

During the eviction the Conservative leader of Basildon Borough Council, Tony Ball, stood at the entrance to the Dale Farm site dressed, like the bailiffs, in a high-visibility jacket, his unruffled speeches to the gathered representatives of the international news media striking a jarring contrast with televised scenes of shocked,

5.1 Riot police at the Dale Farm eviction, October 2011

enraged and weeping residents. A significant number of the viewing public openly tweeted and blogged their hatred for Gypsies and Travellers and their delight at the eviction as it was theatricalized on twenty-four-hour rolling news channels. 'They are filth, scum, thieves. Delinquent paedo wife beating inbreds [sic]. Get them out of this country. I hope they immolate themselves,' wrote one troller on the Dale Farm Solidarity website set up by activists in support of the residents of Dale Farm. As Gypsy Council representative Jo Cowley observed, 'There is this feeling that after Dale Farm, nothing will ever be the same again [...] There is terror in the community, I hear it every day, particularly on those sites that have got temporary planning permission – they just feels like the clock is ticking' (cited in Topping 2011).

Dale Farm: background

It is important to remember that in the case of Dale Farm no criminal laws had been breached by the Travellers; this was a civil planning dispute. Basildon Borough Council contended that approximately half of the Irish Travellers on the Dale Farm site had contravened planning laws by establishing caravans, chalets and mobile-home dwellings on land designated as green belt but which, for many decades, had actually been in use as a scrapyard. In fact, Basildon Borough Council had not only made frequent use of this scrapyard historically, but, according to its former owner, had also contributed to its development by laying down hardcore and concrete over several years (Dale Farm Solidarity 2012; Figure 5.2). The other half of the Dale Farm site, which was designated a brown-field site in planning terms, had been legally inhabited by Gypsies and Travellers since the 1960s. The Travellers on the *illegal* half of the site had applied for retrospective planning permission to stay at Dale Farm several times over the previous decade but had repeatedly been refused on the grounds of the 'alleged harm that may be caused to the Green Belt by the presence of mobile-homes' (Puxon 2010). Indeed, many of these evictees had arrived at Dale Farm in the early 2000s as a consequence of failed planning applications and resulting enforcement actions and evictions against them elsewhere in the south of England. Notable evictions had included those in Woodside in Bedfordshire in 2003, Meadowlands in Essex in 2004, Twin Oaks Caravan Park in Hertfordshire in 2004 and Hovefields in Essex in 2005 (UK Delegation to the European Roma and Travellers 2005). All of these other recent forced evictions were also carried out by the bailiff firm Constant and Co., which specializes

5.2 'If not on a scrap-yard then where?' Dale Farm 2011

in clearing Gypsies and Travellers from their land, profiting from the endless cycle of eviction and occupation.[1]

The forced eviction of people from their homes is recognized as a violent, disturbing and damaging practice. As the Romanian social scientist Michael Cernea has detailed, it impoverishes people in several ways, often resulting in landlessness, joblessness, homelessness, marginalization, health risks including trauma and increased morbidity, loss of access to services and social disarticulation (Cernea 2000). In the case of Dale Farm, people lost homes and access to land in which they had invested a considerable amount of their time, labour and income. They will receive no compensation for damage wreaked by the eviction and, on the contrary, the council will attempt to claim the land legally owned by the evictees, to offset some of the costs of the eviction. The community the residents of Dale Farm had established over a decade had provided filial networks of friendship, care and protection that have been torn asunder. They have lost, or risk losing, stable access to state education and established welfare support systems. The evictees have also been considerably traumatized, the impact of which, both in terms of mental and physical health and also in terms of their faith and trust in the state and state actors, is difficult to measure or comprehend. Many of those evicted from the illegal half of Dale Farm on 19 October 2011 moved what vehicles and caravans they could on to their neighbours' legal plots, but are now threatened with a new wave of evictions for overcrowding the legal half of the site. The other families are, as I write eight months after the eviction, camping in the private road (which is also owned by the Travellers) that leads to the sites of their former homes, without access to mains electricity or running water. As Elly Robson writes, 'It is an unreported refugee camp, just thirty minutes away from London' (Robson 2012). The entire community has been left in a degraded state of perpetual insecurity.

Several international human rights covenants, to which Britain is a signatory, set out the requirements of states to abstain from, and protect against, the forced eviction of people from their homes and land. For example, in 1997, the International Covenant on Economic, Social and Cultural Rights, a multilateral treaty adopted by the United Nations General Assembly, detailed specific covenants vis-à-vis the issue of forced evictions, which include the following statement: 'instances of forced eviction are prima facie incompatible with the requirements of the Covenant and can only be justified in the most exceptional circumstances, and in accordance with the relevant principles of international law' (United Nations 1997a). Not only are signatories legally obligated to ensure that evictions occur only in exceptional circumstances, but they are required to ensure that all alternatives to eviction have been fully explored with the participation of the communities in question. 'Evictions', a further paragraph details, 'should not result in individuals being rendered homeless or vulnerable to the violation of other human rights. Where those affected are unable to provide for themselves, the State party must take all appropriate measures, to the maximum of its available resources, to ensure that adequate alternative housing, resettlement or access to productive land, as the case may be, is available' (United Nations 1997b). While Basildon Council received the permission of the British courts to go ahead with this forced eviction under planning laws, the manner in which they carried out the eviction, and the question of whether they and the government pursued and exhausted all alternatives and offered suitable alternative accommodation to the Travellers, continues to be contested in relation to international law.

As I write, it is estimated that Basildon Borough Council have to date spent £9 million pounds on their eviction of approximately five hundred people (including around eighty-six families and about one hundred children) from this six-acre plot of land. Tony Ball staked his political career on the eviction, promising to stand down if it failed. At the same time, in the face of calls to the British government from a number of national and international human rights organizations including the United Nations and Amnesty International, for the suspension of the eviction, Prime Minster David Cameron personally intervened to ensure that Basildon had access to the additional funding they required to proceed with the action. The government committed £4.65 million of public funds from the Home Office and £1.2 million from the Department for Communities and Local Government towards the total cost of the eviction, which Basildon Council estimated may be as much as £18 million. This would amount to an estimated eviction cost of approximately £117,000 per Traveller family, or £36,000 per woman, man and child. Given that the eviction process is still ongoing, with a second round of evictions likely to begin at any time, it remains unclear what the final costs to the British public will be.

The flagrant double standards of Basildon Council's actions against Dale Farm were made manifest in the fact that at the same time as its ongoing campaign of terror was being conducted against the Traveller community, it granted planning permission for the building of a dogs' home and two houses on green belt land within a mile of the Dale Farm community (Robson 2012), while in February 2012 it set out plans for the development of 850 new homes on a wildlife haven in an area of Basildon called Dry Street. By contrast, this former scrapyard is not situated – as suggested in its portrayal by the council and much of the news media – in an area of environmental significance, but instead lies very close to the A127, a busy arterial road into London. The Dale Farm site is a short distance from the large Mayflower retail park, which is dominated by a giant Tesco superstore, and lies within an industrial area of Basildon, described by the council as the 'A127 Enterprise Corridor'. This area of Essex is at the epicentre of a regeneration project spearheaded by the quango 'Basildon Renaissance Partnership', which, until recently, was funded by central government. Its slogan is 'Basildon is changing perceptions'.

During the coming year (2012) it is expected that 100 Basildon council workers will lose their jobs owing to a cut in its grant from central government creating a £2.3 million shortfall in funding. Some of these job losses will undoubtedly be a consequence of the enormous expenditure on the Dale Farm eviction. So while local councillors had suggested to residents that they might seize the Travellers' land to defray some of the costs of the eviction, and had indicated it might then be developed into community allotments for the local 'settled' residents (Austin 2011), given the current climate of austerity those who have campaigned for the removal of the 'illegal' Traveller families over many years are unlikely to see this former scrapyard restored to green or 'community' space any time soon. Indeed, it has currently been left by the council in a hazardous condition described by advocates as 'a bombsite' (Craig-Greene 2012) and by Channel Four News reporter Alex Thomson in January 2012 as 'An extraordinary morass of earth walls several feet high – "bunding" in council speak – a rampart earthed up around every one of the fifty or so emptied plots [...] Twisted sharp metal and concrete pokes through the earthen walls' (Thomson 2012). On 13 November 2011, Basildon Council's solicitor allegedly told legal observers at the now bulldozed and ravaged site that her job was to make conditions at

Dale Farm 'unlivable' (cited in Austin 2011) and, as one Traveller resident, Daniel Sheridan, told the BBC, 'this isn't home any more. It is cold and like living in a war zone' (BBC News Essex 2011).

Introduction

In what follows, my intention is to situate the forced eviction of Dale Farm within the broader context of state racism and social abjection. To this end, this chapter tracks some of the heightened stigmatization of Gypsies and Travellers, within news media, political rhetoric, policy and popular culture in the decade leading up to events at Dale Farm. As I will detail, the public consent for the Dale Farm eviction was incited and orchestrated, within Conservative Party political rhetoric and, latterly, policies, in concert with the mediating agencies of the tabloid press, over several years. In particular, this forced eviction needs to be understood in the broader context of neoliberal statification and especially the institution of ideologies ('The Big Society') and technologies of 'localism', such as the 2011 Localism Act, which promise to effect the decentralization of central government powers by shifting powers and deepening democracy within local government and the communities they serve. So, while the Dale Farm eviction came after years of legal struggles between the Travelling community and Basildon Borough Council, it was undoubtedly made possible by the formation of a Conservative-led coalition government in 2010. In the final part of this chapter I will consider the forms of activism forged between Travellers and activists from a range of social movements as a consequence of the Dale Farm eviction. I will consider to what extent Dale Farm might mark a new and unpredicted era of political solidarity between Travellers and those activists within settled communities committed to fighting neoliberal governmentality and the forms of disenfranchisement it effects.

One square mile of land

The majority of Gypsies and Travellers in Britain define themselves as English (Romany) Gypsies, with Irish Travellers, Welsh Gypsies (Kales), Scottish Travellers (Nachins), showmen and circus people and New Age Travellers forming smaller, culturally distinct ethnic groups. The majority of Irish Travellers live in Ireland but there have been Irish Traveller communities in the United States, Germany and in Britain since the mid-nineteenth century (Gabhann 2012). It is not known exactly how many people self-defined as Gypsies and Travellers currently live in Britain, but estimates, including those made by the Gypsy and Traveller communities themselves, suggest a population of about 300,000 people. This figure includes those who now live in 'bricks and mortar' housing. Only a small number of Britain's Gypsies and Traveller communities continue to maintain some kind of traditional way of life, such as living together in extended family networks on communal pitches and/or travelling in the spring and summer. As Grayson notes:

> The scale of the Gypsy 'problem' is remarkably modest. We have to remember that Gypsy and Traveller families with a travelling way of life have probably just 3,729 caravans on 'unauthorised' sites in the whole of England, with a further 13,708 caravans on council and private sites. (Grayson 2010)

Since Gypsies and Travellers were barred from camping on the remaining common land in Britain, a ban which was cemented in law in the 1857 Enclosure Act and which has been followed by numerous immobilizing laws and policies, the nomadic, anti-proletarian, autonomous culture of Britain's Gypsies and Travellers has become increasingly precarious. At the same time, processes of industrialization, urbanization and the mechanization of agriculture radically destabilized their access to traditional forms of income, including farm labour and the selling of hand-crafted goods. Processes of enclosure, surveillance and policing intensified with the 1960 Caravan Sites Act, which meant that Gypsies and Travellers were unable even to camp on the private land of the farmers they had traditionally undertaken seasonal work for. Banned from traditional stopping places, and their primary forms of livelihood diminished, in the latter half of the twentieth century successive numbers of Gypsy and Traveller communities began to purchase their own land to settle on, as they had been actively encouraged to do by successive governments. However, approximately 90 per cent of their planning applications to live on that land in caravans and mobile homes are turned down by local and parish councils, often under pressure from aggressively xenophobic campaigning by settled communities (Wilson and Home 1998). In Britain today local authorities spend a staggering £18 million a year evicting the small number of remaining caravanning communities from unauthorized sites rather than allowing more applications for planning permission to succeed (Commission for Racial Equality 2003: 12). Yet it has been estimated that only one square mile of land is needed to address the current shortage of pitches needed to accommodate the 3,500 families currently without a legal pitch (see Ryder et al. 2011).

'If you're a Traveller you're an outcast' (cited in Gabhann 2012: 9)

Gypsies and Travellers are the quintessential outsiders and often lead a parallel shadow existence alongside the settled communities in the areas in which they live, even though they have often remained in or passed through these same areas for several generations. There are many historical reasons for this outsider status, both legal and social, including the long struggle and resistance of Gypsy and Traveller communities to retain their way of life, to remain outsiders in their fight against the forces of integration that have attempted to immobilize them as their nomadic rights have been incrementally 'curtailed by criminal justice legislation, commodification of marginal land, and settled people's resistance to their nomadic way of life' (Powers 2004: 5). Conflict between 'urban settled denizens, municipal authorities, police forces' and Gypsy and Traveller communities has intensified (ibid.: 5), and members of these communities are widely perceived as workless, parasitical welfare dependants, a drain on local and state resources who cheat the system which has, in fact, been *designed to fail* them. Lack of access to sites on which they can settle and access education and welfare support has effected a permanent insecurity within many of these communities. Furthermore, as the state has increasingly made Traveller ways of life 'illegal', this has led to a cycle of criminalization and criminality (Gabhann 2012). Young men in particular find themselves trapped in what have been described as '"Kafka-esque" cycles of recidivism', with one recent report suggesting that 'nearly half of the UK's estimated 400–800 Irish Travellers in jail are young adults' (ibid.). In short, Gypsies and Travellers are imagined as abhorrently unmodern anti-citizens who are antithetical to the self-scripting, flexible, entrepreneurial and individualized notions of selfhood promoted in neoliberal Britain (see Chapter 6). They are in effect an internally displaced migrant population within the state. As one young Irish Traveller in prison noted, 'we are treated as though we are foreign national prisoners' (ibid.: 13).

It is well documented that Gypsies and Travellers are today the most ostracized, hated and feared ethnic minority populations in Britain and are subject to daily racism, including violent attacks and death threats (Commission for Racial Equality 2003). A 2007 Children's Society report detailed that nine out of ten Gypsy and Traveller children have suffered racial abuse, with 63 per cent reporting intensive bullying and physical attacks (Ureche and Franks 2007), while a 2003 MORI poll conducted on behalf of the charity Stonewall found that more than one third of British adults openly admitted to being prejudiced against Gypsies and Travellers (Valentine and McDonald 2004). The disgust and intolerance expressed in relation to Gypsies and Travellers were not only higher than those towards any other minority group in Britain, they were markedly more aggressive and vehement (ibid.). Consequently, in order to navigate racism, many Gypsies and Travellers hide their ethnic identity in schools, universities and other workplaces (Greenfields and Ryder 2010). So deep is the xenophobic hatred of Gypsies and Travellers in Britain that it is also directed towards those who support or work with these populations. For example, Margaret Greenfields, an academic who engages in action research focused on the area of Gypsy and Traveller health, education and housing rights, has described how she has been spat at and verbally abused as a consequence of her research and had been made physically afraid by the threats she had received (Fearn 2010). Depressingly, many of the online responses to this article by academic colleagues reiterate the xenophobic myths about Travellers which her work attempts to challenge.

These cycles of stigma, suspicion and exclusion are intergenerational. Gypsies and Travellers are deeply suspicious and sometimes afraid of settled communities, local authorities and the police force, and have as a consequence found it difficult to access the services, such as education, welfare and legal representation, that might enable them better to defend and represent their interests in the face of deep-seated xenophobia. In a 2009 report, the Equality and Human Rights Commission (EHRC) detailed the multiple and myriad forms of inequality experienced by Gypsies and Travellers, including lack of access to secure accommodation, employment, healthcare services, education, criminal justice and legal services (Cemlyn et al. 2009). (Indeed, one of the many tragedies of the forced eviction of Dale Farm is that many of the children who were born and lived there had been the first in a generation to benefit from a relatively undisturbed primary school education and, as a consequence, were the first literate generation of Dale Farm Travellers.) The report collates new and existing evidence to detail the high levels of mental health problems, significant levels of substance abuse and domestic violence, shockingly high mortality rates, especially among infants, and the short life expectancy within Gypsy and Traveller communities (ibid.). The report notes that:

> One core theme which arises across all topics is the pervasive and corrosive impact of experiencing racism and discrimination throughout an entire lifespan and in employment, social and public contexts. Existing evidence, including from the consultation, high-lights high rates of anxiety, depression and at times self-destructive behaviour (for example, suicide and/or substance abuse). These are, on the face of the evidence, responses to 'cultural trauma' produced by the failings of 21st century British society and public bodies' failure to engage in an equitable manner with members of the communities. (Ibid.: iii)

In short, Gypsies and Travellers are national abjects within the British nation-state, a population symbolically and materially excluded from the body politic proper, people who have been forced either to give up their nomadic way of life or compelled to subsist in often degraded abject border zones within the state. The interpellative effects of racism have, as the EHRC report details, been devastating in multiple ways.

Stamp on the camps

The deep xenophobic hatred against Gypsies and Travellers is fomented within, and incited by, local and national newspapers. Journalists and newspaper editors regularly engage in anti-Gypsy and Traveller campaigns, the most infamous in recent years being the *Sun*'s 'Stamp on the Camp' campaign, which began in March 2005, in the run-up to the May general election (see Bhopal and Myers 2008; Richardson 2010). On 9 March 2005, with the front-page headline 'Sun War on Gypsy Free-For-All', the newspaper encouraged readers to contribute stories about the misery it claimed was inflicted by Traveller communities. As with its 2003 'Stop the Asylum Madness' campaign against asylum seekers, the *Sun* again produced a cut-out petition for readers to sign and send to Downing Street (see Chapter 3). This petition had three major demands to stop what it termed the 'illegal camp madness': 1) that European human rights laws be revoked on British soil, 2) that retrospective planning application be disallowed, and 3) that planning laws be made equal for all.

The 'Stamp on the Camps' campaign focused from the outset on Dale Farm, the largest Traveller site in Britain, employing the now familiar aerial shots of the site, captioned by the title 'Spreading misery' (Sun 2005). This use of long-distance visual shots is a conventional framing device in news media coverage of Gypsy and Traveller issues. This bird's-eye perspective forms part of a longer tradition of representing 'social others', notably the urban working classes, through distancing point-of-view shots that reinforce a sense of 'us' and 'them' (Tyler 2011a). Tabloid newspapers invariably depict Traveller sites as abject and liminal territorial spaces, polluting the landscape of rural Britain, even though many are on the edges of developed urban areas. To reinforce this revolting classification, the florid descriptive writing which accompanies these distancing visual depictions of Gypsy and Traveller sites in newspapers functions to incite readers' disgust for the filthy and squalid conditions in which, it is claimed, Gypsies and Travellers live. The *Sun* described Dale Farm in the following way: 'The sprawling Eighty-Caravan camp boasts top of the range mobile homes and flash motors. But it is a squalid eye-sore – blighting lives of villagers [...] each morning gallons of sewage overflows into the roads. Stray dogs roam in packs, feasting on rats in the makeshift estate' (cited in Bhopal and Myers 2008: 157).

As this quotation demonstrates, Gypsies and Travellers are condemned in equal measure for their perceived excessive and vulgar consumerism and for the imagined revolting sanitary conditions in which they live. This paradoxical juxtaposition, which, as we shall see, is the source of intense public disgust and fascination, extends from a longer tradition of exoticization. Anti-Gypsy and Traveller campaigns are also often accompanied by photographs of Travellers and their homes that have been taken from hidden locations, and which allow readers to assume an 'anthropological' or 'wildlife documentarist's' perspective from which 'to peek in and recoil in horror; via a telephoto lens' (ibid.: 161–2). As the journalist and Learning Editor of the *Traveller Times*, Damian Le Bas, notes:

> To most hacks we are not real people – more like animals. We are definitely not seen as actually being part of whatever their

perception of the 'British public' is. I have many examples of journalists acting weird around Travellers, but one of the most galling and dehumanising is their use of the telephoto lens to get pictures. They hide behind bushes and take photos of us as if we were sheep. (In Irish Traveller Movement in Britain 2012: 11)

Proud to be British

The 'Stamp on the Camps' campaign did not emerge out of thin air but was launched the same month as the seven-point plan of Michael Howard, then leader of the Conservative opposition party, which detailed how the Conservative Party planned to curb illegal Gypsy and Traveller encampments. On 21 March, Howard visited Crays Hill, the village next to Dale Farm, during what he termed his 'Proud to be British' pre-election tour, and spoke with local residents who lived near the Dale Farm site. Notably, he didn't visit or speak to any Dale Farm residents themselves, although he was photographed gazing at the camp 'through the 8ft spiked fence' at the bottom of one resident's garden (Brown 2005). Dale Farm resident Kathleen McCarthy 'described her sense of incredulity at the sight of the Leader of the Opposition gazing through the fence at her. "It was like we were in a zoo"' (ibid.). On his visit to Crays Hill, Howard restated the new Conservative policies for dealing with 'the Traveller problem'. The proposed new legal and policy framework included: 1) removing existing legal duties from local councils to provide sites for Gypsy and Traveller communities; 2) removing the right to make retrospective planning applications (which is virtually the only route through which Gypsies and Travellers have been able to obtain planning permission to dwell on their own land); 3) the introduction of a new criminal offence of intentional trespass (which would make trespass a criminal rather than civil offence and allow police to carry out forced evictions); 4) greater powers of compulsory purchase over Travellers' land; 5) allowing local lobby groups to be involved in decision-making on issues such as Gypsy and Traveller planning applications; and, most radically, 6) reviewing and if necessary scrapping the Human Rights Act (1998), which granted British citizens the judicial means to pursue the fundamental rights and freedoms contained in the European Convention on Human Rights (ECHR) within the British legal system. To publicize this new policy framework Howard took out a series of full-page advertising spots in national newspapers entitled 'I BELIEVE IN FAIR PLAY' with the strapline of the Conservative election campaign, 'ARE YOU THINKING WHAT WE'RE THINKING?' The text of this 'manifesto' was as follows:

> I BELIEVE IN FAIR PLAY.
>
> THE SAME RULES SHOULD APPLY TO EVERYONE.
>
> I DON'T BELIEVE IN SPECIAL RULES FOR SPECIAL INTEREST GROUPS.
>
> WE ARE ALL BRITISH. WE ARE ONE NATION.
>
> TOO MANY PEOPLE TODAY SEEM TO THINK THEY DON'T HAVE TO PLAY BY THE RULES – AND THEY'RE USING SO-CALLED HUMAN RIGHTS TO GET AWAY WITH DOING THE WRONG THING.
>
> IF YOU WANT TO BUILD A NEW HOME YOU HAVE TO GET PLANNING PERMISSION FIRST. BUT IF YOU ARE A TRAVELLER YOU CAN BEND PLANNING LAW – BUILDING WHERE YOU LIKE THANKS TO THE HUMAN RIGHTS ACT.
>
> IT'S NOT FAIR THAT THERE'S ONE RULE FOR TRAVELLERS AND ANOTHER FOR EVERYONE ELSE.
>
> THIS IS ONE OF THE REASONS WHY THE CONSERVATIVE PARTY IS REVIEWING THE HUMAN RIGHTS ACT. AND IF IT CAN'T BE IMPROVED WE WILL SCRAP IT.
>
> FAIRNESS MATTERS. BRITAIN NEEDS A GOVERNMENT THAT STOPS PEOPLE USING HUMAN RIGHTS AS AN EXCUSE FOR BENDING THE RULES.
>
> (Michael Howard, Conservative Party advertisement, 2005)

Given the correlation between the Conservative Party policies and the *Sun*'s 'Stamp on the Camps' petition demands, this was clearly a carefully planned and orchestrated media campaign, similar to the 2003 'Stop the Asylum Madness' assault launched against asylum seekers by the tabloid press in concert with the New Labour government (see Chapter 3).[2] In a speech to launch the Conservative election campaign, Howard declared, 'Some people say I shouldn't talk about difficult issues like the abuse of our asylum system and those travellers who stick two fingers up to the law. But we cannot make Britain a better place if we sweep difficult issues under the carpet' (Howard 2005).

Just as asylum seekers and other migrants were immobilized by racial hatred after the concerted campaigns against them in the same decade, so intensified hostility towards Gypsies and Travellers was incited and unleashed by these political and tabloid campaigns. For example, Roy Bickerstaffe, the former general secretary of public sector union Unison and a noted activist for Gypsy and Traveller rights, noted:

> Since the tabloid and Conservative campaign on Travellers started there has been an increase in racist incidents towards Travellers. According to the Commission for Racial Equality, this includes an arson attack against a Gypsy camp in Lanarkshire and evidence of Traveller children staying away from school because of the stress and fear of the current atmosphere. (Cited in Silvester 2005)

The Conservative Party lost the 2005 general election, but, as we shall see, their plans to target Gypsy and Traveller communities were only temporarily put on hold.

The Big Society

In April 2010, the Conservative Party set out proposals in their 'Big Society' election manifesto to 'give new powers and rights to neighbourhood groups', which they described as 'the "little platoons" of civil society – and the institutional building blocks of the Big Society' (Conservative Party 2010). Two months earlier a Conservative Party press release entitled 'Conservatives pledge to tackle trespass' had relaunched the policies proposed by Howard in 2005 'to address the small minority of travellers who occupy illegal or unauthorised sites' (Conservative Party Press Release 2010). The press release stated that 'travellers are treated with a "soft touch" from some town halls', and that the new legal framework proposed 'will allow councils to tackle the problem of unauthorised sites including both those built on land which is owned by travellers and land which is not' (ibid.). In other words, the devolution of power to communities described in the Big Society programme was specifically imagined as a means of enabling powers to evict and resist Gypsy and Traveller settlements to be significantly increased. Within eight months of the general election the forced eviction of Dale Farm would be carried out in the full gaze of the British public and the international media, and the promises made in the 'Stamp on the Camps' campaign were realized. In 2012, the Local Government Information Unit (LGIU), a think tank which describes its 'mission' as one of strengthening 'local democracy to put citizens in control of their own lives, communities and local services', shortlisted Tony Ball for the award of council leader of the year for his role in spearheading the Dale Farm eviction. The Dale Farm eviction was, in short, *the Big Society in action*.

Social abjection

As I detailed in Chapter 1 of this book, social abjection describes the violent exclusionary forces of sovereign power: those forces that strip people of their human dignity and reproduce them as dehumanized waste, the disposable dregs and refuse of social life (Krauss 1999). The social abjection of Gypsy and Traveller communities describes both the symbolic violence enacted by xenophobic media demands for Travellers to be *stamped out*, and the material violence so vividly evident in forced evictions. It also describes 'the pervasive and corrosive impact of experiencing racism and discrimination throughout an entire lifespan condition' (Cemlyn et al. 2009: iii). That is, it describes what it feels like to be *made abject*. As Thomas McCarthy, an Irish Traveller folk singer, describes in his account of the effects of prejudicial news reports:

> It has a devastating effect on the Travelling people. It eats at your self-confidence, self-image and self-esteem and causes bad health in your mind and your body. When I see the headlines it feels like a physical blow. It feels like we have been knocked backwards when we are trying to step forward. (McCarthy, cited in Irish Traveller Movement in Britain 2012: 17)

Perhaps more than any other population in Britain, Gypsies and Travellers fit the description offered by Georges Bataille of sovereign abjection. They are a population 'represented from the outside with disgust as the dregs of the people, populace and gutter' (Bataille 1993 [1934]: 9). A population that has for centuries resisted being sucked into forms of wage-labour exploitation in order to maintain their freedom and independence and, as a consequence, are deemed the ultimate social parasites, 'disinherited [from] the possibility of being human' (ibid.: 11). Furthermore, it is not only that 'Gypsies and Travellers are likely to experience far-reaching inequality, prejudice, discrimination and racism from politicians, the media, the public, and from services that should be designed [...] to meet their needs', but also that they are 'frequently excluded from the concept of exclusion itself' (Cemlyn et al. 2009: 253). This fact is made manifest in continual claims by politicians and members of the public that the expression of prejudice against Travellers and Gypsies is 'not racism' (Mckenzie-Borev 2012).

The marketization of racism

Just as in the case of asylum seekers (see Chapter 3), the huge amounts of public funds committed by local and national government to manage 'the Traveller problem' at first appear to be anathema to the logic of neoliberal economics, understood as forms of governance that are primarily concerned with the removal of impediments to the 'free market'. Indeed, Ben Pitcher has argued that neoliberal ideologies might be understood to support *anti-racist* politics. As he writes:

> it can be argued that there are sections of certain labour markets in which the banishment of racism has become so expedient that anti-racism might be rightly conceived as entirely concordant with – even an objective of – the neoliberal corporation. The transnational world of new media corporations necessarily embraces diverse forms of expertise and cultural knowledge. The global marketplace is undeniably multicultural and polylingual, and has, whether we like to admit it or not, been at least as important a site of anti-racist practice over the last few decades as the social movements that might profess their ownership of it. (Pitcher 2012: 9)

Pitcher's argument makes sense in respect of some global labour markets, such as entertainment, sport (and in particular football), and to some extent celebrity culture. However, there are also major limitations to his thesis, as the relative absence of minority groups within all levels of government, including local and corporate government, and within the back-room structures of all major British industries, including the media, sports and celebrity industries, and within public bodies such as academic institutions, makes abundantly clear. Neoliberal anti-racism is often a form of 'window-dressing' rather than suggestive of any deeper commitment to social or political justice. A consideration of those subjects deemed unemployable or who have been deliberately cast outside the labour market, such as asylum seekers who are barred from work, the young unemployed people condemned as 'the underclass' (see Chapters 6 and 7) and the Gypsies and Travellers whose entire history has been one of struggle *against* capitalist systems of wage-labour entrapment, reveals a different and more uneven picture of the relationship between neoliberal capitalism and racism. These populations of 'failed citizens' present both a challenge and an *opportunity* for neoliberal forms of governmentality. First, abject populations are frequently capitalized upon by politicians in order to garner public consent for their governmental strategies, and to create votes. In other words, the generation of 'a disgust consensus' enables these populations to be transformed into *political capital*. These are examples of what right-wing political strategist Lynton Crosby, who many claimed was behind the 'Stamp on the Camps' campaign, describes as 'dog whistle' issues which bring voters to heel. Secondly, their status as national abjects also presents opportunities for business enterprise, such as the penetration of international global securities companies into the fabric of the state in response to the 'problem' of migrant illegality, or the sale of newspapers and the generation of work for local and national bailiff companies engaged in the endless cycle of evictions in response to the 'problem' posed by Gypsies and Travellers. Most remarkable, though, in the case of Gypsies and Travellers, is the way their abject status has been capitalized upon spectacularly within the global entertainment industry.

Big fat gypsy weddings

Since 2010 the lives of Gypsies and Travellers, once almost invisible within mainstream media culture apart from when being routinely demonized in local and tabloid newspapers, have become luridly spectacularized on 'reality television' through the hit BAFTA-nominated series *Big Fat Gypsy Weddings* (2010–12). Produced by Firecracker Films and screened on Channel Four, *Big Fat Gypsy Weddings* is one of the channel's highest-rating programmes ever. Viewing figures peaked at 9.7 million for the screening of the second episode of series one in 2010 when, as Mark Soldinger, the founder and managing director of Firecracker, put it, 'Gypsy-mania swept across Britain' (cited in Campbell 2011). *Big Fat Gypsy Weddings* is described by Firecracker as a 'Revealing documentary series that offers a window into the secretive, extravagant and surprising world of gypsies and travellers in Britain today'. However, despite its title, *Big Fat Gypsy Weddings* centres almost exclusively on Irish Travellers and, in particular, on the extravagant weddings of young Irish Traveller women. These young women are depicted as competing to outdo one another in the size and splendour of their wedding dresses and the scale of their weddings. They are largely framed as shallow, naive and gauche tragicomic figures who wear scanty outfits and other forms of clothing coded as vulgar and tasteless. Several episodes feature scenes of Traveller girls and women emulating the sexually provocative dance routines they have copied from American popular music videos, underscoring the programmes' insistence that Traveller femininity is modelled on the excesses of celebrity culture. Journalist Polly Dunbar has claimed that 'producers have rehearsed and reshot scenes and have egged on teenage girls to wear provocative clothing in a process described by insiders as "nurtured reality"' (Dunbar 2012). These claims are denied by Firecracker, but are common practice in reality TV production, as my own research with reality TV participants has revealed (Tyler 2011a). Indeed, a photographer, Elisabeth Blanchet, hired by Channel Four in 2012 to produce advertising images for a new series of *Big Fat Gypsy Weddings*, revealed how she has been sent emails from the television company's creative agency, 4Creative, directing her to go to Traveller sites with the remit of obtaining tackier and more sexualized images for their promotional campaign. The email suggested to Blanchet a series of scenarios in which Travellers might be asked to pose in order to achieve '"the spirit of what we want to get at"', which included: '"A dirty kiss between a couple with tongue. A toilet, ideally an outdoor one. We can see the tail of a wedding dress coming out from it, like a bride has just used it. A very young girl pretending to be a bride. [...] Two guys screaming at the camera with a bottle of Champagne in their hands"' (cited in Taylor 2012: 10).[3] When Blanchet's photographs finally appeared on billboards and hoardings around the UK, she was dismayed to find that they were overlaid by the caption 'Bigger. Fatter. Gypsier', provoking a series of complaints about racism to the Advertising Standards Authority (ASA). In 2012, the ASA determined that one of the billboard images sexualized children and was likely to cause prejudice and harm to Gypsy and Traveller children.

Liesbet van Zoonen (2006) suggests that a shift from an economy of fame (inaccessible to women by virtue of its emphasis on heroic masculine attributes and public speaking) to a culture of celebrity (in which fame depends less on certain forms of achievement and public speech, and more on attributes such as appearance) privileges 'femininity'. However, the forms of celebrity this shift enables are restricted to those who can perform femininities of highly specific kinds. Femininity has never been easily accessible to non-white or working-class women. As Skeggs suggests, 'Both black and white working-class women' have historically been coded 'as the sexual and deviant other against which femininity [is] defined' (Skeggs 2001: 297). It is, perhaps, because 'celebrity femininity', and the conspicuous consumption it implies, is associated with social mobility and the acquisition of cultural and social capital that the Irish Traveller women depicted in *Big Fat Gypsy Weddings* desire to emulate these femininities. As Skeggs argues, socially idealized femininities are often practised and employed by working-class women as a way of 'deflecting associations of pathology, poverty, and pollution' (ibid.: 298). However, the entertainment value of *Big Fat Gypsy Weddings* lies in part in the pleasure the audience can take from the idea that these women are unable to 'do' femininity correctly. As Julia Lawrence reveals, when she writes in the *Mail* of gawping in 'morbid fascination' at the young women on the programme:

> [*Big Fat Gypsy Weddings* invites its] viewing millions [...] on a surreal journey where scantily-clad, perma-tanned, bling-loving gypsy girls – many as young as 16 – subjected themselves to draconian courtship rituals to fulfil their 'dreams' of getting married. The gaudy – some might say comical – excesses of the ensuing wedding days made for unmissable television. (Lawrence 2012)

As Carole Anne Tyler observes, '[A] real woman is a real lady; otherwise, she is a female impersonator, whose "unnaturally bad" taste – like that attributed to working-class women or women of colour – marks the impersonation of such' (Tyler 2002: 61). *Big Fat Gypsy Weddings* revolves around these incompetent or unsuccessful impersonations, and the repeated demonstration of this failure is, I would argue, a key source of spectatorial pleasure for millions of the programme's viewers within the settled community. To direct viewers towards this preferred reading, sequences are frequently assembled to produce a comic effect through such devices as using circus music to accompany the images, or displaying on-screen subtitles as if to translate their speech, although the Travellers all speak in English (Dunbar 2012).

Reality TV programmes such as *Big Fat Gypsy Weddings* draw

on many of the formal techniques of socially committed television documentary, such as the use of hand-held cameras, 'fly-on-the-wall' camera angles, the employment of non-actors and an improvised, unscripted, low-budget 'authenticity' in order to justify the exploitation and voyeurism involved in such programmes through an implied association with 'documentary realism'. However, these kinds of reality TV programmes have none of the aspirations of longer-standing socially critical and politicized traditions of British documentary film and television (Tyler 2011b). On the contrary, contemporary reality TV series such as *Big Fat Gypsy Weddings* are made almost exclusively by independent production companies and are motivated by profit. Firecracker Films has sold the first series of *Big Fat Gypsy Weddings* to broadcasters around the world and saw its profits surge to £11 million in 2011. 'To date, it has generated sales revenues of £3.5 million from deals in 81 territories, including countries in Africa, Central Europe and Latin America' (Dunbar 2012). Of course, as is customary with documentary film and television, none of the participants in the programmes is paid, their free labour adding considerably to the profit margins to be made. Predictably enough, a franchise spin-off, *My Big Fat American Gypsy Wedding*, debuted on the US-based TLC Discovery Channel network in April 2012.

The culturalization of politics

In its annual report to government under the heading 'Celebrating difference and challenging prejudice', Channel Four claimed that '79% of [viewers] polled agreed [*Big Fat Gypsy Weddings*] had taught them something new about the gypsy and traveller communities' (Channel Four 2012). No details were given about what it was that viewers had learnt, although the report relates that the programme generated the most 'buzz' of all Channel Four output in 2011.

It is important not to underestimate the central role of media genres such as reality television in what Boris Buden has described as 'the culturalization' and correlative depoliticization of social conflicts and struggles (Buden 2007). By pretending to enrich democracy by extending visibility to marginal communities, cultural enterprises such as reality TV not only profit from the free labour of participants, but function to elide the political struggles of minority subjects and to incite further social antagonisms (Tyler and Bennett 2010). Detailing the central role of reality TV in this process, Nick Couldry argues:

every system of cruelty requires its own theater. [...] The regime of economic production that, with its associated discourses, is usually called 'neoliberalism,' is a system of cruelty. [...] The 'truths' of neoliberalism would be unacceptable if stated openly, even if their consequences unfold before our eyes every day. Those truths must therefore be translated into ritual that enacts as 'play' an acceptable version of the values and compulsions on which that cruelty depends. 'Reality TV' is a theater where just such an enactment takes place. (Couldry 2008: 3)

The Irish Traveller movement has argued precisely that *Big Fat Gypsy Weddings* is a system of cruelty, which misrepresents, mocks, stigmatizes and exploits Irish Travellers. Moreover, as Traveller activists and spokespeople have detailed, the depiction of Traveller culture in *Big Fat Gypsy Weddings* has played a central role in legitimizing the current groundswell of overt discrimination, prejudice and racial hatred towards Irish Traveller and other Gypsy and Traveller communities within the British Isles. As Brian Foster, chairman of the Advisory Council for the Education of Romany and other Travellers, notes:

'Big fat gypsy' has joined 'pikey' as an acceptable form of address in some schools and girls have been subjected to sexual harassment by boys emulating the dubious practice of 'grabbing' sensationalised by the programme. The tabloids follow the programme assiduously seeking to capitalise on aspects of the portrayal of these communities. (Foster, cited in Irish Traveller Movement in Britain 2012: 15)

In 2012 a seventeen-year-old Romany Gypsy, Pip Mckenzie-Borev, published an open letter to Channel Four about the impact of *Big Fat Gypsy Weddings* on his and his family's life.

I was subjected to physical attacks during your last series of your 'documentary' which ultimately led to my expulsion from school (long story), whilst my 12 year old cousin was beat up on her way home from school by a gang of girls who were calling her a prostitute [...]. Last year, Leeds University Union thought it would be okay to laugh at the Gypsy and Traveller communities by hosting a Big Fat Gypsy Weddings fancy dress party. While the union holds events throughout the year to celebrate other ethnic minorities, your 'documentary' encouraged them to incite ethnic hatred. (Mckenzie-Borev 2012)

In response to this letter, Nick Hornby, the Channel Four commissioning editor accountable for *Big Fat Gypsy Weddings*, claimed that Gypsies and Travellers have 'contacted us to say that they feel the documentaries have portrayed the community in a positive light and had a positive impact on their lives' (Hornby 2012). However, Hornby must have been aware of events that transpired at a Royal Television Society event in May 2011, when the producers of the series were invited to a panel discussion to celebrate and share the secrets of their incredible ratings success. The Royal Television Society had denied representatives from the Traveller and Gypsy community a place on the podium alongside the production team, but twenty Romany Gypsies and Irish Travellers nevertheless travelled to London and proceeded to interrupt the debate. As Jake Bowers, the editor of *The Travellers' Times*, later reported on the testimonies made by the community at the event:

> Romany woman and filmmaker Dee Cooper revealed how racist
> bullying had exploded across the country. Her own daughter who
> had already endured years of abuse was now forced to relive it.
> Thanks to Firecracker Films, Dee's daughter had been punched,
> drawn on and called pikey once again. When, she wondered, would
> Firecracker be donating some of their huge profits from selling this
> series and the next one to the kids whose lives they had ruined?
>
> Gypsy pastor, Jackie Boyd, revealed how his own family also
> now had to hide their identity. 'What you have done,' he told them,
> 'may be a good thing in your community and you've obviously
> made a lot of money out of it. But it has brought great shame and
> fear to mine.' (Bowers 2011)

While Firecracker and Channel Four claim that *Big Fat Gypsy Weddings* 'demonstrates' that 'some Travellers are now ready to open up and speak for themselves', Joseph John, the secretary of the Gypsy Council, stood up in the Royal Television Society event to tell the producers, 'You should be ashamed of yourselves for what you have done' (cited in Khalsa 2011). Interviewed after the Royal Television Society event, an Irish Traveller mother named Margaret stated that while the programme had been 'great for nine million viewers', it had created incredible suffering in the Traveller community: 'it put us back twenty years. We have fought years and years to get where we are. [Thanks to] the racial abuse that has being going on [since the first series was aired] the young girls are terrified' (transcribed from audiovisual clip in Bowers 2011). The racial and sexist abuse incited by the programme continues today. In 2012, during the screening of the second series, Irish Traveller Christine Crawley wrote an article for the *Guardian* describing the levels of bullying Gypsy and Traveller children were enduring at school during the airing of the series: 'My daughter was called a prostitute and eventually left school because of the way girls were portrayed in the series' (Crawley 2012).

We should understand the culturalization of political struggles within popular cultural formats such as reality TV as forms of neoliberal governance in which 'politics' is transferred from 'the "classical" domain of the state apparatuses such as political parties, the parliamentary system and the procedures of the Rule of Law to the dispersed field of competing "cultural options"' (Grlja and Vesić 2007). Hence, when Travellers complain about, and ask for some kind of redress for, their exploitation and stigmatization in *Big Fat Gypsy Weddings*, the response is that the involvement of Travellers in the programme was their choice, and that the programme depicts their lives, and the choices Travellers make in their lives, in a realistic way. Indeed, claims that *Big Fat Gypsy Weddings* is a consensual and therefore an accurate depiction of 'reality' that somehow supports a multicultural programming philosophy, rather than the manufacturing of 'reality' for profit, are not only disingenuous but deny the harm the programme has effected. In this way cycles of stigma and exclusion are reproduced. As liberal civil society has withered, global media companies have extended their power and reach, proliferating within every sphere of social life. As the colonizing of virtual social spaces by corporate companies makes manifest, these global businesses increasingly function as the primary civil or public sphere. As Michael Hardt has argued, the very 'conditions of possibility for civil society have progressively been undermined [...] the society we are living in today is more properly understood as a postcivil society' (Hardt 1995: 27).

Paul Gilroy, in his response to the riots in England in August 2011 (see Chapter 7), argued for the importance of creating alternative media representations and aesthetic practices for imagining alternatives to the images and discourses of stigmatization. He argues that media privatization has led to the contraction and impoverishment of the freedom and diversity of expression, and states that 'our tactics for understanding our defence of our communities have to take those changes into account' (Gilroy 2011). As Gilroy claims, 'one of the worst forms of poverty that's shaped our situation is poverty of the imagination' (ibid.). I understand this poverty of imagination in several ways; as Gilroy suggests, it relates in part to the increasingly central role of mediating agencies such as the corporate news and entertainment media in shaping perceptual realities. As I argue throughout this book, *mediation* is a pivotal part of the neoliberalization of the state. The poverty of imagination which the global corporatization of media industries has effected must be countered through the development of alternative media and aesthetic practices.

A struggle of imagination

In his writing on the politics of aesthetics, Rancière (2004b) argues that the redistribution of visibility is not only a critical element within any programme for social and political change, it *is* change (ibid.). In Rancière's critical lexicon, 'police' is the name for the political, judicial and media establishments and the technologies of surveillance, order, control and classification that shape the borders of the consensual community, while 'politics' is his name for the radical interruption of this consensus. Politics is that which contests the 'conditions for sharing' and the available conditions of visibility that underpin and legitimize inequality. For Rancière, politics is thus not about creating a consensus but rather about generating dissensus within the hegemonic perceptual and aesthetic field.[4] As Davide Panagia explains:

> Dissensus [...] is at once a dissent from inequality and an insensibility (i.e. an inability to be sensed, noticed or accounted for). Democratic politics occurs when certain elements in society that are deemed insensible are challenging the governing political order. The task of political action, therefore, is aesthetic in that it requires a reconfiguration of the conditions of sense perception so that the reigning configuration between perception and meaning is disrupted by those elements, groups or individuals in society that demand not only to exist but indeed to be perceived. (Panagia 2010: 96)

In the case of the Dale Farm eviction, the space granted to Gypsies and Traveller voices within the mainstream news media, particularly within newspapers such as the *Guardian* and the *Independent*, but also in a number of mainstream and marginal media sites, was pivotal in generating a significant dissensus about how these communities are understood and portrayed. While this may not have altered the outcome at Dale Farm, what these counter-media representations enabled was the voices of Travellers to be heard in ways that troubled the reductive framings of Gypsies and Travellers as either abject and subhuman or exoticized and eroticized others. In this regard, Dale Farm may mark the beginning of a significantly new era in news media representations of Gypsy and Traveller communities. As McKenzie-Borev suggests:

> While the travellers may have lost the fight for their homes, they leave behind a legacy and no longer is the plight of the Gypsy and Traveller community a silent one. The media attention that has surrounded the fight for Dale Farm has enlightened Britain to the inequalities faced by the Gypsy and Traveller population, and the eviction signals not the end, but the beginning of a movement for equality. (Mckenzie-Borev 2012)

Yet the struggle of imagination described by Gilroy also relates to the prevailing conditions of 'left melancholia' and to the question of what kinds of political vocabularies of equality are available for larger and more sustainable movements of resistance against neoliberalism to be articulated and understood. As Gilroy observes, the political elites on the left and the right act as a class and in concert, and so, he writes, 'if we want to act as a body, if we want to act in concert, we have to learn something from the way they conduct themselves, even as we challenge what they do' (Gilroy 2011). What Gilroy identifies is the need to be more systematic both in our thinking about, and in our resistance to, neoliberal governmentality, by recognizing the systemic composition of this radically transformatory regime, and the specific ways that 'the role of information, of policing, of deprivation, of inequality' function in concert (ibid.). This is precisely what I have set out to do in this chapter, and in *Revolting Subjects* as a whole.

Conclusion: the tragedy of the commons

> The hard-eyed men who guard the road,
> They bid us choose our way …
> And yet they will not let us go
> Nor will they let us stay

Five hundred years of timeless days,
We wandered through the land ...

But now the guardians of the clocks
Have said our race is damned,
They say our race is damned. (MacColl and Seeger 1964)

The history of the subjugation of Gypsies and Travellers in Britain is a 'tragedy of the commons' in the literal sense that it was the enclosure and privatization of land and property which made their way of life both increasingly untenable and rendered them abject in the eyes of the state (Hardin 1968). For centuries these communities have been fighting against enclosure and eviction in order to defend and sustain themselves but increasingly they have come to lack any proper place within the privatized orders of social hierarchy. For example, even when Gypsies and Travellers buy their own land, and decide it is better to settle and integrate in order to secure their children an education and a better future, they come up against extraordinary levels of ignorance, xenophobia and fear, a hatred sedimented over centuries but today inflamed by the politicians and the news media that seek to capitalize upon that fear and anxiety. At the same time, despite their official recognition as distinct ethnic groups under British law, open expressions of racism pass unremarked.

However, the struggles of the Travellers at Dale Farm in 2011 against their eviction coincided with the emergence of a number of 'space-hacking' social and political movements which contest the effects of neoliberal social and economic policies. Many of these social and political movements draw inspiration from *the philosophy of the commons* and explicitly understand their politics as *a politics of occupation* and their activism as *forms of commoning* against (capitalist) forms of *enclosure*. As George Caffentzis writes:

> In the last decade the concept of the commons has increasingly become the basis of anticapitalist thinking in the antiglobalization [...] movement. It has been politically useful both as an alternative model of social organization against the onslaught of 'there is no alternative' neoliberal thinking and as a link between diverse struggles ranging from those of agricultural workers demanding land, to environmentalists calling for a reduction of the emission of 'hot house gases' into the atmosphere, to writers, artists, musicians

and software designers rejecting the totalitarian regime of intellectual property rights. (Caffentzis 2010)

'Camp Constant', the activist camp built alongside and in solidarity with the Travellers at Dale Farm (named after the bailiff company Constant and Co.), was a notable instance of this new politics of occupation and the forms of commoning activism which it engages. The camp was set up on 9 April 2011, the day after Roma Nation Day, and attracted activists from across Europe from different political affiliations and groups, many of whom had previously had little or no knowledge of, or previous relationship with, the struggles of Gypsies and Travellers. Indeed, given the long histories of stigma, prejudice, distrust and fear, Gypsies and Travellers have historically had notably few political allies among the settled community. Among the activists who gathered at Camp Constant were members of the NoBorders and No One is Illegal networks, which campaign for migrant rights and freedom of movement across Europe and international border zones, activists from the Occupy movement, Climate Camp, trade union representatives and human rights monitors. These individuals and groups came together to work with the Travellers at Dale Farm to create a Traveller Solidarity Network, which today describes itself 'as part of the antifascist movement and the wider struggle against racism and class oppression' (Traveller Solidarity Network 2011). The inhabitants of Camp Constant were engaged in the kinds of practices of collective provisioning and cross-class collaboration that are generating alternative models of capital(ism), sociality and democracy more widely within the Occupy movement. Indeed, these movements draw their inspiration from precisely the histories of struggle against enclosure to which the ongoing struggle of Gypsies and Travellers in Britain belongs. Indeed, the Traveller Solidarity Network is one of the best examples of the ways in which grassroots and direct action movements concerned with forging and thinking new forms of associational politics are garnering resistance to the neoliberal political consensus – and in the process generating new and sometimes unexpected forms of collective political subjects (Badiou 2010: 245).

6 | BRITAIN AND ITS POOR

The Britain of the elite is over. The new Britain is a meritocracy. (Tony Blair 1997)

A child's chances in life are now more determined by where
(and to whom) they were born as compared to any other date
in the last 651 years. (Dorling 2007: 5)

Introduction

During the 1990s the fiscal imperatives of neoliberalism were
becoming visible in Britain in a number of ways. As the electorate
began to see and feel some of the material effects of the marketization of the state they voted in a Labour government in a massive
landslide victory. The Labour Party fought the election with promises
of 'better schools, better hospitals, better ways of tackling crime' and
the 'building [of] a modern welfare state' (Labour Party 1997).[1] In
their rebranding of the party as New Labour they also set out to
uncouple the associations between the Labour Party and the politics
of the labour movement and to 'defang' oppositional class politics. As
they stated in their election manifesto, they wanted to move beyond
'the bitter political struggles of left and right that have torn our
country apart for too many decades' (ibid.). At the very moment
that economic inequalities between populations within the state were
deepening, 'class' was to be expunged from mainstream political
vocabularies.[2] This was illustrated in Tony Blair's speech to the Labour
Party conference in 1999 when he stated that 'The class war is over.
But the struggle for true equality has only just begun' (Blair 1999).
This statement revealed much about the efforts made by New Labour
to decouple economic inequalities from the conceptual and political
language of class. These kinds of rhetorical exertions formed part of
a three-decades-long struggle on the part of the elites to jettison the
language of class struggle as the perceptual framework through which
to perceive social and economic (dis)advantage.

This chapter tells the story of concerted efforts to make class a *revolting subject* in Britain. It will examine how questions of class-based inequalities were repressed, reworked and reformulated within sociological and political discourses and within wider popular and public culture. Drawing on the work of Skeggs, it will examine this abjectification of class politics as a form of *class-making* (Skeggs 2004). At the centre of this account is the grotesque and comic figure of 'the chav' (Tyler 2008; Tyler and Bennett 2010). As I will detail, from around 2002 'chav' became the popular pejorative name for 'the underclass' in Britain and in particular for a generation of young people disenfranchised by neoliberal economic and social policies. Drawing on Jacques Rancière's (2004a) formulation of class as *a struggle over names*, I will consider what lessons we might learn from the polarized debates among social commentators, experts and academics around this figure and what this might teach us about class politics in Britain today. This chapter draws upon an influential body of (predominantly feminist) scholarship which has persisted with class-based research in the face of the constitution of class as a defunct mode of analysis within sociology in the 1990s. I am particularly indebted to the inspirational work of Skeggs.

Sociology and its poor

Britain is often imagined as a nation exceptionally wrought by class hierarchies, antagonisms and tensions: political, cultural and economic. Writing in 1941, George Orwell proclaimed England to be 'the most class-ridden country under the sun'. This is 'a land of snobbery and privilege', he stated, 'ruled largely by the old and silly' (Orwell 2000: 67). Half a century later the British historian David Cannadine observed in the *New York Times* that 'it remains a generally held belief, not just in Britain but around the world, that class, like the weather and the monarchy, is a peculiarly and particularly British preoccupation' (Cannadine 1998: 1). However, as post-industrialization and the outsourcing of industrial labour to the global East and South deproletarianized the British labour market, so the occupational vocabulary inherited from industrial capitalism and from the politicization of the working class within the labour movement became increasingly unstable (Wacquant 2008: 250). Within the state the growing number of economically oppressed but marginalized people grew as industrial labour was replaced by precarious low-paid and often short-term work, a development often derogatively termed the feminization of labour (ibid.: 251, n59). Of course, as feminist and post-colonial scholars have long argued, 'proletariat' had always been an inadequate concept, failing to account for the unwaged, low-paid or forced labours of social reproduction, servitude, imperialism and slavery. However, for many sociologists these transformations in class structure raised 'in a pointed manner the question of the adequacy of the conceptual frameworks and analytical approaches inherited from an era of capitalist organization that is now bygone' (ibid.: 249). At the same time systems for the classification of people within the state proliferated. The marketization of the state goods and services, the rise of a consumer culture built on credit, the financialization of capital and the securitization of borders required multiple and diverse practices and systems of classification and surveillance for managing populations within the state. Within disciplines concerned with mapping this changing social stratification the relationship between 1) 'class' understood as a historical and political (Marxist) name for antagonistic relations of power between groups of people under industrial capitalism and 2) 'class' understood as technologies of measurement – state, corporate and social-scientific systems devised for the classification of populations – was increasingly strained.

For Rancière the term 'class' is a homonym. He ascribes two primary meanings to class. In the first, governmental sense, class is understood as 'a grouping of people assigned a particular status and rank according to their origins or their activity' (Rancière 1999: 83). In the second, political sense, class is 'an operator of conflict, a name for counting the uncounted' (ibid.: 83). Class politics, in the sense Rancière understands it, describes the struggle of the uncounted/exploited against their classification and against the social destinies defined by 'class names'. These struggles are always historically contingent and the names for class mutate and transform. As we shall see, Rancière's definition comes much closer to the understandings of class within cultural studies as practices and process of making.

Class is dead

For many sociologists the response to 'the problem' of class was not, however, to explore its paradoxical status but to 'retreat from class' altogether (Skeggs 2005: 45). 'Class is dead', some esteemed and many less well-known sociologists declared (Pahl 1989; Beck 1992; Clark and Lipset 1991; Giddens 1991). It is useful to consider one influential moment in this attempt to jettison class from the discipline of sociology in the 1990s because it reveals both the conceptual confusion about class within the field, and the neoliberal political investments that shaped the calls for its rejection.

In 1996, the journal *Theory and Society* published a special section on class. The introductory article by Jan Pakulski and Malcolm Waters, 'The reshaping and dissolution of social class in advanced society', argued that class was an outdated historical phenomenon (Pakulski and Waters 1996).[3] Pakulski and Waters chastised sociologists for 'manufacturing class' in the context of global changes which meant that class 'no longer exist[ed] as a meaningful social entity' (ibid.: 667–8). They also argued that the continued focus on class within sociology diverted attention away from more pressing forms of inequality (such as inequalities of race and ethnicity) and from identity-based social movements. This argument assumes that categories such as gender, sexuality, disability, race and ethnicity, migrancy (and illegality) are not 'class categories' (I will return to this below), and that the subjectivities, forms of lived experience and resistant politics these other classifications give rise to are not intertwined with nor indeed can be a consequence of prevailing social and economic relations.

As we shall see, Pakulski and Waters's thesis proceeds from a place of conceptual confusion, as they move between the two meanings of class described by Rancière: namely, class meaning the 'grouping of people assigned a particular status and rank according to their origins or their activity' and class as a form of politics, a name for struggles against social destinies imposed at birth (Rancière 1999: 83). This confusion becomes evident when Pakulski and Waters support their 'death-of-class' thesis by citing empirical data which suggests that public understandings of class identities had decomposed. Unsurprisingly they found that in neoliberal states many people no longer identify with nineteenth-century class names. Their conclusion is that the only place that class is alive and well is within sociology itself. This view was shared by the influential German sociologist Ulrich Beck, who argued that class was a sociological 'zombie category': 'the idea lives on even though the reality to which it corresponds is dead [...] Society can no longer look in the mirror and see social classes. The mirror has been smashed and all we have left are the individualized fragments' (Willms 2004: 51–2). The insistence that inequality cannot be a matter of class, if it is not explicitly named as such by those who might experience (dis)advantage, is forged from the idea that sociological categories *mirror* empirical realities. As we shall see, people are never identical to the categorical versions of themselves that circulate in the public sphere and, indeed, they often actively reject class names and other classifications imposed from outside.-

However, Pakulski and Waters's desire to purge class from sociology wasn't motivated by the fact people disidentify with given class names, or that Marxist theories cannot accommodate the changing economic and social environment of the post-industrial societies (and the deproletarianization of labour effected by neoliberalism). They also scorn attempts by theorists to develop social stratification theories to describe the changing relations of labour and capital, state and market. Staggeringly, they also ignore the many decades of rich feminist and post-colonial scholarship which had developed intersectional approaches to examine social and cultural inequalities. Rather, what Pakulski and Waters want to (make) abject are *the political associations* of class which they perceive to be contaminating the discipline. As they note, '[c]lass belongs to a particularly contentious vocabulary and is anchored in deep ideological commitments and heavy intellectual investments' (Pakulski and Waters 1996: 668):

> Less and less is left of class theory's original seductive emancipatory promise. Its ideological pretensions and its radicalism have faded and with them have also faded a large part of its attractiveness and appeal [...] In the past, class analysis was a paragon of 'progressivism.' A commitment to class analysis was associated with a pro-reformist stance. This association is weakening, and the very notion of progressivism that class analysis implies has become increasingly problematic. (Ibid.: 664)

The implication here is that sociology's partisan political associations had become 'a political straitjacket' which must be cast off. For sociology to survive the transition to neoliberal market economics, which was not only transforming politics and society but was rapidly transforming the university, reshaping academic disciplines and the meaning of scholarly labour, class had to die. It was the unmarketability of class which was for Pakulski and Waters the most decisive nail in 'the coffin of class'. As they write:

> The recent record of class analysis then, its ineffectiveness in

explaining the dynamics of contemporary society, is far from proud. If popularity is taken as a measure of its success, the record is damning. No current social-science best-seller has adopted the class-analytic paradigm, and many specifically reject it. (Ibid.: 683)

The message was clear: class analysis was providing rapidly diminishing intellectual returns. Class no longer sold academic books or made academic careers. Class was a block to the marketization of academic knowledge. Class had become an embarrassing and even shameful topic (Sayer 2002). In place of the conceptual language of class, sociologists developed new theoretical vocabularies which didn't carry the ideological baggage of class politics. Chief among these new concepts were choice, autonomy, reflexivity, consumerism, lifestyle and mobility (see Skeggs 2004).

One of the reasons why sociologists' efforts to cast off class were so significant is that one of the architects of the New Labour project was the sociologist Anthony Giddens. An erstwhile class analyst, Giddens positioned himself at the leading edge of 'class backlash'. His departure from class centred on his belief that globalization and consumerism had transformed understandings of selfhood. In place of the conceptual framework of class, he argued for a mobile, flexible and individualized notion of selfhood in which life-chances related less to birth and more to an individual's ability to script themselves into the neoliberal workplace through the adoption of the 'right' lifestyle choices. As Val Gilles summarizes:

According to Giddens [...], achieving a more meritocratic society requires people to embrace their individualized citizenship and become 'responsible risk takers'. From this perspective, prosperity derives from being the right kind of (middle-class) self, while poverty and disadvantage [are] associated with poor self-management. (Gilles 2005: 837)

Giddens's account was less an empirical analysis and more a political vision, a dream of a 'new egalitarianism' effected by neoliberal market economics. He argued, in concert with New Labour, that 'expanding the productive efficiency of the economy' was the primary route through which to diminish inequalities within the state (Giddens and Diamond 2005: 106). The influence of sociologists such as Giddens shouldn't be understated. As Gilles suggests, Giddens was pivotal in shaping New Labour policies that emphasized 'redistributing possibilities as opposed to wealth' (Gilles 2005: 837).

Aylesbury Estate, Southwark, England, 2 June 1997

Hours after winning the 1997 election, Tony Blair went to the Aylesbury council estate in Southwark, south-east London, to deliver his first address as prime minister.

> I have chosen this housing estate to deliver my first speech as prime minister for a very simple reason. For eighteen years, the poorest people in our country have been forgotten by government. They have been left out of growing prosperity, told that they were not needed, ignored by the government except for the purpose of blaming them. [...] There will be no forgotten people in the Britain I want to build. We need to act in a new way because fatalism, and not just poverty, is the problem we face, the dead weight of low expectations, the crushing belief that things cannot get better. I want to give people back the will to win again. [...] But that cannot be done without a radical shift in our values and attitudes. [...] It will be about how to recreate the bonds of civic society and community in a way compatible with the far more individualistic nature of modern economic, social and cultural life. [...] There is a case not just in moral terms but in enlightened self-interest to act, to tackle what we all know exists – an underclass of people cut off from society's mainstream, without any sense of shared purpose.
>
> Now, at the close of the twentieth century, the decline of old industries and the shift to an economy based on knowledge and skills [have] given rise to a new class: a workless class. In many countries – not just Britain – a large minority is playing no role in the formal economy, dependent on benefits and the black economy. [...] Today the greatest challenge of any democratic government is to refashion our institutions to bring this new workless class back into society. (Blair 1997)

In the years following Blair's stirring maiden speech, the Aylesbury Estate, then the largest social housing estate in Europe, was transformed not into a symbol of a newly inclusive Britain, but into 'journalistic shorthand for inner-city crime, squalor and deprivation, with the *Daily Mail* describing a walk around its precincts as "like visiting hell's waiting room"' (Jones 2010). This speech, and the inauguration of New Labour government, marked a new era in class relations in Britain, an era in which 'the council estate' would come to mark the moral boundaries of the nation-state. Under Thatcher, Britain's decaying social housing estates were already being reconfigured in the public imaginary as 'barracks for the poor' which 'warehoused poverty' and bred a parasitical dysfunctional underclass of failed citizens (Jones 2011: 81). This pathologization of the council estate was used to legitimize 'right-to-buy' policies. However, it was under New Labour that a powerful consensus emerged that council estates were abject border zones within the state which were not only *liminal* with regard to wider societal norms and values but were actively *antisocial* spaces. Dystopian and terrorizing images of council estates became a staple of the British media. Hundreds of news stories, television documentaries, reality TV and comedy programmes contributed to the formation of a moral panic about the 'culture of worklessness' which estates were said to both reproduce and represent. It mattered little that the mushrooming 'discourses of demonization' about estates 'often have only tenuous connections to the reality of everyday life' in them (Mooney 2008). In 2012, the *Guardian* reported that so many journalists, television crews and film-makers flock to the Aylesbury Estate 'looking to portray crime, deprivation and urban decay' that Southwark Council banned filming there at the residents' request (Murray 2012).[4]

'Open the gates and free people from Britain's ghettos' declared Will Hutton in 2003 (cited in Mooney 2008: 14). Perhaps unintentionally, Hutton's words had a double meaning. For, as many urban geographers have detailed, the moral panic about council estates as places in socio-economic exile from the neoliberal state proper was used to legitimize the opening up of social housing to private capital. Local councils mortgaged run-down estates to private property developers and/or financed refurbishment through disastrous public–private finance initiatives (PFIs). This 'urban regeneration' often entailed the bulldozing of homes and the mass eviction of residents (some pushed out by increased rents). These projects were driven by a governmental agenda of eradicating 'the culture of worklessness' through creating 'a social mix', a process which many have argued, given the existing ethnic diversity of people who lived on estates like Aylesbury, was gentrification by another name (Lees 2008).

Failed citizens

New Labour redesigned citizenship around the double axis of inclusion/exclusion and work/worklessness. In the absence of a political vocabulary of class exploitation what emerged was an account in which the poor were outside the domain of the social proper, and had to be 'helped or coerced to become included citizens' (Gilles 2005: 838). Only through work could class abjects find a route back to citizenship and into the bosom of the body politic. The punitive policies deployed to manage these failed citizens were based on limiting financial or material aid in order to make citizens take responsibility for their own welfare (and get a job). As Gilles notes, the White Paper *Respect & Responsibility – Taking a Stand against Anti-Social Behaviour* (2003) contained some of the most severe proposals, 'including benefit cuts for errant families, the removal of persistent young offenders from their families for placement in foster homes, and the committal of parents to residential homes for "re-training"' (ibid.: 840). In total, between 1997 and 2008, Labour introduced 3,605 new criminal offences. Some of these, including the introduction of Anti-Social Behaviour Orders, Parental Orders and Individual Behaviour Orders, targeted the urban poor. These disciplinary policies were premised on two myths. The first of these was that deprived people didn't work or didn't want to work (MacDonald et al. 2010b). The second was that full employment was possible or indeed desirable (Theodore 2007). Neoliberal economics had transformed waged work, making a large sector of the labour market, but particularly low-paid work, precarious, fragile and often short-term. As MacDonald et al. claim, it was precisely the kinds of work available to people at the losing end of the class system which had trapped many people within 'churning low-pay, no-pay careers at the bottom of the labour market' (ibid.: 7). As they argue, '[c]ontrary to the widely held view that "employment is the best route out of poverty", the sorts of [low-paid] work available to our interviewees kept them in poverty rather than lifting them out of it' (ibid.: 5). Nevertheless, within the space of a decade the idea that it was a poverty of aspiration, the failure to make the 'right choices' and an unwillingness to grasp the opportunities gifted by the state which were to blame for intergenerational cultures of worklessness was established as a powerful myth.

Territorial stigma

The council estate became metonymic shorthand for this 'new class of problem people', and the poverty associated with these places was imagined as a self-induced pathological condition. Blair's speech in 1997 signalled how, by drawing on neoconservative theories of welfare dependency and the conceptual categories of underclass, poverty would come to be unshackled symbolically from economic inequalities and reframed as a psycho-cultural problem: 'the dead weight of low expectations' (Blair 1997). It was by stigmatizing and blaming the deficient subjectivities of the workless that New Labour was able to reconfigure poverty as a matter of choice and champion 'hard-working families' in place of the working poor. Indeed, the entire perceptual framework which legitimized the punishment of the poor relied upon the *culturalization* of poverty and disadvantage. At the same time the discourses of meritocracy and choice that saturated public culture and policy documents functioned as an alibi for economic inequalities by 're-branding them as deserved' (Jones 2011: 97).

The moral panic about council estates unleashed pervasive forms of territorial stigmatization, a revolting class discourse that was inscribed upon the bodies of those who lived in these abjectified zones. Drawing on research undertaken by the Joseph Rowntree Foundation, Haylett argues that:

> Whilst some of the many disadvantages of a dilapidated material environment [were] alleviated [by regeneration policies] the stigma associated with the estate as types of places inhabited by types of people has proved much harder to shift. [R]esearch identifies stigma as having deleterious effects on the quality of residents' lives through lower-quality service provision from outside agencies, discrimination by post-code from local employers ('red-lining') and heavy emotional impacts, such as low self-esteem. (Haylett 2003: 68)

This territorial stigmatization was heightened when, during New Labour's second term in office (2001–05), a new popular vocabulary of social class came to saturate British public culture. The word 'chav' alongside its various synonyms and regional variations (including simply 'council') was a pejorative and ubiquitous term of abuse of and abhorrence at Britain's poor. Widely understood to be an acronym for 'Council Housed and Violent' or 'Council-House-Associated Vermin', chav was the popular (con)figuration of that imagined 'underclass of people cut off from society's mainstream, without any sense of shared purpose', which Blair had first bodied forth in his maiden speech (Blair 1997).

The animation of the chav

It was undoubtedly the mediating agencies of popular culture, newspaper journalism, television and the Internet which transformed New Labour's symbolic abjection of class into the figure of the chav. The cumulative effects of many hundreds of thousands of newspaper articles, photographs and online commentaries about chavs constituted this figure as a national abject par excellence. For example, in 2004 the *Independent on Sunday* recorded more than ten thousand references to the word 'chav' in one week, the same week that 'chav' was named by the *Oxford English Dictionary* as the 'buzzword' of the year (Independent on Sunday 2004). In fact, 2004 was the year in which disgust and fascination with chavs peaked in the British press. Writing in the *Edinburgh Evening News* that year, journalist Gina Davidson offers us a typical journalistic account of 'the chav' phenomenon:

> And we will know them by their dress ... and trail of fag ends, sparkling white trainers, baggy tracksuit trousers, branded sports top, gold-hooped earrings, 'sovvy' rings and the ubiquitous Burberry baseball cap. Throw them together, along with a pack of Regal, and you have the uniform of what is being described as the UK's new underclass – the chav. Call them what you will, identifying them is easy. They are the sullen youths in hooded tops and spanking-new trainers who loiter listlessly on street corners and shopping malls, displaying an apparent lack of education and an all too obvious taste for fighting; the slack-jawed girls with enough gold or gold-plated jewellery to put H Samuel out of business. They are the dole-scroungers, petty criminals, football hooligans and teenage pram-pushers. (Davidson 2004: 14)

The repeated association made between 'chavs' and 'dole-scroungers, petty criminals, football hooligans and teenage pram-pushers' vividly recalls Victorian and Edwardian accounts of the dangerous, immoral and libidinal poor. Yet, as I will explore in more detail in Chapter 7, this history of class names is reconfigured through the neoliberal lens of the underclass.

Vicky Pollard

Britain's 'favourite chav', Vicky Pollard, began life as a fictional television character in the phenomenally successful BBC comedy series *Little Britain* (2003–06). The Vicky Pollard sketches are set in the fictional town of Darkley Noone. This character, played in drag by the privately educated comic actor Matt Lucas, is an overweight moody teenage girl who is usually dressed in a pink tracksuit, wearing badly applied make-up with some of her long, bleached-blonde hair pulled up into a 'scrunchy'. Pollard speaks in an incomprehensibly fast regional accent and much of the comedy derives from Lucas's vocal performance. Pollard's 'online c.v.' reveals that Vicky has had 'at least 13 children', and publicity stills for *Little Britain* depict Vicky posing with some of her children framed by a council estate backdrop (Tyler 2008).

The actors and writers of *Little Britain*, David Walliams and Lucas, argue that Vicky is a genuine 'social type', commenting in a newspaper interview that 'you can find her type lurking on every street corner [...] People always say they know a Vicky Pollard. There are even Vicky Pollards on the road where I live and *we always point to them when we see them*' (cited in Jeffries 2005: 3). Many journalists concur, arguing, for example, that:

> The reason Vicky Pollard caught the public imagination is that she embodies with such fearful accuracy several of the great scourges of contemporary Britain: aggressive all female gangs of embittered, hormonal, drunken teenagers; gym slip mums who choose to get pregnant as a career option; pasty-faced, lard-gutted slappers who'll drop their knickers in the blink of an eye. (Delingpole 2006: 25)

Vicky Pollard is, of course, 'a joke', a joke which allows the audience to engage freely in 'the pleasures of hatred' (Billig 2001: 267). However, Pollard is also a joke crafted out of the political ideologies of New Labour, and ideologies always overflow their containment within jokes (ibid.: 286; Finding 2008). Vicky Pollard congealed within political and public culture and within everyday social intercourse as figurative shorthand for 'Broken Britain' and the underclass (see Chapter 7). Take the following examples of newspaper reports in which Vicky Pollard is crafted into the name for a variety of social ills:

This unimaginative redevelopment at the heart of Bristol is

emblematic of the city's Vicky Pollard tendencies. It has been consistently let down by civic leaders who share Vicky's bovine poverty
of ambition. (Observer 2005)

Woman mugged by Vicky Pollard look-alike. (Daily Mail 2005)

Vicky Pollard-style ladettes are bringing more and more booze-
fuelled trouble to our streets, new figures revealed today. (Sunderland 2007)

More than 1500 16 to 18-year-olds in Bradford are living a
Vicky Pollard lifestyle – leaving taxpayers facing a staggering bill.
(Telegraph and Argus 2007)

During the airing of *Little Britain* barely a day went by without the
use of the name or an image of Vicky Pollard in a newspaper story
about the feckless, violent underclass. This figure moved relentlessly
through public culture on a wave of mockery, contempt and disgust.
Social media and the feedback loops offered by the message boards
of online newspapers are a critical part of this process in that they
enable publics to shape and craft the chav as a knowable figure. The
term animation is particularly useful here; to animate something is to
breathe life into an inanimate object or figure. The chav as national
abject is brought to life and vitalized with negative qualities through
interaction. Online publics collaborate in the making of pejorative
class figures, concurring with and elaborating upon the descriptions
proffered. Consider, for example, schoolteachers I came across talk-
ing to one another on the Times Education online bulletin board in
2008, discussing 'the chav dole scum that seem to be on the rise
and causing the trouble'. They describe the schools they work in as
'stinking chav-pit[s]' and problem pupils as 'Vicky SLAPPER Pollards'
(cited in Tyler 2008). We can begin to see here how fictional fabrica-
tions (chavs and chav mums) come to shape perceptual realities at
multiple levels of social interchange. These perceptual realities come
to organize 'public opinion' and incite 'consent' for punishing the poor
through the rollback of welfare systems: *there is a revolting underclass
and we need punitive policies to deal with them*. The hardening of public
opinion into consent is constituted by the accumulation and repetition
of these expressions and beliefs in everyday life: 'conversations between
neighbours, discussion at street-corners or in the pub, rumour, gossip,
speculation' (Hall et al. 1978: 129).

It was not coincidental that my research on the figure of the chav emerged from the university seminar room. If chavs are imagined as revolting subjects conceived in the pathological culture of council estates, then the neoliberal university is the spatial and imaginary antithesis to this abject zone. A figure of sloth, ignorance and welfare dependence stuck in time and place, the chav is the polar opposite of the 'self-scripting' mobile, flexible and individualized selves which the children of New Labour had been taught to embrace. As one schoolgirl explained to me on an access course designed to encourage disadvantaged young people to come to university, 'I used to be a chav, but I want to be a student now.'

It is not simply that many university students define themselves as a group against their excluded peers, 'the chav-nots', but that students have been absolutely instrumental in the *fabrication* and *corporealization* of this figure. For over a decade now, Britain's students have held 'chav nites' in which they dress up as chavs. Female students carrying plastic bags from cut-price food superstores, push cushions under tight tops to feign pregnant chav bellies, and drink cider and cheap lager, enjoying the affect of being imaginary chavs. Photographs of these chav student nights populate Internet sites, and images of students cross-class dressing are reproduced on 'chav hate' websites where they are vilified as 'authentic chavs' (see Tyler 2008). Students at Leeds University went to the lengths of making a comedic feature film, entitled *CHAV!* (Shepherd 2005): the storyline involved the university being invaded by tracksuit-clad chav zombies, who threatened to *infect* the middle-class student protagonists. Echoing Beck's claim that class is a 'zombie category', the chavs are depicted clawing at the doors of the university and pursing students through lecture theatres and seminar rooms (Willms 2004: 51–2). The students defeat the chav-zombies by mesmerizing them with grime music (a British derivative of hip hop). In 2007 schoolboys at the elite private Glenalmond College School in Scotland made a mockumentary film entitled *Class Wars* which depicted pupils dressed as chavs being beaten, hunted and shot by aristocrats on horseback and their hounds. The film begins with a teenager in a baseball cap being pulled out of a river before being subjected to a simulated beating. It finishes with a spectacular 'shoot' after 'chavs' are flushed into open ground by beaters and gunned down with double-barrelled shotguns. The release of the film on YouTube garnered significant news media coverage,

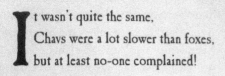

I t wasn't quite the same,
Chavs were a lot slower than foxes,
but at least no-one complained!

6.1 Popular greetings card

which in turn provoked an outpouring of similar home-made films. *Class Wars* was memorialized in popular greetings cards (Figure 6.1), T-shirts, online computer games and game apps (*Chav Hunter, Zombie Chav Hunt*), and social media pages (such as the popular Facebook site '1,000,000 against chavs').

As a neoliberal name for the poor in Britain, 'chav' enables those who use, invoke or indeed perform this name to constitute themselves as 'other than poor'. In this respect, the figure of the chav reveals much more about the imperatives of neoliberal citizenship than it does about the conditions of existence for the poor in neoliberal Britain.

Classificatory struggles

When the term chav was first popularized, it was frequently denied by those who used it that it might be a pejorative 'class name'; many political and expert social commentators still make this claim. When, for example, in May 2011, Baroness Hussein-Ece, a Liberal Democrat peer and a member of the coalition government's Commission for Equality and Human Rights, tweeted, 'Help. Trapped in a queue in chav-land! Woman behind me explaining latest EastEnders plot to mate, while eating largest bun I've ever seen', journalists and political commentators were divided on what the tweeting of the word chav by a government-appointed champion of equality and rights meant. The baroness later attempted to defend herself by counter-tweeting that the word chav is 'endearing in my part of town'.[5] Other frequently cited 'evidence' that chav is not a pejorative word is that working-class people use the term, and that it is frequently directed at rich celebrities as well as poor people. As the journalist Ed West wrote in the *Telegraph* in defence of Baroness Hussein-Ece:

> The reason [chav spread with such speed] was because it so perfectly, and succinctly, described a type of person that almost everyone in Britain recognised [...]. A type of person defined not just by their clothes, speech and mannerism but their lifestyle and attitude. [...] Working-class people use it all the time, understand what it means and, if anything, dislike chavs more than anyone. Why? Because they have to live with them. Being a chav is not about being poor, or unskilled, or any of the traditional markers of the proletariat, but about attitude, and in particular one that lacks civic-mindedness and civility. That's why it's perfectly reasonable for people, of all classes, to mock them. (West 2011)

For those on the left, however, the use of the term chav is indicative of 'social racism' (Burchill 2011) and 'poisonous class bile' (Toynbee 2011). As Toynbee writes on the Hussein-Ece affair:

> She would presumably never say nigger or Paki, but chav is acceptable class abuse by people asserting superiority over those they despise. Poisonous class bile is so ordinary that our future king and his brother played at dressing up and talking funny at a chav party mocking their lower class subjects. Wrapped inside this little word is the quintessence of Britain's great social fracture. Over the last 30 years the public monstering of a huge slice of the population by luckier, better-paid people has become commonplace. This is language from the Edwardian era of unbridled snobbery. [...] The form and style may have changed – but the reality of extreme inequality and self-confident class contempt is back. (Ibid.)

As these two responses to Baroness Hussein-Ece's tweet reveal, the chav has become a symbolic site of polarized struggles between left- and right-wing social commentators and experts.[6] One of the things which characterizes this struggle is the way in which those who are most critical of this pejorative figuration of class disadvantage attempt to denaturalize the chav by positing an authentic and positive working-class figure in its place. For example, in her article Toynbee invokes 'the remarkably strong work ethic of those in jobs paying little more than benefits, the carers and cleaners doing essential work well, despite lack of money or respect' (ibid.). This strategy of revitalizing working-class identities is also central to Owen Jones's best-selling book, *Chavs: The Demonization of the Working Class* (2011).

In his book Jones attempts to trouble the figure of 'the chav mum' by testing its empirical veracity on the streets. As he writes, 'wandering around Ashington [...] it was difficult not to notice a number of young mothers. But were they anything like the popular stereotype of the Vicky-Pollard-style chav teenage mum?' (ibid.: 189). What he finds is young mothers whom he rescripts as 'decent and respectable working-class' women. But what he omits in his descriptions of their responses to his questions is precisely the ways in which these young mothers are compelled to define themselves *against* the interpellative effects of the parasitical figure of Vicky Pollard. Take the following example:

> I spoke to nineteen-year-old Emma, out with her ten-month-old child. She had also brought up a four-year-old, from her partner's previous relationship – 'in case you thought I had him really young!' [...] Emma [...] was determined to work as soon as possible. 'I do plan to go back to work. Definitely. I'd go back now but he's too young.' (Ibid.: 189)

What this quotation reveals is that 'Emma' knows she is pejoratively judged; she carefully clarifies the age at which she had her first child – 'in case you thought I had him really young!' – and insists on her willingness to undertake paid work. If she is asserting a class identity it is not an 'authentic white working-class identity' but an identity produced through a disidentification with a pejorative class name imposed from outside. Indeed, by questioning Emma about her 'willingness to work', Jones unwittingly reproduces the moral distinction between worker/workless which he ostensibly seeks to trouble, but, moreover, Emma is already engaged in work, *the work of social reproduction* (childcare and domestic labour). My intention here isn't to undermine Jones's efforts to shift the terms of the debate. It is, rather, to draw attention to the limits of a methodology that relies upon exposing a mismatch between the 'unreality' of vilifying class names and the 'reality' of working-class dignity.

The positive critical reception to Jones's book, and his subsequent media celebrity, has worked to stabilize the meaning of the term chav on the liberal left as a pejorative name for an indigenous white working class. The creation of authentic working-class culture through the figure of the noble suffering worker has been a central strategy for post-war left politics since the Second World War (see Long 2008). This has been a politically important form of 'strategic essentialism' that enabled the articulation of class solidarities. The politicization of class names is also a critical counter-representational strategy that returns pejorative class names to the elites who fabricated them. While I am sympathetic with these tactics I want to trouble the positing of authentic working-class identities as a 'solution' to the neoliberal political vilification of Britain's poor since, as Deranty notes, '[e]very time emancipatory political action attempts to ground itself in some essential property, it falls into contradictions and paradoxes that make it miss its self-given target [and] transform it into its opposite' (Deranty 2010: 22). In short, the 'essentialist apriorism' of these strategies risks reinforcing the forms of classificatory violence that they might ostensibly seek to contest (Laclau and Mouffe 2001 177). These strategies revolve around the axis of deserving/undeserving poor and, as such, they reproduce the same problematic opposition that Marx conjured up in the figure of the revolting feminized lumpen against which he crafted the gallant muscularity of the proletariat (see Chapter 7). It is this same myth of worthiness which New Labour appeals to in its pitting of 'honest hard-working families' against the parasitical, pathological underclass. Indeed, the use of this strategy by the left often works to the advantage of the right, which (as West illustrates above) also appeals to a mythical 'real working class' in order to legitimize its mockery of the poor.

The critical question here is not whether 'such demonization [...] stand[s] up to scrutiny' (Jones 2011: 220) but rather to understand 'how the representations of self and other – which sustain hierarchy, consensus, or conflict – [are] formed' and how they might be transformed (Rancière 2004a: xxv). Rather, we need to theorize the figure of the chav as '*a figure of consent*' constituted by 'a disgust consensus' (see Chapter 1), a figure through which ideological beliefs (the underclass), economic interests (the erosion of the welfare state) and a series of governmental technologies (media, politics, policy, law) converge to mystify neoliberal governmentality by naturalizing poverty in ways that legitimize the social abjection of the most socially and economically disadvantaged citizens within the state.

Declassificatory politics

In *The Nights of Labor: The Workers' Dream in Nineteenth-century France* (1989), Rancière presented the findings of ten years of archival research on the nineteenth-century labour movement in France. In this book he sought to demonstrate that 'the relationship between the order of things and the desires of those subjugated to it is a bit more complicated than scholarly treatises realize' (Rancière 2004a: xii). Focusing not on the meta-narratives produced by left intellectuals of the social history of labour movements, but on close analysis of the writings of individuals engaged in those movements, what Rancière discovered in the archives was not an indigenous working-class voice, but 'a working class which was more mobile, less attached to its tools and less sunk in its own poverty and drunkenness than the various traditions usually represent it' (ibid.: xii). In place of 'cultural unity', what Rancière found was 'a chronicle of struggles which were countless but on each occasion confined to the particularity of their actors' (Rancière 2011: 22). Alongside these individual accounts he examined the collective and organized expressions of working-class identity in workers' pamphlets and papers. However, as he writes:

> The generality of workers' pamphlets and papers [...] asserted
> a working class identity. It was simply that this assertion was
> completely tied to a denial of the identity imposed by Others.
> The workers spoke to say that they were not those Others, those
> 'barbarians' that bourgeois discourse denounced. (Ibid.: 22)

Rancière discovered that individuals within the labour movement were motivated not by a positive revaluation of working-class labour or culture, or even primarily by economic injustice, but rather by a desire to participate *as equals* within the common social and political life of the nation. So, while Rancière had begun his journey into social history seeking evidence for the 'positive existence' and expression of working-class identity (ibid.: 22), what he found was a negative identity which cohered through collective expressions of rejection of the bourgeois representations of the working class. As he noted:

> the very gap between the wide dissemination of practices of struggle and the grand Sunday speeches about workers' dignity authorized a different definition of working-class identity: a strategic identity in which this discourse of denial crowned the everyday guerrilla practices of resistance. (Ibid.: 22)

If Rancière's thesis, that class struggle was for the workers in the nineteenth-century labour movement a working-class counter-offensive against the imposition of names and the destinies they prescribed, rather than an authentic 'culture', then it is interesting that over one century later we still find those on the losing end of the class system struggling against the imposition of class names.

For example, in *Formations of Class and Gender: Becoming Respectable* (1997), Skeggs's longitudinal ethnography of white working-class women in the north of England, disidentification with 'class names' bestowed from *above* and *outside* is also a recurrent theme. Skeggs's study suggests that while for men, identification with working-class identities might offer strategic and positive identifications (and still retains some of the heroic associations which Rancière identified in the official documents of the nineteenth-century labour movement), for women, often estranged from the history and politics of manual labour, such a positive identification was already impossible. Further, Skeggs's study, which began in the 1990s, tracks the historical moment in which class became a revolting subject. Skeggs uncovers how women daily questioned the (often negative) values associated with 'working-class womanhood' that they were expected to embrace. Critical strategies of disidentification, most notably practices of 'passing', 'self-improvement' and 'respectability', were a way for the women Skeggs worked with to create positive values for themselves in the absence of affirmative social inscriptions of working-class femininities, and against a stigmatizing and judgemental external gaze. Indeed, pathological representations of class and gender are precisely what these women attempted to defend themselves against. As Skeggs notes, 'the women had a clear knowledge about their "place" but they were always trying to leave it', thus 'social and cultural positioning generates denial, disidentification, dissimulation rather than adjustment' (ibid.: 81, 75). This is a study of the political emotions of class, 'of doubt, insecurity and unease', in which 'the real working class for these women is something they are desperately trying to escape' (ibid.: 75, 76). Skeggs theorizes this disidentification as a 'refusal of recognition rather than a claim for the right to be recognized' (ibid.: 74). Strategies of disidentification are employed as a means of resisting negative interpellations. Contrary, then, to the proponents of the 'death of class' thesis, which argues that people's increasing disidentification with class categories is empirical evidence of the redundancy of 'class', what both Rancière and Skeggs suggest is that *class struggle* is *struggle against classification*.

Class as a history of names

The title of this chapter, 'Britain and its poor', makes reference to Rancière's *The Philosopher and His Poor* (2004a), an account of the function of the poor within the history of philosophy and sociology. Rancière uses the term 'poor' rather than, for example, the workers, or the proletariat, advisedly. For Rancière the poor describes not only the economically disadvantaged parts of a population within a given state, but is understood more broadly as 'the category of people who do not count' (Rancière 2001). Focusing his critical attentions on Plato, Marx and Bourdieu, Rancière details the multiple inscriptions and figurations of the poor, the shoemakers, blacksmiths, plebs, common people, proletarians, lumpen, masses, women and slaves within philosophy, political theory and sociology. He argues that the history of European thought is premised on the foreclosure of the poor through practices of naming (class-making). As the diversity of names given to the poor implies, Rancière does not use 'the poor' to describe an existent class of people, but rather uses it as a 'placeholder' for those who are spoken for, described and named by thinkers and experts. The poor in this sense has no referent but describes the fabrication, abstraction and capitalization of *others* in the production of knowledge and culture. The poor are those mute masses who through their abjection constitute the conditions of knowledge itself. The poor are those whose autonomous modes of speech and cultural production are devalued, marginalized and/or silenced. In designating the poor inaudible the philosopher is able to assume an unmarked position of truth outside of history 'in which his own position cannot figure at all' (Rancière 2004a: 33). As Rancière writes: '[The poor are] an ersatz that philosophy cannot do without since, in order to preserve its role in the legislation of legitimate thoughts, it is itself obliged to produce a discourse on non-philosophy, on illegitimate modes of thinking' (ibid.: 131).

'[P]resent as objects rather than subjects of knowledge, appearing only in the guise of philosophy's exempla, the poor enable the philosopher to constitute himself as other than the poor' (Parker, in ibid.: xiii). This inclusive/exclusive logic reveals philosophy to be what Rancière describes as 'the science of truth and lying' and 'the science of speech and silence' (ibid.: 40). For in claiming to speak about and for the poor, the philosopher assumes the position of a liar, a liar who partitions il/legibility in order to legitimize his own knowledge as truth. Rancière's interpretation of the function of the poor in the history of philosophy, as well as his historical research on the nineteenth-century labour movement, led him to the conclusion that the working class should be understood primarily as *a set of names*, rather than as an identity or experience. As he writes, 'those names do not express an awareness of a condition. Their primary function is to construct something, namely a relationship of alterity' (Rancière 1997: 23). The poor are the abject, those who are both excluded from intelligible categories of being but included through their exclusion, securing, constituting and legitimizing the hegemonic politics of the state.

Rancière's argument resonates with the claim made by Raymond Williams in *Culture and Society* that 'the masses don't exist'. The paradox which both Williams and Rancière identify is that naming class makes class. It is worth quoting Williams at some length here:

> The masses are always the others, whom we don't know, and can't know. [...] To other people, we also are masses. Masses are other people. There are in fact no masses; there are only ways of seeing people as masses. In an urban industrial society there are many opportunities for such ways of seeing. The point is not to reiterate the objective conditions but to consider, personally and collectively, what these have done to our thinking. The fact is, surely, that a way of seeing other people which has become characteristic of our kind of society has been capitalized for the purposes of political or cultural exploitation. [...] we mass them, and interpret them, according to some convenient formula. Within its terms, the formula will hold. Yet it is the formula, not the mass, which it is

our real business to examine. The political formula by means of
which it seems possible to convert the majority of one's fellow
human beings into masses, and thence into something to be hated
or feared. (Williams 1960: 319)

Williams details the emergence of the concept of 'the masses' as
a name for the working class under industrial capitalism. The masses
emerged to describe processes of urbanization, factory work and
mass production, and latterly 'the social and political massing' of
the working classes (through unionization, for example) (ibid.: 317).
However, 'the masses', Williams argued, was also just a new word for
the mob, 'and the traditional characteristics of the mob were retained
in its significance: gullibility, fickleness, herd prejudice, lowness of
taste and habit. The masses, on this evidence, formed the perpetual
threat to culture' (ibid.: 318). As Williams argues, the 'conception of
persons as masses springs, not from an inability to know them, but
from an interpretation of them according to a formula' (ibid.: 322).
Williams also reminds us that it is impossible to understand the
political formulas which give rise to 'hatred and fear' of the masses
without a consideration of mass communication and its 'multiple
transmissions' as a technology of governance (ibid.: 319). As he notes,
the institutions of mass communication (newspapers, radio, television,
journalism, advertising) 'were not produced by the working people
themselves. They were, rather, produced for them by others, often
[...] for conscious political or commercial advantage' and often for
'the persuasion of a large number of people to act, feel, think, know,
in certain ways' (ibid.: 326, 322).

If class is a history of names our role, as Williams suggests, is to
consider what these class names 'have done to our thinking' (ibid.:
319). The ways in which elite discourses shape the perceptual frames
of class 'for the purposes of political or cultural exploitation: *The
political formula by means of which it seems possible to convert the majority
of one's fellow human beings into masses, and thence into something to be
hated or feared*' (ibid.: 319). We must also consider the reality effects
of these injurious interpellations, the reworking and the refusal of
these names and the resistant politics which unfold from practices
of social classification and struggles of declassification.

With the assistance of Williams and Rancière, we might interpret
Blair's speech to the residents of the Aylesbury Estate, and to gathered

journalists and television crews, as a moment in the creation of 'Blair's Poor'. The 'new class: a workless class' which he identified as 'the greatest challenge of any democratic government' inaugurated a new political formula in British politics, a neoliberal perceptual frame through which to perceive 'the masses' as 'an underclass of people cut off from society's mainstream, without any sense of shared purpose' (Blair 1997). Through the political art of persuasion and through 'the multiple transmissions' of mass communication technologies, this political formulation came to shape the figure of the chav and the ways in which the British public came to feel, think and act about Britain's poor.

Broken Britain: Little Britain

In 2008 Conservative leader and now prime minister David Cameron shamelessly plagiarized from Blair and launched his own campaign for what he called 'a new morality' to fix 'Broken Britain' (Cameron 2008). Speaking from under a crucifix at a community centre at St Jude's Church in Barlanark in the deprived East End of Glasgow, in the run-up to a by-election, Cameron told the gathered congregation of journalists that 'our mission is to repair our broken society – to heal the wounds of poverty, crime, social disorder and deprivation that are steadily making this country a grim and joyless place to live for far too many people' (ibid.).

> We talk about people being 'at risk of obesity' instead of talking about people who eat too much and take too little exercise. We talk about people being at risk of poverty, or social exclusion: it's as if these things – obesity, alcohol abuse, drug addiction – are purely external events like a plague or bad weather. Of course, circumstances – where you are born, your neighbourhood, your school, and the choices your parents make – have a huge impact. But social problems are often the consequence of the choices that people make. (Ibid.)

As the Scottish newspaper *The Herald* pointed out, hagiography is clearly not Cameron's strong point: St Jude being the patron saint of lost causes, 'hopeless cases and things almost despaired of' (Macdonald 2008). When a journalist asked Father Allan Cameron, the parish priest, whether he would be voting for the Conservative candidate in the by-election, he replied 'definitely not' (ibid.). However, Cameron's underclass verbiage was not intended for the locals in East Glasgow but for an audience south of the border. 'How extraordinary', wrote Conservative MP Michael Fabricant in the *Birmingham Post*, 'that David Cameron should [...] have the political courage and the honesty to say that some of the obese, lazy or poor spend too much time blaming social problems rather than their own lack of moral fibre for their own shortcomings' (Fabricant 2008). To ram the point home Fabricant concluded his article with the sentence '*Little Britain*'s Vicky Pollard – an uneducated, obese, teenage single mother – is not just a comedy character, but a sad observation on part of our society' (ibid.).

Conclusion

> Class distinctions do not die: they merely learn new ways of expressing themselves. Each decade we swiftly declare we have buried class; each decade the coffin stays empty. (Hoggart 1989: vii)

The names by which class is known in Britain today have changed, as Britain has changed from an industrial empire of factories and workers to a post-industrial neoliberal society characterized by new forms of labour and consumption. Class struggles, as struggles over the representations of chavs in media culture make explicit, have not diminished. On the contrary, as neoliberalism wreaks its own brand of exploitation upon the people, class conflicts have heightened. The figure of the chav is the figure of class struggle in neoliberal Britain, which is why attending to this figure, its meanings and effects, is important.

In this chapter I have detailed some of the concerted efforts made by academics, politicians and the mediating agencies of popular culture to transform class into a revolting subject at the very moment that inequalities were deepening and social mobility had stalled. As I detailed in Chapter 1, economic polarization has reached unparalleled depths because *neoliberalism is a class project* (Harvey 2005): an ideology which aimed to restore and consolidate class power, under the veil of rhetoric of individualism, choice, freedom, mobility and border security. It is disappointing, then, that so many social theorists felt class had become a contaminating concept, a 'chav' discourse polluting the academy. Without some understanding of class struggle it is impossible to theorize the politics of global economic restructuring, urban disinvestment, the intensification of resource extraction and ecological crises, the opening up of state borders to flows of capital and migrant labour, the emergence of a new class of super-rich, the deepening precariousness of all labour, the demise of the post-war social contract and the fraying of the welfare state. The figure of the chav reveals precisely how class distinctions continued to be discursively reproduced in Britain at the very moment it was claimed that class had lost its relevance. As Toynbee argues, '[t]here is now no politics to express or admit the enormity of what has happened since the 1980s – how wealth and human respect drained from the bottom to enrich and glorify the top' (Toynbee 2011). However what is perhaps most hopeful about the figure of the chav is the declassificatory struggles – and the forms of dissensus – which this figure is effecting. As I will explore in the next chapter, the abject figure of the chav may yet mark the return of a new political vocabulary of class struggle for these dark times.

7 | THE KIDS ARE REVOLTING

They call you 'council estate'
They call you 'can't go straight'
They call you 'crime rate'

Tricky, 'Council Estate', 2008

We have the riots we deserve. A state in which what is called public order is only a coupling of the protection of private wealth and dogs unleashed on children of working people and people of foreign origin is purely and simply despicable. (Badiou 2006: 114)

England, 6–10 August 2011

Five nights in August 2011 saw the largest and most pervasive scenes of civil unrest in recent British history. On 4 August 2011, Mark Duggan, a twenty-nine-year-old black man and an alleged gang member, was shot dead by police in the north London borough of Tottenham. In the early evening of 6 August, a protest by his family and friends outside a Tottenham police station escalated into a riot. I happened to be staying with friends who lived near by when the riots began. It had been a hot and humid week in London. This was a city notably emptied out of holidaying wealthier residents, filled instead with tourists and those locals unable to escape the August city heat. On the evening of 6 August, police helicopters lit up the sky with searchlights, a bus was set alight on a street near by and sirens keened continuously into the morning. I watched the same short edited sequences of burning vehicles and buildings loop continuously on twenty-four-hour news channels, and observed those citizens who took to social media, tweeting their fear, outrage and excitement at unfolding events. The next day tension crackled in the air, and it felt inevitable that the unrest would proliferate. Over the subsequent five nights several thousand young people joined in and the rioting, arson and looting spread across London and out to the business and shopping districts of several other English cities and towns.

The rioters' destructive and violent activities were targeted primarily at commercial property and the police, but notably directed in some instances at watching journalists and television crews. Frightening, surreal and carnivalesque sequences of young people, often hooded, their faces covered by scarves and masks, flagrantly engaging in what several newspapers described as 'an orgy of looting', saturated the news media and social network sites. Writing on 8 August in the *Telegraph*, in an article titled 'London riots: the underclass lashes out', journalist Mary Riddell described scenes on the streets as 'a Hobbesian dystopia of chaos and brutality' enacted by a 'ruined generation' (Riddell 2012). The spread and scale of the riots, and the surprise and initial reluctance of the police to use force that would aggravate the situation, led to panicked assertions in the news media that the riots were contagious and uncontrollable, and for a while this is how it felt both to the rioters and to the wider public.

There were immediate calls for harsh and exceptional remedies, including shipping water cannon over from Northern Ireland, equipping police with rubber bullets, bringing armed forces on to the streets, the use of unusually punitive detention and prison sentences, the removal of welfare benefits from rioters and their families, and the eviction of families from local authority housing. Many proffered more extreme solutions, such as flogging, conscription, chain gangs, corporal and capital punishment and sterilization; 'I have no problem with armed police or military units hosing down the rioters with machine guns,' commented one blogger (cited in Easton 2011). On 8 August, a Conservative Member of the European Parliament, Roger Helmer, tweeted to followers: 'MEMO TO COBRA: "Time to get tough. Bring in the Army. Shoot Looters and Arsonists on sight."'

By 10 August, five people were dead, by mid-October 2011 4,000 had been arrested (Newburn et al. 2011a and b). If the scale of the unrest shocked the British public, the media coverage of the riots unleashed a torrent of 'underclass' appellations. As Matthew Connolly noted in the *Guardian*, 'Scum, thugs, feral rats, wolves, an army of ants on their BlackBerrys … the dehumanising epithets flew like bricks through a JD Sports window last week' (Connolly 2011). The same hate speech which had systematically mocked, humiliated and shamed disenfranchised young people as 'chav scum' for the preceding decade reached a deafening climax in the immediate and subsequent coverage of these five nights of social unrest. This explosion of visceral hatred was aimed not only at those who had participated in the rioting, but

7.1 Volunteer Haley Miller waits to help with the clean-up operation at Clapham Junction

also at their families and the communities in which they lived. The term 'scum' was the favoured pejorative: 'the scum class', 'verminous waste', 'these scum need to be removed from society permanently by whatever means is necessary', wrote bloggers in a BBC news thread (cited in Easton 2011).

London mayor Boris Johnson was pictured wielding a broom in solidarity with the concerned citizens and campaigners who came out on to the streets to assist local authorities in the post-riot clear-up and to 'reclaim' the streets symbolically by sweeping them clean (see Chapter 1). The news media, keen to capitalize on what Sofia Himmelblau described as 'the thinly veiled symbolism of social cleansing' (Himmelblau 2001), pictured 'broom army' recruits wearing T-shirts proclaiming 'looters are scum' (Figure 7.1). Even before the fires were out and the streets cleansed, the rioters and the public were warned that the proffering and receiving of 'economic and sociological justifications' would be as revolting as the riotous acts themselves

(Boris Johnson, cited in Milne 2011). As Seumas Milne commented in the *Guardian*, 'When [...] Ken Livingstone linked the riots to the impact of public spending cuts, it was almost as if he'd torched a building himself' (Milne 2011).

The article by the BBC's Home Editor, Mark Easton, 'England riots: the return of the underclass' (Easton 2011), drew upon a 2008 policy report by Iain Duncan Smith, the Secretary of State for Work and Pensions, which argued for more early childhood interventions within the '"dysfunctional base" of our society' (Duncan Smith 2008: 11). Duncan Smith contended that there was a 'creeping expansion' of a 'more menacing underclass' which was drawing 'decent' families into the 'code of the street' (Duncan Smith, cited in Easton 2011). He reiterated these claims after the riots at the Conservative Party conference in October 2011, where he characterized this underclass as 'chaos and dysfunctionality [...] governed by a perverse set of values' (Mulholland 2011). This perspective was underscored by Justice Secretary Kenneth Clarke, who used his turn on the conference podium to make the claim that 'Our feral underclass is too big, has been growing, and needs to be diminished' (Daily Telegraph 2011). Indeed, in the aftermath of the riots the underclass 'explanation' was reproduced by the vast majority of mainstream politicians and 'expert' pundits and even by some on the far left, such as the minor political party the Independent Working Class Association (IWCA), which posted an article in response to the riots which stated that the rioters were not 'alienated working class youth' but 'lumpen elements [that] represent a grouping that is quite separate from, and actively hostile to, the interests and well-being of the working class proper' (IWCA 2011). 'Even for Marx,' one IWCA member commented, 'for whom all history is the history of class struggle, the lumpen-underclass was worthy of contempt, not compassion' (ibid.).

Introduction

In Chapter 5 I detailed how the conceptual frame of the underclass, and its popular reconfiguration in the figure of chav, functioned as part of wider efforts by the political elites to expunge the political vocabulary of class from the public domain. In this chapter I develop this argument through an analysis of the August 2011 riots and their representation. I will consider how the conceptual and perceptual frame of the underclass was operationalized as a means of explaining

7.2 'The riots are not political'

and containing the meaning of the August riots as apolitical, while also usefully serving as 'definitive proof' of the existence of a population defined by their 'antisocial behaviours' (Wacquant 2008: 24).

First, tracing the longer revolting history of the underclass and its eugenic origins, I will examine how and why this concept became the dominant perceptual frame through which to perceive poverty and inequality. I will argue that the underclass is a polluting and racializing category, which is employed to legitimize punitive forms of neoliberal governmentality. Secondly, I will detail how the discursive frame of the underclass legitimized the use of exceptionally vindictive judicial and economic punishments. Notably, the riots were also used to generate greater public consent for the shift from protective liberal forms of welfare to penal workfare regimes. Indeed, one of the first responses to the riots was a call for rioters to be forced into work, along with calls for the removal of welfare support and social housing, not only from those who had participated in the riots but also from their families. On 11 August, a government e-petition calling for rioters to lose welfare benefits hit 100,000 signatures and made British history as the first of such petitions to be considered for debate in Parliament. Finally, drawing on empirical data from the LSE/*Guardian* 'Reading the Riots' research, I will consider how stigmatizing discourses of the underclass produce the 'wasted populations' which they describe. My central claim in this final chapter is that if we want to fight neoliberalism – to *defend society* – it is essential to prise open and fracture the concept of the underclass. It is only then that we can begin to make another sense of the August riots as one part of a deepening and global *neoliberal legitimation crisis*. This chapter does not seek to romanticize the criminal behaviour of those who participated in the riots but it insists that we understand these riots as a political event (Figure 7.2).

The lumpen history of the underclass

As John Welshman (2006) details in his excellent history, the asinine concept of the 'underclass' has been the source of intensive debate and critique over three decades. The underclass is broadly understood in political, policy and popular culture as a term that refers to a population 'distinct from the working class – [...] a rootless mass divorced from the means of production – definable only in terms of social inefficiency, and hence not strictly a class in the neo-Marxist sense' (Macnicol, cited in ibid.: xii). While Marxist understandings of class are historically contingent and relational, where classes are formed through antagonism and struggle, the concept of the underclass describes an adjunct class divorced from the body politic proper. The underclass are imagined as being in *excess* of class relations 'with neither chance nor need of readmission', and 'beyond redemption' (Bauman 1998: 66). In this sense, as the IWCA argued, the underclass conceptually corresponds to those whom Marx designated the lumpenproletariat, his pejorative name for those populations that are liminal to the majority moral and political community.

In the *Manifesto of the Communist Party* Marx defines the lumpen as the '"dangerous class", the social scum, that passively rotting mass thrown off by the lowest layers of the old society' (Marx 1848). In *The Eighteenth Brumaire of Louis Bonaparte* (Marx 1852), Marx explores the political crisis in France between 1848 and 1851, reflecting on why revolutionary movements might succeed or fail at different historical moments. His conclusion in the case of France in this period was that the failure of the workers' uprising was a consequence of the fluid social-economic conditions, an effect of the epochal transition from feudalism to industrial capitalism. Labour in France wasn't yet bonded to industrial capital, 'the bricks and mortar of factory walls' (Bauman 2000: 116) and, as a consequence, there were many heterogeneous class fractions in play, too many to permit a proletariat revolutionary mass. In short, he suggests that it was because industrial capitalism was not yet the overriding economic force in French society that a second French revolution was impeded (Hayes 1988). To make this complex argument Marx extends his use of the lumpen to describe the 'scum, offal, refuse' of all social classes, offering an account of how this scum were recruited by Louis Bonaparte, with the support of the equally lumpen 'finance aristocracy', to liquidate the workers' uprising. Marx's loathing for this 'indefinite, disintegrated mass' of tricksters, prostitutes and ex-slaves is tangible:

> Alongside decayed roués with dubious means of subsistence and of dubious origin, alongside ruined and adventurous offshoots of the bourgeoisie, were vagabonds, discharged soldiers, discharged jailbirds, escaped galley slaves, swindlers, mountebanks, lazzaroni, pickpockets, tricksters, gamblers, maquereaux [pimps], brothel keepers, porters, literati, organ grinders, ragpickers, knife grinders, tinkers, beggars – in short, the whole indefinite, disintegrated mass, thrown hither and thither [...] from this kindred element [...] Bonaparte constitutes himself chief of the lumpenproletariat [...] recognizes in this scum, offal, refuse of all classes the only class upon which he can base himself unconditionally. (Marx 1852)

Let us be clear: Marx is ostensibly concerned in this essay with better understanding the contingencies of class, 'class as an unstable yoking together, through political rhetoric, of heterogeneous groups' and 'class as shaped and transformed by state processes' (Stallybrass 1990: 70). Yet it is Marx (not 'the state') that lumps together all liminal, displaced, criminal and disenfranchised peoples into a singular revolting political foe. In his hands this 'overflowing heterogeneity' of foul and exotic others is reformed as a 'coagulating mass', a scapegoat for Bonaparte's *coup d'état* (ibid.: 72, 74). The paradox here is that in order to explain the failure of political efforts of the urban proletariat and their bourgeois supporters to effect a second French revolution Marx found himself compelled to invent a new abject 'classless class'.

The terms lumpenproletariat and 'underclass' function to lump together an entire plethora of disenfranchised people into one stigmatizing category, denoting dangerousness and expendability. Indeed, we might conclude that in Marx's lumpen we have found the rhetorical origins of the underclass. However, 'lumpen' was the fashionable class pejorative in Germany at the time and it was also English slang for the workhouse. As Stallybrass argues, Marx's disgusted description of the poor cites both 'the structure and the content of the descriptions of the street people of nineteenth-century Paris and London that fill the pages of novelists, journalists, and social analysts' (ibid.: 75). Marx was drawing, then, upon an existing 'political formula' for the undeserving poor as fabricated in the popular culture of the time (Williams 1960: 319). The citational history of the lumpen reveals

Marx to be caught up in the prevailing 'hysteria of naming' (Stallybrass 1990: 72). Indeed, describing Marx's depiction of the lumpen as a 'hateful' myth, Rancière argues that Marx becomes complicit with bourgeois fascination and disgust for the poor even while he sought to theorize the contingencies of class formation and the politics of class struggle (Rancière 2004a: 96). Wacquant similarly describes the neoliberal concept of underclass as a 'demonic legend' (Wacquant 2008: 204). Like the lumpen, the underclass functions to distinguish the deserving from the undeserving, and 'hard-working families' from a parasitical 'feckless underclass'.

If the lumpen is the abject of the proletariat, the feral underclass are the abject of neoliberal subject-citizens, the entrepreneurial, individualized, self-managing and flexible workers of 'liquid societies' and neoliberal states (Bauman 2000). As Bauman argues, in his critique of the term, the underclass are 'the aggregate product of wrong individual choices; proof of the "choice incompetence" of its members' (Bauman 1998: 71). The difference between the lumpen and the underclass is that while the concept of the lumpen is employed by Marx to fashion factory workers as the proletariat par excellence, the underclass is a distinctly neoliberal concept, designed to expunge class struggle from political vocabulary. As Westergaard suggests, the 'underclass' is reminiscent of a much older 'culture of poverty' hypothesis, '[b]ut this newer variant is distinct by *the resoluteness of its conception of class as a matter of voluntarily adopted lifestyles* – good versus evil – *essentially unconditioned by economic structure*' (Westergaard 1995: 117).

Paradoxically, Marx's vision of a 'permanent revolution' which would effect the abolition of class distinctions was adopted as the rallying cry of the neoliberal political classes as they scoured class from the political lexicon (see Chapter 5). Over and again we have been told that 'the class war is over'. In actuality the invention of the underclass signals not the death of class but rather 'the ongoing capitalist "revolution from above," commonly called neoliberalism' (Wacquant 2010: 211). For it is through the institution of the conceptual paradigm of the underclass that the ruling elites have been able to claim that there are no classes and legitimize the punishment of the poor.

The lumpen history of the underclass reveals that pejorative class epithets, whatever ideological project they serve, do not describe existing classes of people, as it is often and variously claimed.[1] This is not to say that 'underclass' does not have significant 'reality effects'. Indeed, we might go so far as to say that the arrival of the concept of the underclass in Britain in the 1980s, courtesy of the American political theorist Charles Murray (and the *Sunday Times*), incited public consent for the decomposition of the welfare state. As Hall et al. argue, power is secured through 'democratic' consent in ways which not only seem 'to be universal (what everybody wants) and legitimate (not won by coercive force)', but work to mystify relations of exploitation – which consequently *disappear from view* (Hall et al. 1978: 216).

> Consensus is not the opposite – it is the complementary face of domination. It is what makes the rule of the few disappear into the consent of the many. It actually consists or is founded on the conjunctural mastery of class struggle. But this mastery is displaced, through the mediating form of 'the consensus', and reappears as the *disappearance* or pacification of all conflict; [...] 'the end of ideology'. No wonder, when Harold Macmillan won his third successive electoral victory for the Conservatives in 1959 [...] he announced (no doubt hoping it would become a self-fulfilling prophecy) that 'The class struggle is over'. Perhaps he added, *sotto voce*, 'and we have won it'. (Ibid.: 216)

In neoliberal Britain, with class struggle expunged and inequality reconceived as *a matter of will*, the underclass – the mediating figure of consent – would henceforth be included through their exclusion.

Economic Darwinism

As Ruth Lister argues, in her excellent book *Poverty*, the term underclass is 'an exercise in conceptual contamination' (Lister 2004: 110). It is a racializing epithet for a class which is not a class but rather a 'jobless caste' (Gans 1990: 277). In the USA underclass theory was designed to constitute disenfranchised urban black and Hispanic populations as the abject others of citizenship proper. By way of contrast, Lister suggests that in the UK the racial/racist connotations of the underclass 'have tended to be more subterranean' (Lister 2004: 110). However, one of the things Lister fails to consider is that whiteness is a racializing discourse, and that the underclass discourse propagates categories of contaminated whiteness, as underclass guru Charles Murray made explicit in his essay 'White welfare, families, "white trash"' (Murray 1986).

Speaking on the BBC's flagship politics programme *Newsnight* on 13 August 2011 alongside journalist Owen Jones, historian David Starkey claimed that the involvement of white youths in the riots was evidence that 'the whites have become black'. Echoing Enoch Powell's infamous 1968 'Rivers of Blood' speech, Starkey's comments galvanized popular sentiments that indigenous white British youth had become 'infected' with the corrupting alien values of black migrants, an imported 'black culture' which was antithetical to Britishness:

> What's happened is that a substantial section of the chavs that you [Owen Jones] wrote about have become black. The whites have become black. A particular sort of violent, destructive, nihilistic, gangster culture has become the fashion. And black and white, boy and girl, operate in this language together, this language which is wholly false, which is this Jamaican patois that has been intruded in England, and this is why so many of us have this sense of literally a foreign country [...] It is about black culture, that is the enormously important thing, it is not skin colour, it is culture.
> (David Starkey, BBC *Newsnight*, 13 August 2011)

Starkey's racist remarks were greeted in public with a mixture of condemnation and congratulation. What is notable about his comments is that they are an explicit articulation of the racializing function of underclass discourses: an ideology which, as I argued in Chapter 6, had been vitalized in popular culture through the figure of the chav. From its first appearance in British media culture, the 'chav' was a racialized figure constituting a 'sullied urban underclass' situated 'at the borders of whiteness' (Nayak 2003: 82, 103). While the term chav is pejorative, ordinarily directed towards the white poor, the chav bodies forth a whiteness polluted by poverty and contaminated by territorial proximity to poor black and migrant populations. 'Blame Black Culture! Blame the Chavs!', summarized one student blogger the day after Starkey's claims were aired.

It is because the underclass are imagined as a *race* and not a class that poverty and disadvantage can be conceived as not economic or even properly political issues, but as a *hereditary condition*, a *disease*. As journalist Melanie Phillips 'explains', the August riots were '[a]n explosion of elective lone parenthood and dysfunctional behaviour *transmitted down through the generations* at the very bottom of the social heap' (Phillips 2011). 'The underclass is not something that you can fix. They need to be bred out,' commented one blogger in response to the riots; 'that is not an underclass, those are untermenschen [subhuman]', replied another. This use of the term 'untermenschen' returns us to the other citational history of the underclass: eugenicist thinking. As one blogger on a 'riot thread' expressed themselves:

> Having just seen some of the most repugnant vile 'human' excremental detritus in Salford, who look like something off Jeremy Kyle, leads me to believe a policy of ethical [sic] cleansing is in order. This country needs to rid iteslf [sic] of the 1,000,000 untermenschen by all means necessary and that my friends, means the charming but necessary use of unfettered brutal force. We need a Waffen SS to clean the streets off [sic] this dirt, with tins of Zyklon B at the ready. ('Bob', riot blog, 10 August 2011)

Bob's comments weren't unusual; this is but one of many thousands of similarly fascistic responses to the riots. In this context, it is also important to take note of the background presence of the far-right English Defence League who massed on the streets of north London to 'defend their communities' against the rioters on 11 August. Of course, we can simply reject these kinds of views as repugnant, extremist outbursts, but I would argue that it is critical to examine both the scale and the content of the hateful eugenicist discourse which came out of political quarantine during the riots. For, as we shall see, eugenicist thinking shapes the discourse of underclass.

'Untermenschen' was a term popularized by the Nazis. However, it was first coined by the American eugenicist Lothrop Stoddard in his racist treaty 'The revolt against civilization' (Stoddard 1922). For Stoddard the term 'under-man' was used to describe 'civilization's "inner barbarians"', 'degenerate' races and 'defective classes' (ibid.: 27, 79, 93):

> The rapidity with which feeble-minded stocks spread, and the damage they do, are vividly illustrated by numerous scientific studies which have been compiled. Both in Europe and America these studies tell the same story: feeble-minded individuals segregating in 'clans,' spreading like cancerous growths, disturbing the social life and infecting the blood of whole communities, and thriving on misguided efforts to 'better their condition,' by charity and other forms of 'social service.' (Ibid.: 94)

As charitable support for the poor was responsible for the growth of 'the under-man', Stoddard argued that the withdrawal of welfare support from these populations was an essential first step in effecting a solution to the 'vast hordes of congenital inferiors, incapable, unadaptable' who threated the future of civilization itself. The final solution proposed by Stoddard to the 'prodigious spawning of inferiors' (ibid.: 254) was 'race cleansing' (ibid.: 254). As he suggests, race cleansing is dependent on *race thinking*: 'The great thing [...] is *to get people thinking racially* [...] To cause not to exist those who would be doomed from birth to give only unhappiness to themselves and those about them; [to] decrease [...] the number of the antisocial and defective' (ibid.: 256–7, emphasis added).

Racist ideologies of social hygiene had a profound influence on political thinking in the twentieth century, and attracted support in Britain from among 'an eclectic group of scientists, Fabians, upper-class conservatives, and civil servants', as well as the literary and cultural elites (Hansen and King 2001: 224). As Dennis Sewell has argued, the political classes in this period 'harboured a savage contempt for the poorest of the poor' (Sewell 2009). Despite the seemingly opposing political views of those involved in promoting eugenics, it was a notably consistent and unifying ideology which was shaped by two central beliefs: 1) that mental and physical disabilities and 'deficiencies' were hereditary in origin, and 2) that this genetic 'fact' should be used to engineer social policies in ways that would strengthen national gene pools (see Hansen and King 2001). As Hansen and King detail, the major outcomes envisaged by eugenicist social policies were a massive decrease in the fertility rates among poor and 'mentally defective' populations, the reduction or elimination of a need to provide charitable or state-funded poor relief, and a proliferation of insane asylums, detention centres and prisons (ibid.: 245). The overall result of these policies was imagined as a reinvigoration of the national economy in the face of imperial decline (ibid.: 245).

The 'father' of the welfare state, William Beveridge, also advocated eugenic solutions to poverty. In 'The problem of the unemployed', an essay printed in the journal *Sociological Papers* in 1907, Beveridge stated that:

those men who through general defects are unable to fill such a whole place in industry, are to be recognised as 'unemployable'.

They must become the acknowledged dependents of the State [...] but with complete and permanent loss of all citizen rights – including not only the franchise but civil freedom and fatherhood. (Cited in Brignell 2010)

As I argued in Chapter 3, citizenship is not simply a description of status, but a productive concept which pivots on a distinction between the 'deserving' and the 'underserving' and endlessly produces 'moral abjects' at the periphery of the body politic. At the very origins of the incredible vision of a universal welfare state for all, there was a proviso that it was not intended for those who couldn't make the basic requirements of citizenship, that social residuum of unemployable 'human vermin'. As Foucault argued, while Nazism was exceptional in taking the logic of eugenics as a mechanism of biopower to the nth degree of industrialized murder, state racism is inscribed in the mechanisms of all states (Foucault 2003).

The new government of poverty

While the tone and the severity of the solutions proffered by advocates of eugenist thinking were tempered by the horrors of the Nazi holocaust, genetic explanations and eugenicist ideas continue to shape political and public debates about welfare provision, worklessness and the underclass. In particular, I will argue that eugenics *underpins* the form of (bio)politics that has emerged in the epochal transition from industrial to neoliberal capital, as the state and the market combine to deregulate labour markets and dismantle the welfare regimes (which eugenicist politicians such as Beveridge had put in place to act as a buffer between the volatilities of the market and the 'deserving poor'). Wacquant terms this neoliberal transition 'the new government of poverty' (Wacquant 2010: 204).

The deproletarianization of labour (the liquidification – or, indeed, the liquidation – of job security and the resurgence in inequality that results from this) generates widespread social insecurity. This insecurity is an essential component of neoliberal governmentality as it introduces competition (marketization) into every sphere of social life. This insecurity also operates to classify populations by drawing on longer histories and vocabularies of moral deservedness. In particular, hostility is directed towards welfare recipients and migrants who are figured as 'defamed categories that sap the social order' (ibid.: 204).

Once again the poor are mobilized to do the dirty ideological work of the ruling classes, as they become both the symbolic and material scapegoats for the social decomposition effected by market deregulation and welfare retrenchment. As Wacquant writes, 'the new government of poverty invented [...] to enforce the normalization of social insecurity thus gives a whole new meaning to the notion of "poor relief"' (ibid.: 204).

My argument is that eugenicist discourses of the underclass underpin and legitimize this process of neoliberal statification. The underclass – and we need to include here all those caught in the internal borders of the state including the migrant 'failed citizens' I discussed in previous chapters on asylum and migrant illegality – are those whose lives are imagined as a parasitical drain upon state resources, blocking the open road of 'welfare rollback'. They are not 'human capital' but 'human waste' and are transformed into national abjects who 1) incite the public consent necessary for welfare cuts, and 2) allow for waste populations to be recycled as a resource, for example by the massive expansion of privatized for-profit penal industries. In Chapter 3 I detailed how this works in terms of the global business of immigration detention. Here it is important to highlight the massive increase in civilian (citizen) incarceration rates in England and Wales. In 1992 there were 88 prison inmates per 100,000 residents. By 2008 this had jumped to 150 per 100,000, even though crime rates receded continually for much of this period. As Wacquant notes, this is the 'largest absolute increase in the prison population in British history' (ibid.: 215).

Political artistry, however persuasive or spectacular, is insufficient on its own to generate public consent for the punishment of the poor. What the invention of the underclass provides is not only a political and popular figure for class hatred but a pseudo-scientific rationale for the new government of poverty. In 1989 the *Sunday Times* invited Charles Murray to Britain 'to investigate whether Britain had an "underclass"' (Green, cited in Murray 2001). In the article he wrote for the newspaper 'he described himself as a visitor from a plague area who had come to see whether the disease was spreading' (ibid.). A decade later Murray was invited once again to outline his 'fundamental thesis' to readers of *The Times*, namely that there is a growing 'class of violent, unsocialised people who, if they become sufficiently numerous, will fundamentally degrade the life of society'

(Murray 2001: 3). In his essay 'Genetics of the right', Murray traces a direct line from eugenics to genomics. Murray argues that, if the eugenicist thinkers of the early twentieth century had no 'hard science' on which to ground and affirm their ideological beliefs, the new genetic science was providing or would provide the missing proof. The evidence science will unfurl, he argued, will effect a radical shift in political thinking as the poor would finally be proved to have significantly different genes to the affluent. Murray argued this would lead to new, massive social programmes in genetic engineering aimed at 'improving' the poor. On 10 May 2000, Murray came to Britain to debate his eugenic-genetic thesis with the media and political elites in a public debate sponsored by the *Sunday Times* and entitled 'The growing threat of the underclass'. The Home Secretary, Jack Straw, took his place on the debating panel, despite calls from anti-racist activists for him to decline the invitation to participate. Murray later appeared on BBC TV's *Newsnight*, where he stated: 'We have had the scientific community denying the obvious [...] We've had people saying that IQ is virtually all determined by the environment and we can change it by the proper social interventions and a whole bunch of other things that simply are not true' (Murray 2000). The implication is always that it is not deprivation and inequality which need to be 'reduced', but the poor themselves.

In his manifesto, *What It Means to Be a Libertarian* (1997), Murray outlines his political solution to the underclass, proposing that all social security and welfare be abolished, and that all civil rights and racial discrimination legislation be repealed. His vision of government reduced to the barest essentials (defence, law and order and environmental protections) in which welfare and social security would be replaced by forms of 'localism' such as voluntary-sector support is the neoliberal vision of the denuded state par excellence (the 'Big Society'). The figure that organizes and legitimizes this entire political field is the revolting figure of the profligate, criminalized welfare recipient. If the neoliberal object of repulsion is the welfare state, the underclass (or chav) is the popular name for this abject(ion).

Penal pornography

The eugenicist underpinnings of discourses of underclass were given popular physiognomical expression in the rogues' galleries of CCTV images of accused rioters, circulated by the police in the

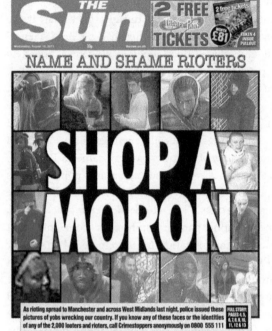

7.3 Front cover of the *Sun*, 10 August 2011

aftermath of the riots and featured on the front covers of many national newspapers and on numerous vigilante social media pages. 'Shop a Moron' was the headline on the front page of the *Sun* on 10 August 2011 (Figure 7.3), as it launched a campaign encouraging readers to 'Name and Shame Rioters'. Its front page invited readers to examine the faces and bodies (as captured on CCTV) of those pictured for evidence of inherent signs of physical, mental and moral defects. News media journalists were transformed into vigilante crime fighters, inviting the public to assist them in cleaning up the streets: 'Let's all nail the scum by joining the army of police and disgusted members of the public who have started identifying the rioters,' wrote the journalist Ross Kaniuk in the *Daily Star*. 'If you also have a picture to put out or can identify yobs in others' photos, then help put the filth who brought terror to our streets in the dock' (Kaniuk 2011). The police toured their rogues' galleries through British cities and towns on digital display vans. Parked in riot-affected shopping areas, these public exhibitions of alleged offenders were used to encourage passing shoppers to identify those who had taken part. As Wacquant argues, the proliferation of these kinds of 'law-and-order pornography' suggest that 'the death of the "spectacle of the scaffold" has been greatly exaggerated' (Wacquant 2010: 206).

The riots and the extraordinary media and judicial responses they prompted are also indicative of the wider acceleration and inflation of 'penal activity conceived, represented, and implemented for the primary purpose of being displayed in ritualized form by the authorities' (ibid.: 206). As Wacquant writes:

> The 'redistribution' of 'the whole economy of punishment' in the post-Fordist period has entailed not its disappearance from public view [...] but its institutional relocation, symbolic elaboration, and social proliferation. [...] In the past quarter-century, a whole galaxy of novel cultural and social forms, indeed a veritable industry trading on representations of offenders and law enforcement, has sprung forth and spread. The theatricalization of penality has migrated from the state to the commercial media and the political field [...] Everywhere the law-and-order guignol[2] has become a core civic theatre onto whose stage elected officials prance to dramatize moral norms and display their professed capacity for decisive action. (Ibid.: 206)

In order to police the riots mediating agencies worked to orchestrate public opinion by transforming these events into a 'moral panic'. Moral panics are always the terrain through which crises are 'experienced and fought out' (Hall et al. 1978: 221). Indeed, in the case of the riots, their cause was identified immediately as a moral deficiency. Cameron made his first public response to the riots on 15 August 2011 in a speech at a youth centre in his Witney constituency. He attributed the riots to a 'slow-motion moral collapse that has taken place in parts of our country these past few generations', arguing that 'these riots were not about poverty' but rather 'about behaviour', and 'Young people smashing windows and stealing televisions is not about inequality' (Stratton 2011). The media spectacle of the riots understandably generated fear in the public, a fear which in turn enables the state to garner public support for the suspension of juridical norms and deployment of exceptional punitive measures. It is in this way that the riots were transformed into 'ideological conductor[s]', mechanisms for 'the construction of an authoritarian consensus' and 'a conservative backlash' (Hall et al. 1978: viii). This is a process that takes place within what Hall termed the 'Exceptional State' (ibid.: 221).

'Will alleged rioters get a fair trial?' wondered media law consultant David Banks on 12 August 2011 in the *Guardian* (Banks 2011). A few days after its 'Shop a Moron' headline, the *Sun* crafted a 'Shop an Edwardian Moron' feature, composed of police mugshots of 'petty pilferers' detained, shamed and punished a century earlier for minor crimes (Sun 2011). The irony, uncommented upon in the *Sun*, was the dramatic differences in punishment meted out to the Edwardian 'petty pilferers' and the petty looters in 2011. While one Walter Glenson was jailed for a week for stealing two packets of cocoa in 1907, Nicolas Robinson was jailed for six months for stealing a £3.50 case of bottled water during the riots. Sixteen-year-old Ricky Gemmell was sentenced to sixteen weeks in prison for uttering the phrase 'I'd smash you if you took your uniform off' to a police officer (Addley et al. 2011). In 2010, the government estimated that it costs on average £50,000 a year to keep a petty criminal in prison, and about £2,800 to administer a community sentence over the same period (McFarlane 2010). Dane Williamson, misidentified and apprehended as he shopped with friends in Manchester city centre and then wrongfully charged and imprisoned for setting fire to a shop, had his flat burnt down in a revenge attack while he was detained.

Penal humiliation

'Constant identity checks and questioning by police.' Of all the complaints made by the youth of this country in revolt, the omnipresence of police checks and being arrested in their everyday lives, this harassment without respite, is the most constant, the most widely shared. Do we really realize what this grievance means? The dose of humiliation and violence it implies? (Badiou 2006: 111)

The findings of the *Guardian*-LSE research project *Reading the Riots: Investigating England's summer of disorder* (Lewis et al. 2011), the only research to date which has interviewed a significant number of those who participated in the rioting (270 people), suggests that it was the intrusive and excessive penal activities of the state which many rioters were expressing their anger about. In particular, the riots were perceived as an opportunity for revenge on the police; these were '"anti-police" riots' (Prasad 2011). In an echo of the riots in 1982, the police represented 'regiments of occupation and control' (Rushdie 1982; see Chapter 2). Seventy-three per cent of people interviewed in *Reading the Riots* had been stopped and searched at least once in the previous year: 'the frequent complaint of a sense of harassment by those interviewees on the receiving end of stop and search was made in every city the research took place and by interviewees from different racial groups and ages' (Lewis et al. 2011: 19). There was an overwhelming resentment among the rioters that the police subjected them to unwarranted suspicion and invasive surveillance. Even within the spaces of their own communities they cannot escape from a penetrating, stigmatizing underclass gaze, as two rioters express:

> I'm angry and frustrated. I feel the same as them. Angry with everything – society, police, the way they treat us. They don't treat us like human beings. (Cited in Hegarty 2011)

> we violate [them] like they violate us, this was our way of getting revenge ... For once we had the police and government scared, for once they felt like we felt. (Cited in Lewis et al. 2011: 25)

Neoliberal citizenship

Reading the Riots suggests that the riots were motivated by a sense of 'poverty, injustice and a visceral hatred of the police' (Lewis 2011a). Further, those interviewed made clear that it was not economic deprivation alone which led to the rioting but a sense of invisibility, of alienation and frustration rooted in feelings of abandonment by the state:

> When rioters were asked if they felt 'part of British society', only 51% said they agreed with the statement, against 92% of the population as a whole. For the young in particular – and more than four-fifths of those we interviewed were aged 24 or under – what came across was a profound sense of alienation. This sense of being invisible was widespread. (Lewis et al. 2011: 25)

This sense of disconnection from the state is a 'product of an active process of institutional detachment and segregation (in the etymological sense of "setting apart")' (Wacquant 2008: 224). The rioters' sense of alienation is symptomatic of the abject politics of citizenship I described in Chapter 3, in which citizenship is redesigned as a technology of neoliberal governance. This marks a displacement of liberal understandings of citizenship, as a universal status that offers rights and protections, by categories of 'active' and 'earned' citizenship. We can trace this shift in the implementation of compulsory citizenship education within the national curriculum in England aimed at children and teenagers and the introduction of policy agendas such as the New Labour 'Respect Agenda', which ushered in laws, social policies and environmental redesigns that targeted young people and made them subject to hitherto unimaginable levels of direct policing, pseudo-legal controls and political governance.[3] The agenda of inclusion was in fact one of exclusion which functioned to make it almost impossible for young people to gather together in urban spaces without being subject to vilification and being perceived with fear and mistrust. Neoliberal citizenship is a productive category which actively constitutes 'failed people' marginalized by, excluded or disqualified from, the social body.

Un/employment

As I argued in Chapter 5, New Labour redesigned citizenship around the axis of work/worklessness, whereby poverty and disadvantage have become associated with 'poor self-management' (Gilles 2005: 837). The public was told that it was only through work that people could find a route back to citizenship and the protective bosom of the state. This is an underclass narrative in which workless people are designated as outside the domain of the social proper and have to be 'helped or coerced to become included citizens' (ibid.: 838).

Reading the Riots estimated that 75 per cent of those who rioted were under twenty-four, about half were in full-time education either at school or college/university, and among the rest a considerable minority were unemployed (Ball et al. 2011). One in five young people in Britain between the ages of sixteen and twenty-four are currently defined as NEETS (an acronym for people currently not in education, employment or training), although this is higher in many of the urban areas affected by riots. This represents about one million young people for whom everyday life is shaped by a crisis of possibility – the idea of a future in which their ability to participate actively in the social life of the state is radically uncertain (Berlant 2011). Many of those who participated in the riots described their actions as a specific response to increasing inequalities of opportunity felt most acutely in the closing of youth centres and services, the slashing of the Educational Maintenance Allowance, the tripling of university fees and rising youth unemployment. As one rioter explained: 'I literally went there to say, "All right then, well, everyone's getting free stuff, I'm joining in", like, 'cos it's fucking my area. These fucking shops, like, I've given them a hundred CVs … not one job. That's why I left my house' (Lewis et al. 2011: 26).

However, in his response to the riots, Cameron argued that a *culture* of worklessness was to blame:

> [There] is a moral hazard in our welfare system – people thinking they can be as irresponsible as they like because the state will always bail them out. [...] I want us to look at toughening up the conditions for those who are out of work and receiving benefits and speeding up our efforts to get all those who can work back to work. (Cited in Stratton 2011)

Similarly, the historian Andrew Roberts commented in the aftermath of the riots, '[t]he violence in England's streets is no working-class insurrection but the uprising of the non-working, anti-working, would-do-anything-sooner-than-work class' (Roberts 2011). The perversity of these political responses to the riots lies in their relentless promotion of the idea that welfare support systems are responsible for workless-ness. As I argued in Chapter 5, penal responses to unemployment are premised on two myths. The first is that a significant group of people don't want to work and prefer a life of welfare dependence and poverty (MacDonald et al. 2010b). The second is that full employment is achievable in a deproletarianized market economy. It isn't (Theodore 2007); labour insecurity and the vertiginous inequalities it effects are a direct consequence of neoliberal economic and social policies. The disintegration of secure forms of waged labour and the falling apart of effective agencies of political representation and collective action (such as unions) are the constitutive conditions of neoliberal governmentality. This is the policy of deliberate 'precarization' which Bauman describes in *Liquid Modernity*:

> 'Flexibility' is the slogan of the day, and when applied to the labour market it augurs an end to the 'job as we know it', announcing instead the advent of work on short-term contracts, rolling contracts or no contracts, positions with no in-built security but with the 'until further notice' clause. Working life is saturated with uncertainty. (Bauman 2000: 147)

That those who cannot even enter into this market, 'the most expendable, disposable and exchangeable parts of the economic system' (ibid.: 152), have diminished aspirations and little hope reveals not a culture of anti-work, but a lack of expectations born out of experience. For the political classes to argue that work is the solution to the criminal behaviour of rioters exculpates their own responsibility for 'the material deprivation, family hardship, temporal uncertainty and personal anxiety' which neoliberal governmentality has effected (Wacquant 2008: 25). Since the riots the government has accelerated its £5 billion workfare programme. 'The Work Programme' is targeted at young people in receipt of welfare benefits, and under the scheme they are forced to work without pay, in the voluntary sector and private sector, in order to retain meagre benefit entitlements. Among the private contractors paid to deliver the new workfare regimes are the global securities companies G4S and Serco, which run immigration detention centres in the UK.[4]

For some of the rioters it was precisely the abject feelings of worthlessness induced by long-term unemployment which they used to attempt to legitimize their participation in violent disorder. As one rioter put it: 'All I can tell you is that me, myself and the group I was in, none of us have got jobs, yeah? I been out of work now coming up two years ... and it's just like a depression, man, that you sink into ... I felt like I needed to be there as well to just say "Look, this is what's gonna happen if there's no jobs offered to us out there"' (Lewis et al. 2011: 25).

Many have commented that the intensive focus on looting set these riots apart from previous episodes of civil unrest, leading to speculations that these were simply opportunistic riots: 'these are shopping riots', stated Zoe Williams in the *Guardian* (Williams 2011). This assertion is used to legitimize claims that the riots were 'apolitical'. Žižek, recycling a phrase he used to describe the riots in the *banlieues* in 2005, insisted that the riots represented 'a zero-degree protest, a violent action demanding nothing' (Žižek 2011). However, the rioters have been articulate in explaining that acts of looting were not so much an expression of 'the absence of material things' but rather 'how they felt they were treated compared with others' (Lewis et al. 2011: 24). Smashing up shops and looting goods was for many an expression of social inequality in a society in which the ability to work and consume are primary markers of social belonging. As Bauman argues, within a consumer society 'non-shopping' represents 'the jarring and festering stigma of a life un-fulfilled – and of [one's] own nonentity and good-for-nothingness. Not just the absence of pleasure: absence of human dignity. Of life meaning' (Bauman 2011). Or, as youth worker and former gang member Sheldon Thomas puts it, 'If you ask how we became a society where young people think it's OK to rob and loot, I respond how did we get to a society that cares more about shops and businesses than the lives of young people?' (cited in Plan B 2012a).

Social abjection

In all the revolted responses to the riots there has been insufficient effort made to examine why it might be difficult to sustain social norms of behaviour in the face of stigmatizing and dehumanizing appellations. The riots must be understood in part as a response to the 'intensity of the stigma' directed at the poor and the 'virulence of its negative effects in the context of the mass unemployment and political marginalization' (Wacquant 2008: 175). As Tom Slater argues, we need what he describes as 'a double nexus' which connects 'these eruptions to urban marginality in British society', not only to 'material conditions of deprivation' but also to 'the denial of dignity' (Slater 2011: 107). One story, related by Paul Lewis in the *Guardian*, illustrates the ways in which rioters understood their actions as a retort to indignity:

> 'Firstly, it was just running into shops, pulling clothes off the
> hangers and running out again,' said Omar, 16, from the suburb of
> Erdington. He had got the train into the city centre with friends.
> 'We seen some windows being smashed in. We just thought, every-
> one else is doing it. It just seemed like a good idea really.' He wore
> a mask. Omar said he hated the police. 'They call us little shits and
> little bastards and everything,' he said. 'They're not what you see
> on the TV and that – acting all good and that.'
>
> He said he stole Nike tracksuit bottoms to make him feel like
> 'people with money, good families', who he said look down on
> him. 'I hate feeling like people are judging me. They don't know
> about me and then they just look at you and I hate it, I absolutely
> hate it.'
>
> Before the riots, Omar said his clothes were all ripped or dirty.
> 'And when I get new clothes I feel better,' he said. 'Then they will

have to look down at someone else.' He added: 'I have gone to
loads of jobs with my CV. But I've got no qualifications so people
just don't want me – there's people better than me.' (Lewis 2011b)

Omar's story relates what Wacquant describes as 'the curse of
being poor in the midst of a rich society in which participation in
the sphere of consumption has become a sine qua non of social
dignity – a passport to personhood if not citizenship' (Wacquant
2008: 29). If the acquisition of consumer goods is 'indispensable for
acceding to socially recognized existence', for many the riots presented an irresistible opportunity to acquire goods through criminal
means (ibid.: 30).

In 'The scaling of bodies and the politics of identity', Young
develops Frantz Fanon's work to explore the ways in which the concept
of abjection can be employed to deepen understanding of practices
and experiences of racism, sexism and associated forms of exploitation and marginalization (Young 1990). What Young suggests is that
'marginalization' fails as a categorical description, to account for how
'being [made] marginal' shapes self-worth. Abjection, Young suggests,
might help us understand the ways in which negative inscriptions
and interpellations are internalized. Developing Joel Kovel's concept
of 'aversive racism', Young focuses on the mundane and everyday
interactive contexts in which 'unconscious fears and aversions of
despised groups' materialize (ibid.: 123). As she writes:

> Pulses of attraction and aversion modulate all interactions, with
> specific consequences for experience of the body. When the domi-
> nant culture defines some groups as different, as the Other, the
> members of those groups are imprisoned in their bodies. Dominant
> discourse defines them in terms of bodily characteristics, and con-
> structs those bodies as ugly, dirty, defiled, impure, contaminated,
> or sick. Those who experience such an epidermalizing of their
> world, moreover, discover their status by means of the embodied
> behaviour of others: in their gestures, a certain nervousness that
> they exhibit, their avoidance of eye contact, the distance they keep.
> (Ibid.: 123)

Like Fanon, Young's analysis focuses on experiences of abjection
and, in particular, on what it feels like to occupy a body which is
constituted, in interactions with others, as 'ugly, fearsome, or loath-

some' (ibid.: 124). Omar describes this for us: 'I hate feeling like people are judging me. They don't know about me and then they just look at you and I hate it, I absolutely hate it.' Abjection describes here a phenomenology of oppression which not only shapes perceptual fields but materializes in subjectivities: 'people just don't want me – there's people better than me'. What Omar understands is that he is not 'human capital', he has nothing to trade, he is 'human waste': *'They call us little shits'*. In putting on his stolen clothes he attempts to re-epidermalize himself, to defend himself against abjection.

Carnival

According to the data collected by *Reading the Riots* researchers (Lewis et al. 2011) the rioters came from a broad range of ethnicities, even putting aside existing tensions between different groups during the riots, temporarily constituting a new class, as they made their way en masse to local high streets, shopping precincts and business districts to wreak chaos. The riots were an opportunity for young people to be together in public space, a form of massing now virtually criminalized, and to cast off temporarily the divisions between them:

> All the gangs left the beef for a day just to riot, so there is a cause [for] the rioting innit [...] everybody was rioting together, enemies next to each other rioting [...] Everybody knew they was fighting for a cause. (Fenn and Owen 2011)

> Unity, yeah, that's what I'd call it, unity ... It brought unity to certain classes ... so there was a lot of unity involved in the riots ... that's the only good thing I saw. (Newburn et al. 2011b)

> I couldn't believe and I was happy that there was actually standing together and I was thinking, why would it cause something like this for these people to get together? [...] For that day, they would have been my friend ... Everyone's aiming for the government today. Everyone's voices needs to get heard. And that's what it was. (Ibid.)

As the *Reading the Riots* research revealed, 'unity' was frequently cited in the interviews with rioters, who experienced events as a new form of collectivity. In this way, the riots created a temporary space of negative freedom, a seemingly autonomous zone in which young people were able to make their rage visible and enjoy themselves in the process. As one rioter stated, 'people who have got nothing wanted to show that they had nothing' (Fenn and Owen 2011). What the rioters experienced was a collective insurgency against authority in its myriad forms, the police, the government, 'the rich', all those whom they blamed for their inaudibility, their powerlessness.

> The government hates us. [...] We hate the police, hate the government, got no opportunities [...] I became involved in the riots in Salford because it was a chance to tell the police, tell the government, and tell everyone else for that matter that we get fucking hacked off around here and we won't stand for it. (Lewis et al. 2011: 20)

Indeed the riots were experienced by many who participated as a carnivalesque moment of counter-control, in which it felt as if the relations of power were not only disturbed but switched. As one rioter noted:

> What I really noticed that day was that *we had control*. It felt great. We could do what we wanted to do. We could do as much damage as we can, and we could not be stopped. Normally the police control us. But *the law was obeying us*, know what I mean? (Ibid.: 23)

> You feel euphoric, you know. Because it's one of the best buzzes personally I've ever had in my life. Better than any drug. And you know it was just that ... It was a feeling of standing up straight against an institution. (Fenn and Owen 2011)

Conclusion: dissensus

We have seen how for many of the rioters it was their sense of being invisible, of being stigmatized, of having no future prospects, which motivated their disorderly behaviour. They wanted to be seen and heard. However, as I have detailed, the violence and criminality unleashed in the riots do not effect an alternative aesthetics. The public don't appear to have come to perceive Britain's disenfranchised youth differently. On the contrary, the representation of the riots entrenches and legitimizes the perceptual frame of the underclass and further stigmatizes the impoverished communities from which the vast majority of rioters came (Hall et al. 1978: 396). In other words, the rioters became the abjects they had been told they were, and in so doing confirmed the consensus that they were the product of their own, and their families', 'chaos and dysfunctionality' (Duncan Smith, cited in Mulholland 2011).

However, the riots came after the global banking crises, the MPs' expenses crises, and public outrage at the grotesque levels of pay awarded to workers in the finance industries. This accumulation of crises had exposed the fact that the neoliberal state was not being managed in the interests of citizens, but for the economic benefits of a minority. Few serious responses to the riots could fail to draw attention to the gross inequalities between the sentences meted out to rioters in the courts and the punishments given to politicians found guilty of expenses fraud or the bankers who had looted the economy. As Judith Revel and Toni Negri argue, '[t]o the mugshots of youth in rebellion posted on the walls and the screens of England's cities one should really juxtapose large sized prints of the swinish faces [...] of the bankers and financial corporate bosses that have turned entire communities to that condition, and keep fattening their profits out of this crisis' (Revel and Negri 2011).

Today politicians of all political persuasions argue that there is no alternative to the austerity effected by the collapse of financial capitalism. What the riots exposed is that the consensus for austerity was founded on an increasingly unstable base. It is not clear that the myth, which was inaugurated with the creation of British citizenship in the post-war era, that majority class interests have been absorbed within a democratic 'national interest' and that class struggle is over, can be sustained. Certainly, the August riots were a manifestation of class conflict on a scale not seen in Britain for a generation. This brings us back to the importance of 'class' as a political vocabulary of struggle, as it is class which describes the efforts of people to contest the social and economic destinies and identities which have been imposed upon them; a situation which the rap artist and singer Plan B beautifully expresses in his post-riots song 'Ill Manors' (2012) – as he explains:

> The point being made in my song 'Ill Manors' is that society needs to take some responsibility for the cause of these riots. Why are there so many kids in this country that don't feel they have a future, or care about having a criminal record?
>
> I think one of the reasons is that there is a very public prejudice in this country towards the underclass. These kids are ridiculed in

the press as they aren't as educated as others, because they talk and dress in a certain way ... but they're not as stupid as people think. They are aware of the ill feelings towards them and that makes them feel alienated. I know because I felt it myself growing up. These kids have been beaten into apathy. They don't care about society because society has made it very clear that it doesn't care about them. (Plan B 2012b)

AFTERWORD

People do revolt; that is a fact. And that is how subjectivity (not that of great men, but that of anyone) is brought into history, breathing life into it. (Foucault 2002: 452)

The London Olympic Stadium, 29 August 2012

On the evening of 29 August 2012, the opening ceremony of the London Paralympic Games saw thousands of performers and volunteers stage a spectacular commemoration of the historical achievements of the disability rights movement in Britain. The highlight for many viewers was a raucous mash-up of Ian Dury's 1981 punk disability anthem 'Spasticus Autisticus' performed by the electronic dance duo Orbital and the Graeae Theatre Company. During this exhilarating routine dozens of disabled performers enacted an abstract montage of disability rights protests, holding up placards which spelled out 'RIGHTS', 'Equality', 'Look Beyond Appearances' and 'Don't Judge a Book by its Cover'. The sequence culminated in the inflation of a forty-foot reproduction of Marc Quinn's sculpture of the disabled artist Alison Lapper, 'Alison Lapper Pregnant' (2005), at the centre of the stadium, while a young woman was simultaneously lifted into the air, smashing a symbolic glass ceiling with her walking stick. The ceremony finally ended with fireworks and a rendition of the musical number 'I Am What I Am', which has become a queer anthem. Many commentators hailed this opening ceremony, which attracted UK television audiences of 11 million, as a watershed moment in the history of disability rights in Britain that promised to challenge stigmatizing cultural perceptions and attitudes to disability. Yet, earlier in the day, hundreds of disability activists had taken to the streets to stage the first of a series of rather different protest performances to make manifest their rage that the Paralympics were being sponsored by ATOS, an information technology and health multinational.

ATOS is currently in receipt of a £100-million-a-year contract from the government Department for Work and Pensions to undertake 'Work Capability Assessments' (WCAs) with those claiming or seeking disability-related welfare benefits. These 'points-based' tests

– comprising a combination of computer-based questionnaires, short face-to-face interviews and minimal physical examinations – determine whether people are fraudulently claiming benefits when they are 'fit for work'. The Paralympic protesters, from Disabled People Against the Cuts and UK Uncut, sought to draw attention to the thousands of people who died after ATOS tests determined them capable of finding and undertaking paid employment – approximately one thousand people declared 'fit for work' died between January and August 2011 alone, 'an average of 32 people every week' (Fund 2012). Protests began on 29 August with the staging of a memorial service outside ATOS's London headquarters and continued with 'die-in' protests outside ATOS buildings in Cardiff, Glasgow, Belfast and Hull. The following day they escalated the direct action, staging a 'Closing ATOS Ceremony' which culminated in the occupation of Caxton House, the home of the government Department for Work and Pensions. Activists used wheelchairs to lock themselves into the lobby of Caxton House, while hundreds of protesters on the street, carrying 'ATOS kills' placards and chanting 'shame on you' and 'you can stick your work assessment up your arse', created a human barricade to stop riot police from gaining access to the building.

WCAs were introduced in 2008 as part of a package of austerity-driven welfare reforms which, to date, have seen £18 billion worth of cuts made to the UK benefits system. As part of these cuts the existing benefits system for the long-term sick and the physically and mentally disabled has been replaced with what the government describes as 'an active benefits system where individuals are provided with greater support and in return take greater responsibility for their own circumstances' (Department for Work and Pensions 2009: 1). A series of independent reports by charities, trade unions and medical associations,[1] the collection of hundreds of personal testimonies by activist groups[2] and two investigative television documentaries, *Don't Hate Us!* (ITV 2012) and *Disabled or Faking It?* (BBC 2012), have variously detailed the devastating impact which WCAs are having on the lives of people with disabilities in Britain, driving many thousands into poverty and despair.[3] While the policy rhetoric centres on the presentation of 'evidence' of the health benefits of paid work (Department for Work and Pensions 2009), disability activists and their allies have questioned not only the testing procedures but the ideology of a policy agenda which determines welfare entitlement by assessing individuals' *capability* for work in the absence of suitable employment opportunities for people with disabilities. Writing on the impact of these changes, Richard Hawkes, the chief executive of disability charity Scope, notes:

> We have seen evidence of declining mental health, exacerbated by fear for the future; of physical and emotional strain [...] we are seeing it become increasingly difficult for disabled people to participate in everyday family and civic life. This has all taken place against a backdrop of growing hostility towards those who claim disability and welfare support. (Hawkes, cited in Wood 2012: 10)

In 2011, researchers from Strathclyde University's Centre for Disability Research and Glasgow University's 'Media Unit' analysed changes in the way the newspapers reported and represented disability and the impact of stigmatizing coverage on public attitudes (Briant et al. 2011). Comparing their data against a similar study undertaken five years earlier, they found a 'significantly increased use of pejorative language to describe disabled people, including suggestions that life on incapacity benefit had become a "Lifestyle Choice"' (ibid.: 5). They also noted a surge in the number of newspaper articles that invoked 'the "burden" that disabled people are alleged to place on the economy – with some articles even blaming the recession itself on incapacity benefit claimants' (ibid.: 5). By undertaking a series of focus groups, what this research further detailed is how this pejorative visibility has created a consensus within the British public that the majority of disability benefits claims are fraudulent (ibid.). Indeed, as I detailed in Chapter 1, since the disability welfare reform programme began in 2008, there has been a massive increase in disability hate crimes on the streets of Britain. Official police data reveal that recorded incidents of disability hate crime grew by 60 per cent between 2009 and 2011 and are now at their highest levels since records began (Guardian 2012). By 2012 it was estimated that disability hate crimes had risen to 65,000 per year as a consequence of the continued and incessant portrayal of people with disabilities as 'welfare scroungers'. It was in the context of enforced destitution, stigma and growing public antipathy that activists set out to wreck ATOS's ability to capitalize on any positive publicity generated by their Paralympic sponsorship.

There is much more that could be said about the London

Paralympic and Olympic Games and what these events and the protests against them reveal about the shifting relationship between the state, corporate capitalism and citizenship. For example, in the Olympic opening ceremony director Danny Boyle and scriptwriter Frank Cottrell Boyce paid homage to Britain's National Health Service (NHS) with a dazzlingly theatrical sequence of 800 dancing nurses, a vision that one US news commentator described as 'a bizarre tribute to socialized medicine' (Fund 2012). Yet a few months before the Olympic Games began the Health and Social Care Act (2012) had paved the way for the evisceration of the NHS, the last major edifice of the British post-war welfare state, by private healthcare, pharmaceutical and insurance companies. It is also important to draw attention to the enclosure of public land and the forced evictions of people from their homes and business which preceded these games, the as yet unrealized 'legacy' of jobs and affordable housing, the use of flying drones, ground-to-air missiles and extraordinary surveillance measures to 'secure' the event, the estimated £24 billion cost of the games to the British taxpayer, and the excessive profiteering of multi-national corporations – including BP, the Dow Chemical Company, Coca-Cola, McDonald's and G4S[4] (the global securities company which has featured throughout *Revolting Subjects*). Yet in the midst of all the greed and corruption and in the face of the escalation of government programmes to privatize public services and the deepening impact of austerity-driven cuts to welfare, it was difficult not to be cheered by the joyfulness of the ceremonies and the melodramatic spectacle of the sport. The critical question is what kind of 'sense' we might make of these spectacular dramatizations of the paradoxes of the political present.

Disaster capitalism

In *The Shock Doctrine: The Rise of Disaster Capitalism*, Naomi Klein details the ways in which 'the policy trinity' of neoliberalism, 'the elimination of the public sphere, total liberation for corporations and skeletal social spending', has been enabled through the invention and/or exploitation of crises, be they natural disasters wrought by hurricanes or earthquakes, terrorist attacks on civilian populations or the collapse of international banks (Klein 2007: 16). In the context of contemporary Britain, the fear and anxiety generated by the 'shock' of the current economic crisis provides one explanation for how public consent has been procured for the current programme of seismic welfare reforms that 'punish the poor' (Wacquant 2008) while allowing the amassing of wealth in the hands of individuals and corporations through the privatization and 'asset-stripping' of public institutions, infrastructure and natural resources. However, my intention in *Revolting Subjects* has been to develop a 'thick' account of the ways in which neoliberal modes of governance operate in everyday life, not only by capitalizing upon 'shocks' but through the daily, pervasive production and mediation of 'social insecurity' (Wacquant 2010). In short, my aim has been to produce a rich and textured account of the everyday political and media technologies engaged by state and corporate agents of *disaster capitalism* in the relentless manufacture of poverty and inequality and to capture some of the practices and processes through which *public consent* for the disenfranchisement that unfolds from neoliberal ideologies and policies is procured. In particular, I have attempted to capture some of the ways in which social and cultural, emotional and affective economies combine with neoliberal economic policies to produce 'national abjects': scapegoats that enable 'the structures, mechanisms, and justifications of power to function' (Foucault 2008: 85). To this end *Revolting Subjects* has explored how the social insecurity generated by neoliberal governmentality has given rise to novel modes of (re)classification – refugees transformed into bogus asylum seekers, unemployed young people into feckless chavs, people with disabilities into welfare cheats – that cut deep into popular consciousness, and the book has examined how those unfortunate enough to be classified as abject are mobilized to do the dirty ideological work of neoliberalism. They are transformed into symbolic and material scapegoats for the social decomposition effected by market deregulation that has a negative, degrading impact upon us all.

The chapters in this book detail the common origins, in political rhetoric, policy documents and news media, of stigmatizing depictions of marginal populations and groups. However, as Stuart Hall and his colleagues elaborated over thirty years ago, *the hardening of public opinion into consent* relies upon the repetition and accumulation of expressions and beliefs 'on the streets', in 'conversations between neighbours, discussion at street-corners or in the pub, rumour, gossip, speculation' (Hall et al. 1978: 129). Increasingly in twenty-first-century Britain, 'the streets' include the informal technologies of social media such as blogs, wall posts, text messages and tweets. What I hope to have impressed upon the reader is that the production and media-tion of these revolting subjects are not simply an effect of neoliberal ideologies and policies but are 'a core organ' of neoliberal govern-mentality (Wacquant 2010: 200). Stigmatization operates as a form of governance which legitimizes the reproduction and entrenchment of inequalities and injustices which impact upon us all. Indeed, the 'selec-tive and aggressive deployment' of strategies of social abjection is not only 'constitutively injurious to the ideals of democratic citizenship', but has perverted the very meaning of democracy and citizenship (ibid.: 200). As Arundhati Roy puts it:

> Until quite recently, right up to the 1980s, democracy did seem as though it might actually succeed in delivering a degree of real social justice. But modern democracies have been around for long enough for neo-liberal capitalists to learn how to subvert them. They have mastered the technique of infiltrating the instruments of democracy – the 'independent' judiciary, the 'free' press, the parlia-ment – and moulding them to their purpose. [...] Free elections, a free press, and an independent judiciary mean little when the free market has reduced them to commodities on sale to the highest bidder. (Roy 2003)

One argument of this book is that national abjects, and the com-munication media which create and sustain them, are in a very material sense the vehicles for the political production of the neoliberal doctrine that *there is no alternative*. As David Graeber argues in his wonderful book *Debt: The First 5,000 Years*, 'the last thirty years have seen the construction of a vast bureaucratic apparatus for the creation and maintenance of hopelessness, a giant machine designed, first and foremost, to destroy any sense of possible alternative futures' (Graeber 2011: 382). So, while historians would be right to question the extent to which the production of scapegoats to further capitalist agendas is a 'new' strategy for policing populations – we need think only of the role played by witch-hunts in paving the way for mass industrialization in early modern European history (Federici 2004) – what is peculiar to our times are the ways in which the language of democracy, fairness and equality is invoked *to justify* the channelling of public hostilities towards vulnerable and/or disadvantaged populations. It is this paradox which the opening ceremony of the Paralympic Games made manifest in its *dramatization* of the importance of rights and democratic protest at a historical moment when people's ability to protest against the dramatic curtailing of these rights has been severely curtailed (Atkins 2007). As Klein writes:

> [f]or those inside the bubble of extreme wealth created [by neoliberalism], there can be no more profitable way to organize a society. But because of the obvious drawbacks for the vast majority of the population left outside the bubble, other features of the corporatist state tend to include aggressive surveillance [...], mass incarceration, shrinking civil liberties and often, though not always, torture. (Klein 2007: 18)

What Klein means by torture in this passage is that which we ordinarily understand by the term, namely the physical detention, abuse and punishment of 'suspects' by the state and/or private police or military actors working on behalf of state and/or corporate interests – as seen in the mass rendition and torture of 'enemy combatants' in the global war on terror. Yet torture is also, as Klein argues, 'a metaphor of the shock doctrine's underlying logic' (ibid.: 15). *Revolting Subjects* is concerned with torture in this second sense. That is, with the everyday forms of torture visited on those populations constituted as *human waste* within and by the state (Bauman 2002, 2004). To this end, I have explored some the ways in which national abjects become enmeshed within the interpellative fabric of everyday life as I have sought to understand a little of what it means to be made abject – to be tortured by words, images, policies and mechanisms of policing and control which continuously produce you as less than human. The common refrain of so many of those people whose words I have collected, in the course of researching this book, is the insistence that *they are human*. This refrain was common among asylum seekers protesting against their detention and/or deportation – 'I took my clothes off because they treat us like animals. We are claiming asylum, we're not animals' (cited in Dugan 2008) – Travellers protesting their forced eviction – 'if you live in a caravan you are scum' (Freeman 2011) – and the disenfranchised young people who joined in with rioting on the streets of London – 'I'm angry and frustrated. I feel the same as them. Angry with everything – society, police, the way they treat us. They don't treat us like human beings' (cited in Hegarty 2011).

Homi Bhabha writes that 'stereotyping is an everyday drama', the site of 'fantasy and desire', and a scene of 'subjectification and power' (Bhabha 1983: 23). What concerns Bhabha, and has been central also to the project of *Revolting Subjects*, is the 'processes of subjectification made possible (and plausible) through stereotypical discourse' (ibid.: 19). As the work of Fanon most clearly articulates, negative and discriminatory stereotypes are not simply 'the fabrication of false images, which in turn enable discriminatory practices', but are also a *subjectifying force* (ibid.: 19). The work of critique thus entails shifting our attention from 'the identification of images as positive or negative', to more nuanced understandings of 'the processes of subjectification made possible (and plausible) through stereotypical discourse' (ibid.: 18). It is the endeavour of *Revolting Subjects* to understand more fully how this process works – that is, how the tortures of stigma are produced, mediated, embodied and lived. To this end I have sought to refashion the psychoanalytic concept of abjection. The theory of social abjection which emerges across the course of this book extends Fanon and Bhabha's analysis of the techniques of colonial and post-colonial subjectification, to the forms of governmentality in operation within contemporary Britain.

In *Revolting Subjects* I wanted to begin to think about the implications of revolt as a subjectifying force – that is, as a means through which those made abject attempt to reconstitute themselves not only as citizens with rights, but as *subjects of value*. I wanted to map how abject figures come to function as technologies of consent and how abjectified populations refuse and revolt against the disenfranchising effects of their classification. It is my hope that the conceptual paradigm of social abjection will prove useful to others engaged in thinking both about the ways in which representational forms work to 'get inside' people – instructing, correcting, regulating and shaping subjectivities (Gill 2008) – and the practices of resistance in which revolting subjects engage to survive stigma and disenfranchisement: people's attempts to remake themselves and draw attention to the state we are in, which I have described in this book as forms of 'declassificatory politics'.

I would like *Revolting Subjects* to be a testament to people's capacity for revolt. But further, as I have attempted to demonstrate, what matters is not only acts of resistance themselves but the images and the stories of revolt and resistance that emerge 'as outsiders attempt to recast their identity as politically legitimate subjects of justice' (McNevin 2006: 138). It is my contention that the documentary afterlife of protests, the political parables which I stage in *Revolting Subjects*, has the capacity to fracture the consensus in ways that enable us to question how and why we consent to the degradation of rights and justice so hard fought for.

The importance of cultural studies

Davide Panagia states:

> Democratic politics occurs when certain elements in society that are deemed insensible are challenging the governing political order. The task of political action, therefore, is aesthetic in that it requires a reconfiguration of the conditions of sense perception so that the reigning configuration between perception and meaning is disrupted by those elements, groups or individuals in society that demand not only to exist but indeed to be perceived. (Panagia 2010: 96)

Panagia is drawing, as have I throughout *Revolting Subjects*, on the work of Jacques Rancière to articulate the important claim that aesthetics is central to all projects of social and political change. Which is why cultural studies – a history of critical scholarship concerned with 'unlearning the norms of intelligibility' (Berlant, cited in Tyler and Loizidou 2000: 498) – has always focused on questions of representation and mediation and in particular on what John Berger famously described as 'ways of seeing' (Berger 1972). So, finally, while *Revolting Subjects* draws inspiration from a diverse body of scholarship, both theoretical and empirical, it pays homage in particular to the political and critical tradition of British cultural studies best exemplified by the work of Stuart Hall.[5] At a time when the formative foci of cultural studies are more urgent and relevant than ever, I would like to imagine *Revolting Subjects* as a backlash against some of the current forms of 'post-ideological' scholarship, often expressed in more or less overt ways as a 'fatigue with issues of "race, class, and gender"' (Berlant 1997: 4). My hope is that this book reads as an unashamed return to the critical vocabularies, energy and oppositional politics that shaped the emergence of cultural studies as a field of study.

NOTES

1 Introduction

1 I have been fortunate enough to discuss the autonomy of migration scholarship with Dimitris Papadopoulos during the editorial process of working through revisions of his and Vassilis Tsianos's excellent contribution to a special issue of the journal *Citizenship Studies* on the theme 'Immigrant Protest' (forthcoming in 2013). I am grateful for the conversations this opportunity provided. Their article for this special issue, 'After citizenship: autonomy of migration, organisational ontology and mobile commons', extends and develops some of the ideas formulated in *Escape Routes* but with an emphasis on affective cooperation, mutual support and care between migrants on the road.

1 Social abjection

1 Subjectivization is taken to mean the process of becoming a subject in and through power, while subjugation describes the modes of power and governance which control, limit and shape the appearance and forms of subjectivity (Butler 1997).

2 Noting the resurgence of historical accounts of French colonialism in the wake of the headscarf ban in 2004 and race riots provoked by Sarkozy in the *banlieues* in 2005, Stoler argues that aphasic cycles of 'forgetting' and 'rediscovering' colonialism characterize contemporary French intellectual and political life.

3 Debra Ferreday (2012) makes a similar argument in her important work on 'Anorexia and Abjection'.

4 On the theme of 'immigrant rage', see also Marciniak (2006).

5 Doug Ireland, *Guardian*, 8 November 2008, www.guardian.co.uk/news/blog/2005/nov/08/inflammatoryla.

6 In March, 2010, MIR became an official political party, Parti des Indigènes de la République.

7 'Melancholic States' was the title of a conference which I co-organized with Anne-Marie Fortier, Gail Lewis, Maureen McNeil, Nayanika Mookherjee, Celia Roberts and Jackie Stacey, at the Institute for Gender and Women's Studies at Lancaster University, 27–29 September 2007. I am grateful to my colleagues for the opportunity to be part of this conference; I learnt much from the many reading groups and discussions which preceded the main event.

2 Politics of British citizenship

1 The spectre of top-down EU governance is frequently invoked by the political right to produce fears of de-nationalization in the face of European federalism.

2 Both Foucault and Hall were influenced by Fanon's 'mixed thinking' about race and class. Indeed, the title of Fanon's final book, *The Wretched of the Earth*, is drawn from the first line of the nineteenth-century socialist anthem 'The Internationale' ('Stand up, damned of the Earth'), an acknowledgement of the common roots of declassificatory struggles.

3 In the UK, the criminologist Mary Bosworth is currently undertaking the first comprehensive ethnographic study of immigration detention centres.

3 The asylum invasion complex

1 Khalkhali was known as the 'hanging judge' in reference to the relish with which he condemned an estimated eight thousand Iranians to death by execution in his role as head of the revolutionary courts.

2 A team from the charity Medical Foundation for the Care of Victims of Torture had documented in detail Amini's extensive physical injuries and scars.

3 There have been dozens of protests like Amini's by asylum seekers in Britain, including many by other Iranian men, but few of them have received any significant mainstream media coverage. For example, shortly after Amini's protest Shahin Portohfeh, a twenty-three-year-old Iranian living in Coventry, undertook a 'copycat' protest, stitching up his eyes, mouth and ears when his asylum application was rejected. Portohfeh claimed he faced a fatwa in Iran after a gay love affair had been discovered. In July 2003, a young Iranian man endeavoured to hack himself to death with a knife outside a refugee support agency office in Newcastle's Bigg Market shopping centre after his asylum application was refused. He scrawled a message before his attempted suicide which stated: 'You have to kill yourself in this country to prove that you would be killed in your own country' (Moorehead 2005: 138). Passing shoppers intervened to save his life.

In April 2011, six Iranian men, Ahmad Sadeghi Pour, Morteza Bayat, Kiarash Bahari, Keyvan Bahari, Mahyar Meyari and Mehran Meyari, all of whom had fled to Britain after being imprisoned and tortured for their participation in the anti-regime protests that swept Iran in 2009, began a hunger strike after their applications for political asylum were refused. The men set up two street camps, occupying pavements outside Lunar House immigration centre in Croydon and outside the Amnesty International building in central London. Four of the men sewed up their lips with fishing line. Paradoxically, these men had come to Britain because of vocal British government support for the 2009 anti-regime demonstrations. Indeed, the then Foreign Secretary, David Miliband, saluted the 'great courage' of supporters and expressed grave concerns for the fate of those rounded up by the Iranian police.

4 I have developed the concept of 'invasion complex' from the work of Papastergiadis (2006).

5 Empirical evidence suggests that even though a minority of asylum claims are indeed weak and even deceitful, the substantive majority of migrants seeking asylum have come from countries 'where human rights violations and conflict are pervasive' (Schuster, cited in Gibney 2011).

6 Between 2001 and 2004 the then prime minister Tony Blair held more meetings about the issue of asylum than any other single issue except Iraq (which was invaded by the USA and the UK in 2003) (Gibney 2011).

7 After the 7 July 2005 London bombings, the *Daily Express* ran with the headline 'Bombers are all spongeing asylum-seekers'; the sub-headline read: 'Britain gave them refuge and now they want to repay us with death'. In actuality, none of the bombers was or had been an asylum seeker.

8 This report was commissioned by the Asylum Coalition and the Transport and General Workers' Union in response to the 2004 Bill.

9 In 2003, at the behest of Blair, the Italian government entered into an agreement with Libya in which it provided boats, helicopters, arms and cash to build and run detention centres, army and security personnel and thousands of body-bags to the Libyan government on the understanding that it become a 'regional protection zone'

which would ostensibly work to limit the flow of sub-Saharan migrants into Europe and specifically from Libya to Italy. It is estimated that several tens of thousands of Africans attempt to cross the Mediterranean each year. By 2009, Libya was holding migrants in twenty-eight immigrant prisons, including in both regular prisons and specially built remote camps which could hold many thousands of migrants. An EU arms embargo on Libya was lifted in return for this 'favour' and a new Libyan–Italian business venture also saw the opening of a massive undersea pipeline (ironic-ally named 'Greenstream') to transport gas into Italian homes.

10 Indeed, as Gibney suggests, 'the amount of money spent by European governments annually on determining refugee claims dwarfs the yearly budget of the UNHCR [US$3 billion in 2010], the organization tasked with responding to almost all of the world's refugees' (Gibney 2011).

11 A 2008 report entitled 'Asylum matters' by the conservative think tank the Centre for Social Justice opened with a preface by Duncan Smith which began, 'Historically the UK has a proud tradition of helping asylum seekers and in return they have contributed to the culture and achievement of this country. Isambard Kingdom Brunel, Isaiah Berlin and Sir Tom Stoppard were all from refugee families in their time. The evidence gathered for this report shows that the welcome offered today falls far short of our traditional standards' (Centre for Social Justice 2008: 4). Drawing upon the language of refugee activism, this report decries 'the irrational policy making' of the previous decade and dispels the myth of soft-touch Britain by detailing how welfare and employment opportunities were not primary asylum 'pull factors' (ibid.: 12). It also describes how policies of destitution keep asylum

seekers captive in unbearable states of limbo within the state. The political stress within this report is on how to better effect voluntary return, and on the lost economic opportunities created by no-work destitution policies.

12 'Third space' was a concept developed in post-colonial studies as a way of understanding the capacity of subaltern populations for resistance and counter-political speech (see, for example, Bhabha in Rutherford 1990).

13 The immigration judge who approved Shiri's removal described his sexuality as a 'predilection', referred to 'his coterie' of fellow gay men and spoke of 'unseemly activity'. Iranian gay rights groups estimate that the Iranian government has executed at least four thousand gay men and women since 1979 (Lupin 2005).

14 *Fram* draws on the extraordinary life of Fridtjof Nansen, the Norwegian explorer and humanitarian campaigner who became the first High Commis-sioner for Refugees for the League of Nations in 1921.

4 Naked protest

1 The title of Waugh's report makes a reference to an important qualitative study of the experiences of women dur-ing the asylum process: *Mothers in Exile: Maternity Experiences of Asylum-Seekers in England* (Mcleish 2002).

2 In his history of capital punish-ment in London, Peter Linebaugh also documents the changes in demographic and reproductive policies and the intensification of punishments against women for reproductive crimes during this transitional period in the history of capitalism. He argues that 'the increased numbers of hangings for infanticide sug-gest that capital punishment was part of the preparation for a new organisation of reproduction in the London Labour market' (Linebaugh 1992: 149).

3 Nigerian state violence was highlighted in the international media by the execution of environmental activist, author and political representative of the Ogoni people in the Delta region Ken Saro Wiwa in 1995.

4 This formulation of Arendt's work is developed out of joint research with Lisa Baraitser on maternal publics.

5 I am grateful to Amy Russell for bringing Long's wonderful article (which like this chapter thinks Agamben, Kristeva and the maternal together) to my attention.

5 The Big Society

1 In one of a series of High Court judicial reviews carried out before the Dale Farm eviction, the violent and terrorizing conduct of Constant and Co., in carrying out the Twin Oaks eviction in 2004, led Mr Justice Andrew Collins to state that: 'I have seen a video which shows how the bailiffs employed by the Council [...] acted. The conduct was unacceptable and the evictions were carried out in a fashion which inevitably would have led to harm to those affected. I have no doubt that the Council must reconsider the use of the firm in question and ensure that any eviction [...] is carried out in as humane a fashion as possible' (Royal Courts of Justice 2008).

2 It was notable that the Conservative Party's 2005 election campaign was being run by the political strategist Lynton Crosby, the erstwhile adviser to the Australian Conservative leader John Howard, who ran for re-election during the notorious Tampa asylum affair – many suggested that Howard's election success was derived from his 'tough stance' on refugee issues. The Norwegian freighter MV *Tampa* was refused entry to Australian waters in August 2001 as it was carrying 438 Afghans it had rescued from a sinking vessel.

3 Thanks to Ken Barlow for directing me to Rebecca Taylor's article.

4 The term dissensus is today almost solely attributed to Rancière but was developed by Stuart Hall and colleagues in *Policing the Crisis* (1978).

6 Britain and its poor

1 New Labour did build many new schools and hospitals, largely funded by mortgaging off public assets through disastrous public–private initiatives (PFIs).

2 Owen Jones also recounts the Thatcher government's determination to scrub 'class' from political vocabulary. He tells the story of how in the 1990s the social classification index used in national statistics, and then termed 'Social Class on Occupation', was renamed the 'National Statistics Socio-Economic Classification'. When the sociologist, whose research formed the basis for the revisions being made, asked why the title had been changed, he was told that 'New Labour had vetoed any mention of class' (Jones 2011: 98).

3 Pakulski and Waters expand on their class thesis in their book *The Death of Class* (1996).

4 In 2011 a new Channel Four ident was filmed on the Aylesbury Estate which depicted the estate as a broodingly violent abject space.

5 On the use of the word chav as a term of endearment the rap artist and singer Plan B recently stated, 'What does the word chav mean? The term may have its origins in the Romany word "chavi", meaning child. My godfather used to call me chav, but it was affectionate. I used to enjoy it. So what does that word mean now? I believe it stands for "council house and violent". It's a word that is used to ridicule and label people who come from a less educated background than the rest of society. For me, it's no different from similar words used to be prejudiced towards race or sex. The dif-

ference is, in this country we openly say the word chav' (Plan B 2012a).

6 For academic debates about the chav, see, for example (Hayward and Yar (2006), MacDonald et al. (2010b), Hollingworth and Williams (2009), Sutton (2009), Raisborough and Adams (2008) and Nayak (2006).

7 The kids are revolting

1 As Welshman argues, despite its invention and reinvention over 120 years, the empirical data for the existence of the underclass is of course always elusive; the flexibility of the underclass as a 'lumping device' is precisely its value (Welshman 2006: 210).

2 Guignol takes its name from French puppetry and means dramatic entertainment featuring gruesome characters and events.

3 Some examples of the targeting of controlling 'citizenship policies' at young people under New Labour include the introduction of curfews, Anti-Social Behaviour Orders (ASBOs) and Acceptable Behaviour Contracts (ABCs), the redesign of public spaces to stop young people 'loitering' by, for example, designing park railings that cannot be sat on and bus shelters which cannot be sat in, the use of ultraviolet lighting in areas in which young people gather (which highlights skin blemishes) and the deployment of devices originally designed to scare away vermin such as mosquitoes which emit a very high-frequency buzzing sound discernible only to those under twenty-five. The campaign group Liberty has worked with young people to protest against these technologies of surveillance and control: www.liberty-human-rights.org.uk.

4 See the campaign group Boycott Workfare for details of the workfare schemes in Britain and the companies sponsoring them: www.boycottworkfare. org.

Afterword

1 In July 2012 the British Medical Association conference voted unanimously for an end to the WCAs in their current form.

2 See the websites of www.atos victimsgroup.co.uk, www.thefullfacts. com/esa/forum/ and www. thebrokenof britain.blogspot.co.uk for the collected testimonies of people affected by the WCA regime.

3 Many hundreds of thousands of people whom ATOS has reclassified as 'fit for work' (around 40 per cent) have had that decision overturned on appeal (Gentleman 2012). However, as well as being expensive, the appeals system often takes several months during which time poverty and stress often have a serious impact on the health of appellants. There is also growing evidence of a rise in the number of suicides and attempted suicides by mentally disabled people whose benefits have been withdrawn.

4 In the run-up to the Olympic Games G4S were scandalously exposed for failing to deliver on their multimillion-pound security contract for the Olympic Games. Despite this, they continue to win new government contracts, including, at the time of writing, contracts to run the 'back office' work of some regional British police forces. Activist opposition to G4S is mounting with the emergence of a 'Stop G4S' network in 2012.

5 Birmingham University's Centre for Contemporary Cultural Studies (CCCS), in which Hall worked from 1968 until 1979, was pivotal in the emergence of a generation of scholars in Britain whose research focused on new social movements, class, immigration, racism, feminism, queer and youth subcultures. The Centre was closed controversially in 2002.

BIBLIOGRAPHY

Addley, E., J. Vasagar and J. Coleman (2011) 'UK riots: in courtrooms across country, there was little room for leniency', *Guardian*, 11 August, www.guardian.co.uk/uk/2011/aug/11/uk-riots-courtrooms-country, accessed 1 March 2012.

Agamben, G. (1995) 'We refugees', *Symposium*, 49(2): 114–19.

— (1998) *Homo Sacer: Sovereign power and bare life*, trans. D. Heller-Roazen, Stanford, CA: Stanford University Press.

— (2000) *Means without End: Notes on Politics*, Minneapolis: University of Minnesota Press.

Ahmed, S. (2003) 'In the name of love', *borderlands ejournal*, 2(3).

— (2004) *The Cultural Politics of Emotion*, Edinburgh: Edinburgh University Press.

Amadiume, I. (1987) *Male Daughters, Female Husbands: Gender and Sex in an African Society*, London: Zed Books.

— (2000) *Daughters of the Goddess, Daughters of Imperialism: African Women, Culture, Power and Democracy*, London: Zed Books.

Anon. (1981) 'Background – British racism', *Race and Class*, 23(1/2): 232–44.

Arendt, H. (1958) *The Human Condition*, Chicago, IL: Chicago University Press.

— (1973 [1951]) *The Origins of Totalitarianism*, New York: Harcourt, Brace.

Armstrong, J. (2006) 'Beyond "flexibility" and "juggling": theorising classed and gendered practices of employment and motherhood', *Sociological Research Online*, 11(2).

Asylum Coalition (2004) *Asylum City: An independent review of the government's proposed accommodation centres for asylum seekers*, Asylum Coalition.

Atkins, C. (dir.) (2007) *Taking Liberties (since 1997)*, Motion picture.

Austin, J. (2011) 'Council allotment idea for future of Dale Farm', *Basildon Echo*, 12 November, www.echo-news.co.uk/news/9359391.Council_allotment_idea_for_future_of_Dale_Farm/, accessed 9 June 2012.

Aynsley-Green, A. (2010) *The Children's Commissioner for England's follow up report to: The arrest and detention of children subject to immigration and control*, London: Office of the Children's Commissioner.

Badiou, A. (2006) *Polemics*, trans. S. Corcoran, London and New York: Verso.

— (2008) *The Meaning of Sarkozy*, trans. D. Fernbach, London and New York: Verso.

— (2010) *The Communist Hypothesis*, trans. D. Macey and S. Corcoran, London and New York: Verso.

Bailey, R. (2009) 'Up against the wall: bare life and resistance in the camp', *Law and Critique*, 20(2): 113–32.

Ball, J., M. Taylor and T. Newburn (2011) 'Who were the rioters?', *Guardian*, 5 December, www.guardian.co.uk/uk/2011/dec/05/who-were-the-rioters.

Banks, D. (2011) 'Will alleged rioters get a fair trial?', *Guardian*, 12 August, www.guardian.co.uk/law/2011/aug/10/rioters-fair-trial-contempt-of-court, accessed 2 May 2012.

Baraitser, L. (2009) *Maternal Encounters: The Ethics of Interruption*, London and New York: Routledge.

Barclay, F. (2010) 'Kristeva's stranger within: the question of the foreigner in Daniel Prévost's *Le Passé sous silence*', *Paragraph*, 33(1): 1–19.

Barkham, P. (2000) 'Are our politicans racist?', *Guardian*, 19 April, www.guardian.co.uk/uk/2000/apr/19/race.world, accessed 10 June 2012.

Bataille, G. (1993 [1934]) 'Abjection and miserable forms', in S. Lotringer and S. Lotringer (eds), *More & Less 2*, trans. Y. Shafir, Los Angeles, CA: Semiotext(e).

Baucom, I. (1999) *Out of Place: Englishness, Empire and the Locations of Identity*, Princeton, NJ: Princeton University Press.

Bauman, Z. (1998) *Work, Consumerism and the New Poor*, Maidenhead: Open University Press.

— (2000) *Liquid Modernity*, Cambridge: Polity.

— (2002) 'The crisis of the human waste disposal industry', *Tikkun*, 17(5): 41–7.

— (2004) *Wasted Lives: Modernity and Its Outcasts*, Cambridge: Blackwell.

— (2011) 'The London riots – on consumerism coming home to roost', *Social Europe*, 9 August, www.social-europe.eu/2011/08/the-london-riots-on-consumerism-coming-home-to-roost/, accessed 3 June 2012.

BBC (1977–80) *Citizen Smith*.

— (2003–06) *Little Britain*.

— (2012) *Panorama: Disabled or Faking It?*

BBC News (2000) 'Public view of refugees "misinformed"', 23 October, news.bbc.co.uk/1/hi/uk/985597.stm, accessed 10 June 2012.

— (2002) '"Deal reached" in Nigeria oil protest', news.bbc.co.uk/1/hi/world/africa/2129281.stm.

— (2003) 'Stitches removed from asylum protester', 30 May, news.bbc.co.uk/1/hi/england/nottinghamshire/2949896.stm, accessed 10 June 2012.

BBC News Essex (2011) 'Families return to Dale Farm travellers' site', 16 November, www.bbc.co.uk/news/uk-england-essex-15760161, accessed 16 June 2012.

Beck, U. (1992) *Risk Society: Towards a New Modernity*, London: Sage.

Berger, J. (1972) *Ways of Seeing*, London: Penguin.

Berlant, L. (1997) *The Queen of America Goes to Washington City: Essays on Sex and Citizenship*, Durham, NC: Duke University Press.

— (2007) 'Nearly utopian, nearly normal: post-Fordist affect in La Promesse and Rosetta', *Public Culture*, 19(2): 273–301.

— (2011) *Cruel Optimism*, Durham, NC: Duke University Press.

Beveridge, W. (1942) *Social Insurance and Allied Services*, news.bbc.co.uk/1/shared/bsp/hi/pdfs/19_07_05_beveridge.pdf, accessed 6 January 2010.

Bhabha, H. (1983) 'The other question: the stereotype and colonial discourse', *Screen*, 24(6): 18–36.

— (1994) *The Location of Culture*, London and New York: Routledge.

Bhopal, K. and M. Myers (2008) *Insiders, Outsiders and Others: Gypsies and Identity*, University of Hertfordshire Press.

Bigo, D. (2002) 'Security and immigration: towards a critique of the governmentality of unease', *Alternatives: Global Local Political*, 27(1): 63–92.

Billig, M. (2001) 'Humour and hatred: the racist jokes of the Ku Klux Klan', *Discourse and Society*, 12(3): 267–89.

Blair, T. (1997) Speech at the Aylesbury Estate, Southwark, 2 June.

— (1999) BBC News, 28 September, news.bbc.co.uk/1/hi/uk_politics/460029.stm, accessed 3 March.

Blitz, B. K. (2006) 'Statelessness and the social (de)construction of citizenship: politic restructuring and ethnic discrimination in Slovenia', *Journal of Human Rights*, 5(4): 453–79.

Bouteldja, H. (2012) 'Mohamed Merah et moi', *Les Indigènes de la République*, trans. I. Tyler, 6 March, www.indigenes-republique.fr/article.php3?id_article=1637, accessed 11 June 2012.

Bowers, J. (2011) 'Shooting the messenger?', www.travellerstimes.org.uk/blog.aspx?c=f1b1c82c-of3c-4edf-98cd-502ea8oed8fa&n=347ca453-b298-4ae9-8bbb-a52a2be7e280, accessed 10 June 2012.

Boycott Workfare (2012) 'The profiteers', www.boycottworkfare.org/, accessed 16 June 2012.

Branigan, T. (2003) 'Kurdish poet finds his voice', *Guardian*, 31 May, www.guardian.co.uk/uk/2003/may/31/immigrationandpublicservices.immigration, accessed 10 June 2012.

Briant, E., N. Watson and G. Philo (2011) *Bad News for Disabled People: How the newspapers are potraying disability*, Glasgow: Inclusion London, University of Glasgow.

Brignell, V. (2010) 'The eugenics movement Britain wants to forget', *New Statesman*, 9 December.

Brown, G. (2008) 'Managed migration and earned citizenship', Speech to members of the third sector and local government representatives in North London, www.astrid-online.it/Immigrazio/Studi--ric/GORDON-BROWN-Managed-Migration-and-Earned-Citizenship-20_02_08.pdf, accessed 1 April 2009.

Brown, J. (2005) 'Crays Hill: two communities divided by a fence', *Independent*, 22 March, www.independent.co.uk/news/uk/this-britain/crays-hill-two-communities-divided-by-a-fence-6150109.html, accessed 10 June 2012.

Brown, W. (2005) *Edgework: Critical Essays in Knowledge and Politics*, Princeton, NJ: Princeton University Press.

Brysk, A. and G. Shafir (eds) (2004) *Globalization, Human Rights and the Citizenship Gap*, New York and London: Routledge.

Buckel, S. and J. Wissel (2010) 'State Project Europe: the transformation of the European border regime and the production of bare life', *International Political Sociology*, 4: 33–49.

Buden, B. (2007) 'The post-Yugoslavian condition of institutional critique: an introduction on critique as countercultural translation', *transversal*, eipcp.net/transversal/0208/buden/en, accessed 10 June 2012.

Burchill, J. (2011) 'It's time to tackle the chav-baiters', *Independent*, 29 July, www.independent.co.uk/opinion/columnists/julie-burchill/julie-burchill-its-time-to-tackle-the-chavbaiters-2327824.html, accessed 1 May 2012.

Butler, J. (1990) *Gender Trouble: Feminism and the Subversion of Identity*, New York: Routledge.

— (1993) *Bodies That Matter: On the Discursive Limits of Sex*, London and New York: Routledge.

— (1997) *The Psychic Life of Power: Theories of Subjection*, Stanford, CA: Stanford University Press.

— (2004) *Undoing Gender*, London and New York: Routledge.

— (2006) *Precarious Life: The Powers of Mourning and Violence*, London and New York: Verso.

Butler, J. and G. C. Spivak (2007) *Who Sings the Nation State? Language, Politics, Belonging*, Calcutta: Seagull Books.

Byrne, L. (2007) *Border Security and Immigration: Our Deal for Delivery in 2008*, UK Border Agency, www.ukba.homeoffice.gov.uk/sitecontent/

documents/news/Milestones_final_speech_14.1.pdf, accessed 1 April 2009.

Caffentzis, G. (2010) 'A tale of two conferences: globalization,the crisis of neoliberalism and the question of the commons', *the commoner*, December.

Cameron, D. (2008) 'David Cameron: fixing our broken society', 7 July, www.conservatives.com/News/Speeches/2008/07/David_Cameron_Fixing_our_Broken_Society.aspx, accessed 12 June 2012.

— (2010) 'Big Society', 18 May, www.number10.gov.uk/news/big-society/, accessed 9 June 2012.

Campbell, L. (2011) 'Firecracker Films: our Big Fat Gypsy success', *Broadcast*, 3 March, www.broadcastnow.co.uk/news/firecracker-films-our-big-fat-gypsy-success/5024428.article, accessed 1 June 2012.

Cannadine, D. (1998) *Class in Britain*, London: Penguin.

CARF (1999) 'Racism and the press in Blair's Britain', *Campaign Against Racism and Fascism*, 48, February/March, www.irr.org.uk/carf/feat22.html, accessed 10 June 2012.

Carter, H. (2011) 'Teenager cleared of setting fire to Miss Selfridge during Manchester riots', *Guardian*, 21 August, www.guardian.co.uk/uk/2011/aug/21/dane-williamson-cleared-manchester-riots, accessed 1 May 2012.

Cecil, N. (2003) 'Detain all asylum seekers', *Sun*, January, www.thesun.co.uk/sol/homepage/news/154238/Detain-all-asylum-seekers.html, accessed 10 June 2012.

Cemlyn, S., M. Greenfields, S. Burnett, Z. Matthews and C. Whitwell (2009) *Inequalities Experienced by Gypsy and Traveller Communities: A review*, Equality and Human Rights Commission.

Centre for Social Justice (2008) *Asylum Matters: Restoring Trust in the UK Asylum System*, Asylum and Destitution Working Group chaired by Julian Prior, London: Centre for Social Justice.

Cernea, M. (2000) 'Impoverishment risks, risk management and reconstruction: a model of population displacement and resettlement', in M. Cernea and C. McDowell (eds), *Risks and Reconstruction: Experiences of Resettlers and Refugees*, World Bank, pp. 11–55.

Channel Four (2012) *Television Corporation Report and Financial Statements 2011*, Channel Four.

Chanter, T. and E. P. Ziarek (eds) (2005) *Revolt, Affect, Collectivity: The Unstable Boundaries of Kristeva's Polis*, New York: SUNY.

Clark, T. N. and S. M. Lipset (1991) 'Are social classes dying?', *International Sociology*, 6(4): 397–410.

CodePink (2002) 'Codepink: women for peace', www.codepinkalert.org/article.php?list=type&type=3%20ref, accessed 1 June 2012.

Cohen, W. (2005) 'Introduction: Locating filth', in W. Cohen and R. Johnson (eds), *Filth: Dirt, Disgust, and Modern Life*, Minneapolis: University of Minnesota Press, pp. vii–xxxvii.

Collins, P. (2003) 'abbas amini' Lightjet print on Fuji Crystal Archive paper, 60×70 cm.

Commission for Racial Equality (1999) 'Memorandum from the Commission for Racial Equality', 22 March, Parliamentary Standing Committee on the Immigration and Asylum Bill, www.parliament.the-stationery-office.co.uk/pa/cm199899/cmstand/special/st990326/90325s25.htm#end, accessed 10 June 2012.

— (2003) *Common Ground: Equality, good race relations and sites for Gypsies and Irish Travellers*.

Connolly, M. (2011) 'Do riots show that tensions of earlier decades still smoulder?', *Guardian*, 16 August, www.guardian.co.uk/society/2011/aug/16/riots-tensions-previous-decades-smoulder, accessed 1 June 2012.

Conservative Party (1979a) *Winter of Discontent*, Conservative Party Political Broadcast.

— (1979b) *Crisis? What Crisis?*, Conservative Party Election Broadcast, 23 April.

— (2010) *Big Society: Not Big Government*, Conservative Party.

Conservative Party Press Release (2010) 'Conservatives pledge to tackle trespass', 12 February, conservativehome.blogs.com/local-government/2010/02/conservatives-pledge-to-tackle-trespass.html, accessed 10 June 2012.

Couldry, N. (2008) 'Reality TV, or the secret theater of neoliberalism', *Review of Education, Pedagogy, and Cultural Studies*, 30(1): 3–13.

Craig-Greene, S. (2012) 'Five months on from the Dale Farm eviction: it's not too late to find a long-term solution', Advocacy Project, 22 March.

Crawley, C. (2012) 'My Big Fat Gypsy Wedding exploits our community for cheap laughs', *Guardian*, 14 February, www.guardian.co.uk/commentisfree/2012/feb/14/big-fat-gypsy-wedding-exploits-community, accessed 10 June 2012.

Crawley, H. (2006) 'Child First, Migrant Second: Ensuring that every child matters', Immigration Law Practitioners' Association.

Crawley, H., J. Hemmings and N. Price (2011) *Coping with Destitution: Survival and livelihood strategies of refused asylum seekers living in the UK*, Centre for Migration Policy Research (CMPR), Swansea University/Oxfam.

Cutler, S. and S. Ceneda (2004) 'They took me away: women's experiences of immigration detention in the UK', Bail for Immigration Detainees, www.biduk.org/pdf/women/women_in_detention_in_word_02Sep04.doc, accessed 4 January 2010.

Daily Mail (2000) 'Soft-touch Britain', *Daily Mail*, 28 August, www.highbeam.com/doc/1G1-168114434.html, accessed 1 June 2012.

— (2005) 'Woman mugged by Vicky Pollard look-alike', *Daily Mail*, 24 August, www.dailymail.co.uk/news/article-402120/Woman-mugged-Vicky-Pollard-look-like.html, accessed 1 June 2012.

Daily Telegraph (2011) 'Conservative Party Conference 2011: we must tackle "feral underclass", says Ken Clarke', *Daily Telegraph*, 4 October, www.telegraph.co.uk/news/politics/conservative/8806128/Conservative-Party-Conference-2011-we-must-tackle-feral-underclass-says-Ken-Clarke.html, accessed 1 May 2012.

Dale Farm Solidarity (2012) 'Dale Farm concreted-over by Basildon Council', Press release, 16 September, dale-farm.wordpress.com/2011/09/16/dale-farm-concreted-over-by-basildon-council/, accessed 16 June 2012.

Darling, J. (2009) 'Becoming bare life: asylum, hospitality, and the politics of encampment', *Environment and Planning D: Society and Space*, 27(4): 649–65.

Das, S. K. (2008) 'Ethnicity and democracy meet when mothers protest', in P. Banerjee (ed.), *Women in Peace Politics*, New Delhi and London: Sage, pp. 54–77.

Davidson, G. (2004) 'Sites to check out if you chav what it takes', *Edinburgh Evening News*, 4 February, p. 14.

Day, G. (2001) *Class*, London and New York: Routledge.

De Genova, N. (2007) 'The production of culprits: from deportability to detainability in the aftermath of "Homeland Security"', *Citizenship Studies*, 11(5): 421–48.

— (2009) 'Conflicts of mobility, and the mobility of conflict: rightlessness, presence, subjectivity, freedom', *Subjectivity*, 29(1): 445–66.

— (2010) 'The queer politics of migration: reflections on "illegality" and incorrigibility', *Studies in Social Justice*, 4(2): 101–26.

— (2011) 'Nicholas de Genova in conversation with Rozalinda Borcila', *AREA Chicago*, 11, www.areachicago. org/p/issues/immigrations/image-our-future/, accessed 1 May 2012.

De Haas, H. (2007) 'The myth of invasion: irregular migration from West Africa to the Maghreb and the European Union', International Migration Institute, www.hein dehaas.com/Publications/de%20 Haas%202007%20-%20Migration% 20and%20Development%20in%20 Southern%20Morocco.pdf, accessed 1 June 2012.

— (2008) 'The myth of invasion: the inconvenient realities of African migration to Europe', www. hein dehaas.com/Publications/de%20 Haas%202008%20-%20inconvenient %20 realities.pdf, accessed 1 June 2012.

Dean, M. (2012) *Democracy under Attack: How the Media Distort Policy and Politics*, London: Policy Press.

Delingpole, J. (2006) 'A conspiracy against chavs? Count me in', *The Times*, 13 April, p. 25.

Dell'Olio, F. (2005) *The Europeanization of Citizenship: Between the Ideology of Nationality, Immigration and European Identity*, Aldershot: Ashgate.

Department for Work and Pensions (2009) *Work Capability Assessment Internal Review*, London: Department for Work and Pensions.

Deranty, J.-P. (2003) 'Jacques Rancière's contribution to the ethics of recognition', *Political Theory*, 31(1): 136–56.

— (2010) 'Logical revolts', in J.-P. Deranty (ed.), *Jacques Rancière: Key Concepts*, Durham: Acumen, pp. 17–24.

Diop, A. (1997) 'The struggle of the "sans-papiers": realities and perspectives', trans. I. Nappier, 4 April, www. bok.net/pajol/sanspap/sptextes/ ababacar2.en.htm, accessed 7 January 2012.

Dixon, D. (1981) 'Constitutionalising racism: the British Nationality Bill 1981', *Critical Social Policy*, 1(2): 94–100.

— (1983) 'Thatcher's people: the British Nationality Act 1981', *Journal of Law and Society*, 10(2): 161–80.

Doran, D. (2002) 'Crushing poverty spurs Nigerian village women into oil standoff', Urhobo Historical Society, www.waado.org/environment/ OilCompanies/Women/Women-2002Rebellion/July15.html.

Dorling, D. (2007) *A Think Piece for the Commission on Integration and Cohesion*, Commission on Integration and Cohesion, Wetherby: Communities and Local Government Publications.

Douglas, M. (1966) *Purity and Danger: An Analysis of Concepts of Pollution and Taboo*, London: Routledge & Kegan Paul.

Dugan, E. (2008) 'Mothers detained in immigration centre hold "naked" protest', *Independent*, 11 April, www. independent.co.uk/news/uk/ home-news/mothers-detained-in-immigration-centre-hold-naked-protest-807802.html.

Dunbar, P. (2012) 'Big Fat Gypsy goldmine: behind the scenes claims that TV company has exploited travellers to make it very rich indeed', *Mail*

Online, 26 February, www.dailymail.co.uk/news/article-2106498/Big-Fat-Gypsy-goldmine-How-TV-company-exploited-travellers-make-rich-indeed.html, accessed 10 June 2012.

Duncan Smith, I. (2008) 'How can we mend a broken society?', in G. Allen and I. Duncan Smith (eds), *Early Intervention: Good Parents, Great Kids, Better Citizens*, London: Centre for Social Justice and the Smith Institute.

Easton, M. (2011) 'England riots: the return of the underclass', BBC News, 11 August, www.bbc.co.uk/news/uk-14488486, accessed 1 June 2012.

Editorial (2011) 'Dale Farm evictions: pitch battle', *Guardian*, 19 October, www.guardian.co.uk/commentisfree/2011/oct/19/editorial-dale-farm-pitch-battle, accessed 9 June 2012.

Edkins, J. (2001) 'If no story is possible: trauma, testimony and biopolitics after Auschwitz', ISA, isanet.ccit.arizona.edu/paperarchive.html.

Edkins, J. and V. Pin-Fat (2004) 'Introduction: Life, power, resistance', in J. Edkins, V. Pin-Fat and M. J. Shapiro (eds), *Sovereign Lives: Power in Global Politics*, New York: Routledge.

— (2005) 'Through the wire: relations of power and relations of violence', *Millennium: Journal of International Studies*, 34(1): 1–24.

Ehrenreich, B. (2001) *Nickel and Dimed: On (Not) Getting By in America*, New York: Metropolitan Books.

Ekine, S. (2000) *Blood and Oil: Testimonies of Violence from Women of the Niger Delta*, London: Centre for Democracy and Development.

— (2008) *The Curse of Nakedness: Women in Nigeria Threaten to Bare It All to Better Their Communities*, International Museum of Women, www.imow.org/wpp/stories/viewStory?storyId=1098.

— (2009) 'Women's responses to state violence in the Niger Delta: violence as an instrument of governance', Pambazuka News, pambazuka.org/en/category/features/54174.

Engels, F. (1887) *The Condition of the Working Class in England*, www.marxists.org/archive/marx/works/1845/condition-working-class/, accessed 10 June 2012.

Escobar, M. (2006) *Violent Intersections: The role of prisons and welfare in the exclusion of Mexican immigrant women*, Unpublished.

— (2009) 'Understanding the roots of Latina migrants' captivity', *Social Justice*, 36(2): 7–20.

Fabricant, M. (2008) 'Little Vicky Pollard is a part of our sad society', *Birmingham Post*, 15 July, www.michael.fabricant.mp.co.uk/paper-0030.ihtml, accessed 6 May 2012.

Fanon, F. (2004) *The Wretched of the Earth*, trans. R. Philcox, New York: Grove Press.

— (2008) *Black Skin, White Masks*, trans. C. L. Markmann, London: Pluto.

Fearn, H. (2010) 'Backup is needed for those under fire in the field, abused lecturer says', 27 May, www.timeshighereducation.co.uk/story.asp?storyCode=411721&sectioncode=26, accessed 16 June 2012.

Federici, S. (2004) *Caliban and the Witch: Women, the Body and Primitive Accumulation*. New York: Autonomedia.

— (2011) 'Feminism and the politics of the commons', *The Commoner*, http://www.commoner.org.uk/wp-content/uploads/2011/01/federici-feminism-and-the-politics-of-commons.pdf.

Fekete, L. (2005) 'The deportation machine: Europe, asylum and human rights', *Race and Class*, 47(1): 64–91.

Fenn, C. and P. Owen (2011) 'Rioters in their own words – interactive', *Guardian*, 5 December, www.

guardian.co.uk/uk/interactive/2011/dec/05/rioters-in-own-words-interactive, accessed 2 June 2012.

Ferreday, D. (2012) 'Anorexia and abjection: a review essay', *Body and Society*, 18(2): 139–55.

Finding, D. (2008) '"I can't believe you just said that": figuring gender and sexuality in Little Britain', *Media@lse*.

Foucault, M. (2002) 'Useless to revolt?', in M. Foucault and J. Faubion (eds), *Power: The Essential Works of Michel Foucault 1954–1984*, trans. R. Hurley et al., London: Penguin.

— (2003) *Society Must Be Defended: Lectures at the Collège de France*, trans. D. Machey, New York: Picador.

— (2008) *The Birth of Biopolitics: Lectures at the Collège de France, 1978–1979*, ed. M. Senellart, trans. G. Burchell, New York: Palgrave Macmillan.

Freeman, R. (2011) 'Dale Farm: a community with nowhere to go', *Guardian*, 19 October, www.guardian.co.uk/commentisfree/2011/oct/19/dale-farm-community-nowhere-to-go, accessed 9 June 2012.

Fund, J. (2012) 'Britain's NHS: no fun and games', 29 July, www.nationalreview.com/articles/312573/britain-s-nhs-no-fun-and-games-john-fund, accessed 30 August 2012.

Fuss, D. (1994) 'Interior colonies: Frantz Fanon and the politics of identification', *Diacritics*, 24: 20–42.

G4S (2012) *Securing Your World*, www.g4s.com, accessed 1 April 2012.

Gabhann, C. M. (2012) *Voices Unheard: A Study of Irish Travellers in Prison*, Irish Chaplaincy in Britain.

Gans, H. J. (1990) 'Deconstructing the underclass: the term's dangers as a planning concept', *Journal of the American Planning Association*, 56(3): 271–7.

Geddes, A. (2005) 'Chronicle of a crisis foretold: the politics of irregular migration, human trafficking and people smuggling in the UK', *British Journal of Politics and International Relations*, 7: 324–39.

Gentleman, A. (2012) 'GPs call for work capability assessment to be scrapped', *Guardian*, 23 May, www.guardian.co.uk/society/2012/may/23/gps-work-capability-assessment-scrapped.

Gibney, M. J. (2004) *The Ethics and Politics of Asylum: Liberal Democracy and the Response to Refugees*, Oxford: Oxford University Press.

— (2011) 'Asylum policy', Oxford Migration Observatory Policy Primer, March, migrobs.vm.bytemark.co.uk/policy-primers/asylum-policy, accessed 10 June 2012.

Giddens, A. (1991) *Modernity and Self-Identity*, Stanford, CA: Stanford University Press.

Giddens, A. and P. Diamond (2005) 'The new egalitarianism: economic inequality in the UK', in A. Giddens and P. Diamond (eds), *The New Egalitarianism*, Cambridge: Polity, pp. 87–100.

Gill, N., D. Conlon, C. Oeppen and I. Tyler (2012) *Networks of Asylum Suport in the UK and USA: A Handbook of Ideas, Strategies and Best Practice for Asylum Support Groups in a Challenging Social and Economic Climate*, University of Exeter.

Gill, R. (2008) 'Culture and subjectivity in neoliberal and postfeminist times', *Subjectivity*, 25(1): 432–45.

Gilles, V. (2005) 'Raising the "meritocracy": parenting and the individualization of social class', *Sociology*, 39(5): 835–53.

Gilroy, P. (2011) 'Paul Gilroy speaks on the riots, August 2011, Tottenham, North London', *the dream of safety: to surrender to the dream of safety*, dreamofsafety.blogspot.co.uk/2011/08/paul-gilroy-speaks-on-riots-august-2011.html, accessed 10 June 2012.

Giroux, H. A. (2007) 'Violence, Katrina, and the biopolitics of disposability', *Theory, Culture and Society*, 24(7/8): 305–9.

Graeber, D. (2011) *Debt: The First 5,000 Years*, New York: Melville House.

Grayson, J. (2010) 'Playing the gypsy "race card"', Institute of Race Relations, 4 June.

— (2012a) 'First they came for the asylum seeker …', Institute for Race Relations, 8 March, www.irr.org.uk/news/first-they-came-for-the-asylum-seeker/, accessed 10 June 2012.

— (2012b) 'Mobilising outrage: campaigning with asylum seekers against security industry giant, G4S', *OurKingdom: Power and Liberty in Britain*, 12 April, www.opendemocracy.net/ourkingdom/john-grayson/mobilising-outrage-campaigning-with-asylum-seekers-against-security-industry, accessed 10 June 2012.

Greenfields, M. and A. Ryder (2010) 'The Traveller Economic Inclusion Project: an inclusive and intercultural approach to research combining policy, practice and community in action research', *Proceedings of cAIR10, the first Conference on Applied Interculturality Research*, Graz, Austria, 7–10 April 2010, Graz: cAIR10.

Grlja, D. and J. Vesić (2007) 'The neoliberal institution of culture and the critique of culturalization', *transversal*, eipcp.net/transversal/0208/prelom/en, accessed 10 June 2012.

Gross, B., K. Moore and T. Threadgold (2007) *Broadcast News Coverage of Asylum April to October 2006: Caught between Human Rights and Public Safety*, Cardiff School of Journalism, Media and Cultural Studies.

Guardian (2005) 'Inflammatory language', *Guardian*, 8 November, www.guardian.co.uk/news/blog/2005/nov/08/inflammatoryla, accessed 4 June 2012.

— (2012) 'Disability hate crime is at its highest level since records began', *Guardian*, 14 August, www.guardian.co.uk/news/datablog/2012/aug/14/disability-hate-crime-increase-reported-incidents-data?mobile-redirect=false, accessed 31 August 2012.

Guterres, A. (2006) 'Victims of intolerance', *Refugees*, p. 3.

Hague, W. (2001) 'Hague's "foreign land" speech', *Guardian*, 4 March, www.guardian.co.uk/politics/2001/mar/04/conservatives.speeches, accessed 10 June 2012.

Hall, S., C. Critcher, T. Jefferson, J. N. Clarke and B. Roberts (1978) *Policing the Crisis: Mugging, the State and Law and Order*, London and Basingstoke: Macmillan.

Hancock, A.-M. (2004) *The Politics of Disgust: The Public Identity of the Welfare Queen*, New York: New York University Press.

Hansen, R. and D. King (2001) 'Eugenic ideas, political interests, and policy variance: immigration and sterilization policy in Britain and the U.S.', *World Politics*, 53(2): 237–63.

Hardin, G. (1968) 'The tragedy of the commons', *Science*, 162(3859): 1243–8.

Hardt, M. (1995) 'The withering of civil society', *Social Text*, 45: 27–44.

Hardt, M. and A. Negri (2000) *Empire*, Cambridge, MA: Harvard University Press.

— (2005) *Multitude, War and Democracy in the Age of Empire*, London and New York: Penguin.

Harman, C. (1981) 'The summer of 1981: a post-riot analysis', *International Socialism*, 14(1): 1–43.

Harrison, T. (2008) *Fram*, London: Faber and Faber.

Harvey, D. (2005) *A Brief History of Neo-liberalism*, Oxford: Oxford University Press.

Hayes, P. (1988) 'Utopia and the lumpenproletariat: Marx's reasoning in "The Eighteenth Brumaire of Louis Bonaparte"', *Review of Politics*, 50(3): 445–65.

Haylett, C. (2003) 'Remaking labour imaginaries: social reproduction and the internationalising project of welfare reform', *Political Geography*, 22: 765–88.

Hayward, K. and M. Yar (2006) 'The "chav" phenomenon: consumption, media and the construction of a new underclass', *Crime, Media, Culture*, 2(1): 9–28.

Hegarty, S. (2011) 'London riots: young people voice their frustrations', *Guardian*, 16 August, www.guardian.co.uk/society/2011/aug/16/london-riots-young-people-voice-anger, accessed 5 May 2012.

Himmelblau, S. (2011) *#riotcleanup or#riotwhitewash?*, University for Strategic Optimism, 10 August, universityforstrategicoptimism.word press.com/2011/08/10/riotcleanup-or-riotwhitewash/, accessed 1 June 2012.

HM Government (2004) *Every Child Matters: Change for Children*, London: Department for Education and Skills.

HMIP (2005) *Report on an announced inspection of Yarl's Wood Immigration Removal Centre (28 February–4 March 2005)*, London: HMIP.

Hodge, N. (2004) 'Britain: asylum seekers protest persecution', World Socialist website, 28 January, www.wsws.org/articles/2004/jan2004/asyl-j28.shtml, accessed 10 June 2012.

Hoggart, R. (1989) 'Introduction', in G. Orwell, *The Road to Wigan Pier*, London: Penguin.

Hollingworth, S. and K. Williams (2009) 'Constructions of the working class "other" among urban white middle class youth: "chavs", subculture and the valuing of education', *Journal of Youth Studies*, 12(5): 467–8.

Home Office (2007) *Enforcing the Rules: A strategy to ensure and enforce compliance with our immigration laws*, London: Home Office.

— (2008) *Handling of Suspected Health Tourists*, www.homeoffice.gov.uk/about-us/freedom-of-information/releasedinformation/.

— (2012) *Leave to Remain*, UK Border Agency, www.ukba.homeoffice.gov.uk/asylum/outcomes/successfulapplications/leavetoremain/, accessed 20 June 2012.

Hornby, N. (2012) 'An open letter to @pipogypopotamus', 20 February, Channel Four website, www.channel4.com/4viewers/editors-blog/an-open-letter-to-pipogypopotamus, accessed 10 June 2012.

Howard, M. (2005) 'Mr Blair's Labour government has lost the plot', *Guardian*, 6 April, www.guardian.co.uk/politics/2005/apr/06/uk.conservatives, accessed 3 June 2012.

Huang, P. (2008) 'Anchor babies, over-breeders, and the population bomb: the reemergence of nativism and population control in anti-immigration policies', *Harvard Law and Policy Review*, pp. 385–406.

Hussey, A. (2012) 'France: a country at war with itself', *New Statesman*, 30 March, www.newstatesman.com/europe/2012/03/hatred-banlieue, accessed 5 June 2012.

Hyndman, J. (2000) *Managing Displacement: Refugees and the Politics of Humanitarianism*, Minneapolis: University of Minnesota Press.

ICAR (2004) *Media Image, Community Impact: Assessing the impact of media and political images of refugees and asylum seekers on community relations in London*, London: ICAR.

Ifekwunigwe, J. (2004) 'Recasting Black Venus in the new African diaspora', *Women's Studies International Forum*, 27(4): 397–412.

ILPA (Immigration Law Practitioners' Association) (2007) *Submission to Lord Goldsmith for the Citizenship Review: The Different Categories of British Nationality*, Ministry of Justice, www.justice.gov.uk/docs/ilpa-citizenship.pdf, accessed 10 February 2009.

Independent on Sunday (2004) 'Media: the week in numbers', *Independent on Sunday*, 24 October.

Irish Traveller Movement in Britain (2012) *Submission by the Irish Traveller Movement in Britain to the Leveson Inquiry*, Irish Traveller Movement in Britain.

Isin, E. (2004) 'The neurotic citizen', *Citizenship Studies*, 8(3): 217–35.

Isin, E. F. and B. S. Turner (2007) 'Investigating citizenship: an agenda for citizenship studies', *Citizenship Studies*, 11(1): 5–17.

Isin, E. and K. Rygiel (2007) 'Abject spaces: frontiers, zones, camps', in E. Dauphinée and C. Masters (eds), *The Logics of Biopower and the War on Terror: Living, Dying, Surviving*, Basingstoke: Palgrave Macmillan, pp. 181–203.

ITV (1984–96) *Spitting Image*.

— (2012) *Don't Hate Us!*

IWCA (2011) 'The lumpen rebellion', www.iwca.info/?p=10184, accessed 6 May 2012.

Jeffers, A. (2012) *Refugees, Theatre and Crisis: Performing Global Identities*, London and New York: Palgrave Macmillan.

Jeffries, M. (2005) 'Grate Brits: there's a Vicky on every corner, say comic show stars', *Daily Star*, 19 December, p. 3.

Jones, A. (2009) 'Performing the wounded body: pain, affect and the radical relationality of meaning', *Parallax*, 15(4): 45–67.

Jones, O. (2011) *Chavs: The Demonization of the Working Class*, London: Verso.

Jones, S. (2010) 'You're stigmatised if you live on a council estate', *Guardian*, 27 January.

Kaniuk, R. (2011) 'UK riots: let's shop a looter', *Daily Star*, 10 August.

Kawash, S. (1999) 'Terrorism and vampires: Fanon's spectral violence of decolonization', in A. C. Alessandrini (ed.), *Frantz Fanon: Critical Perspectives*, New York: Routledge, pp. 234–57.

Kear, A. (2008) 'Intensities of appearance', *Performance Research*, 12(4): 16–24.

Kearns, I. and K. Gude (2008) *The New Front Line: Security in a changing world*, IPPR, www.ippr.org/images/media/files/publication/2011/05/the_new_front_line_1623.pdf.

Kennedy, H. (2005) *Just Law: The Changing Face of Justice and Why It Matters to Us All*, London: Vintage.

Keynes, J. M. (1936) *The General Theory of Employment, Interest and Money*, London: Macmillan.

Khalsa, B. (2011) 'Gypsy Weddings producers come under fire', *Broadcast*, 1 April, www.broadcastnow.co.uk/home/complaints-log/gypsy-weddings-producers-come-under-fire/5025654.article, accessed 10 June 2012.

Khanna, R. (2006) 'Post-palliative: coloniality's affective dissonance', *Postcolonial Text*, 2(1)

— (2009) 'Disposability', *Differences: A Journal of Feminist Cultural Studies*, 20(1): 181–98.

— (2011) 'Racial France, or the melancholic alterity of postcolonial studies', *Public Culture*, 23(1): 191–9.

Khiari, S. (2006) *Pour une politique de la racaille: Immigré·e·s, indigènes et jeunes de banlieues*, Paris: Textual.

Kipfer, S. (2011) 'Decolonization in the heart of empire: some Fanonian echoes in France today', *Antipode*, 43(4): 1155–80.

Klein, N. (2007) *The Shock Doctrine: The Rise of Disaster Capitalism*, New York: Metropolitan Books.

Knowsley, J. (2003) 'Luxury for migrants in new centre', *Mail on Sunday*, 23 August, www.highbeam.com/doc/1G1-106874678.html, accessed 10 May 2009.

Korsmeyer, C. and B. Smith (2004) 'Visceral values: Aurel Kolnai on disgust', in A. Kolnai, C. Korsmeyer and B. Smith (eds), *On Disgust*, Peru: Open Court.

Krahmann, E. (2009) *Private Security Companies and the State Monopoly on Violence: A Case of Norm Change?*, Peace Research Institute Frankfurt (PRIF).

Krauss, R. (1996) '"Informe" without conclusion', *October*, 78: 89–105.

— (1999) 'The destiny of the Informe', in Y.-A. Bois and R. E. Krauss (eds), *Formless: A User's Guide*, New York: Zone Books, pp. 234–52.

Kristeva, J. (1982) *The Powers of Horror: An essay on abjection*, trans. L. S. Roudiez, New York: Columbia University Press.

— (1989) *Black Sun: Depression and melancholia*, trans. L. S. Roudiez, New York: Columbia University Press.

— (1991) *Strangers to Ourselves*, trans. L. S. Roudiez, New York: Columbia University Press.

— (1993) *Nations without Nationalism*, trans. L. S. Roudiez, New York: Columbia University Press.

— (1995) *New Maladies of the Soul*, trans. R. Guberman, New York: Columbia University Press.

— (2002) *Revolt, She Said*, trans. B. O'Keeffe, Los Angeles and New York: MIT Press.

— (2010) *Hatred and Forgiveness*, trans.

J. Herman, New York: Columbia University Press.

Labour Party (1997) *New Labour because Britain deserves better*, www.labour-party.org.uk/manifestos/1997/1997-labour-manifesto.shtml, accessed 2 June 2012.

Laclau, E. and C. Mouffe (2001) *Hegemony and Socialist Strategy: Towards a Radical Democratic Politics*, 2nd edn, London: Verso.

Lawrence, J. (2012) 'My Big Fat Gypsy divorce', *Mail Online*, 4 February, www.dailymail.co.uk/femail/article-2096185/My-Big-Fat-Gypsy-Wedding-Joan-Fureys-fairytale-ended-divorce-tears-tantrums.html, accessed 6 June 2012.

Lees, L. (2008) 'Gentrification and social mixing: towards an inclusive urban renaissance?', *Urban Studies*, 45(12): 2449–70.

Lentin, R. (2004) 'Strangers and strollers: feminist notes on researching migrant m/others', *Women's Studies International Forum*, 27: 301–14.

— (2011) 'Palestinian women from Femina Sacra to agents of active resistance', *Women's Studies International Forum*, 34(3): 165–70.

Lewis, P. (2011a) 'Reading the riots: "It was a war, and we had the police scared"', Video, 5 December.

— (2011b) 'A fire lit in Tottenham that burned Manchester: the rioters' story', *Guardian*, 5 December, www.guardian.co.uk/uk/2011/dec/05/tottenham-manchester-rioters-story-england?INTCMP=SRCH, accessed 6 December 2011.

Lewis, P., T. Newburn and D. Roberts (2011) *Reading the Riots: Investigating England's Summer of Disorder*, London: Guardian/London School of Economics.

Linebaugh, P. (1992) *The London Hanged: Crime and civil society in the eight-*

eenth century, Cambridge: Cambridge University Press.

Lister, R. (2004) *Poverty*, London: Polity.

Liu, C. (ed.) (1992) 'The abject America', *Lusitania*, 1(4).

Long, J. (2006) 'Border anxiety in Palestine–Israel', *Antipode*, 38(1): 107–27.

Long, P. (2008) *Only in the Common People: The Aesthetics of Class in Post-War Britain*, Newcastle: Cambridge Scholars Publishing.

Lord Goldsmith (2008) *Citizenship Our Common Bond*, Ministry of Justice, www.justice.gov.uk/docs/citizenship-report-full.pdf, accessed 1 April 2009.

Lord Scarman (1982) *The Scarman Report: The Brixton Disorders 10–12 April 1981*, London: Penguin.

Lotringer, S. (1993) 'Les Miserables', in S. Lotringer and C. Kraus (eds), *More and Less*, Cambridge, MA: Semiotexte.

— (2000) 'Julia Kristeva in conversation with Sylvère Lotringer', trans. J. Herman, *Semiotexte*, semiotexte. com/?p=123, accessed 11 June 2012.

Luibhéid, E. (2004) 'Childbearing against the state? Asylum seeker women in the Irish Republic', *Women's Studies International Forum*, 27(4): 335–49.

— (2006) 'Sexual regimes and migration controls: reproducing the Irish nation-state in transnational contexts', *Feminist Review*, 83: 60–78.

Lupin, W. (2005) *Blood on Our Hands – Remembering Hussein and Israfil*, goinguphill.blogspot.co.uk/2005/08/blood-on-our-hands-remembering-hussein.html, accessed 1 June 2012.

Lyall, S. (2003) 'A hunger strike puts spotlight on British asylum policy', *New York Times*, 29 May, www.nytimes.com/2003/05/29/world/a-hunger-strike-puts-spotlight-on-british-asylum-policy.html?pagewanted=all&src=pm, accessed 20 June 2012.

Lyddaird, A. (2005) '1001 Nights Now', devised and directed by Alan Lyd-

daird from stories by Abas Amini, Maziar Bahari, Fadia Faqir, Johan Bergman Lindfors/Reza Parsa, Paul Mattar, Shazia Mirza, Murathan Mungan and Atiq Rahimi.

MacColl, E. and P. Seeger (1964) *Travelling People*, www.setintosong. co.uk/downloads/PDF/rb_website_ travelling_ people.pdf, accessed 23 August 2012.

Macdonald, C. (2008) 'Cameron takes moral stance on the trouble society faces', *The Herald*, 8 July, www. scottishpolitics.org/glasgoweast/ glasgoweast130.html, accessed 10 June 2012.

MacDonald, R., T. Shildrick and S. Blackman (eds) (2010a) *Young People, Class and Place*, London and New York: Routledge.

MacDonald, R., T. Shildrick, C. Webster and K. Garthwaite (2010b) *The Low-pay, No-pay Cycle: Understanding recurrent poverty*, York: Joseph Rowntree Foundation.

Malone, C. (2003) 'Stunt is a stitch-up', *Sunday Mirror*, 1 June.

Manchester Evening Chronicle (1905) 'Editorial', *Manchester Evening Chronicle*, 19 April, p. 2.

Marciniak, K. (2006) 'Immigrant rage: alienhood, "hygienic" identities, and the Second World', *differences: A Journal of Feminist Cultural Studies*, 17: 33–63.

— (forthcoming) 'Legal/illegal: protesting citizenship in Fortress America', *Citizenship Studies*.

Marshall, T. H. (1950) *Citizenship and Social Class and Other Essays*, Cambridge: Cambridge University Press.

Marx, K. (1848) *Manifesto of the Communist Party*, www.marxists. org/archive/marx/works/1848/ communist-manifesto/, accessed 1 May 2012.

— (1852) 'The Eighteenth Brumaire of Louis Bonaparte', 1 May, www.

marxists.org/archive/marx/works/1852/18th-brumaire/.

— (1853) 'Forced emigration', *New York Daily Tribune*, 22 March, www.marxists.org/archive/marx/works/1853/03/04.htm, accessed 20 June 2012.

— (1870) 'Letter to Sigfrid Meyer and August Vogt', 9 April, www.marxists.org/archive/marx/works/1870/letters/70_04_09.htm, accessed 1 June 2012.

Marx, K. H., F. Engels and A. Willich (1850) 'The Prussian refugees: letter to the editor', 18 June, www.marxists.org/archive/marx/works/1850/06/15.htm, accessed 11 June 2012.

McClintock, A. (1995) *Imperial Leather: Race, Gender, and Sexuality in the Colonial Contest*, New York: Routledge.

McFarlane, A. (2010) 'Can community sentences replace jail?', *BBC News*, 16 August, www.bbc.co.uk/news/magazine-10725163, accessed 3 May 2012.

Mckenzie-Borev, P. (2012) 'An open letter to Channel 4', *Pipopotamus*, 18 February, pipopotamus.blogspot.co.uk/, accessed 10 June 2012.

Mcleish, J. (2002) *Mothers in Exile: Maternity Experiences of Asylum-Seekers in England*, London: Maternity Alliance.

McNevin, A. (2006) 'Political belonging in a neoliberal era: the struggle of the sans-papiers', *Citizenship Studies*, 10(2): 135–51.

— (2007) 'The liberal paradox and the politics of asylum in Australia', *Australian Journal of Political Science*, 41(4): 611–30.

Meagher, M. (2003) 'Jenny Saville and a feminist aesthetics of disgust', *Hypatia*, 18(3): 23–41.

Menninghaus, W. (2003) *Disgust: Theory and History of a Strong Sensation*, trans. H. Eiland and J. Golb, Albany, NY: SUNY.

Mezzadra, S. (2004) 'Citizenship in motion', *Generation Online*, www.generation-online.org/t/tmezzadra.htm, accessed 10 June 2012.

— (2011) 'The gaze of autonomy. Capitalism, migration and social struggles', in V. Squire (ed.), *The Contested Politics of Mobility: Borderzones and Irregularity*, London and New York: Routledge, pp. 121–42.

Midnight Notes Collective and Friends (2009) 'Promissory notes: from crisis to commons', www.midnightnotes.org/mnpubarticles.html, accessed 11 June 2012.

Miller, W. (1997) *The Anatomy of Disgust*, Cambridge, MA: Harvard University Press.

Milne, S. (2011) 'These riots reflect a society run on greed and looting', *Guardian*, 10 August, www.guardian.co.uk/commentisfree/2011/aug/10/riots-reflect-society-run-greed-looting, accessed June 2012.

Mirzoeff, N. (2005) *Watching Babylon: The War in Iraq and Global Visual Culture*, New York: Routledge.

Misri, D. (2011) '"Are you a man?": performing naked protest in India', *Signs*, 36(3): 603–25.

Molé, N. (2008) 'Precarious subjects: anticipating neoliberalism in northern Italy's workplace', *American Anthropologist*, 112(1): 38–53.

Mooney, G. (2008) 'Urban nightmares and dystopias, or places of hope?', *Variant*, 33: 14–16.

Moorehead, C. (2005) *Human Cargo: A Journey among Refugees*, Vintage.

Mountz, A. (2010) *Seeking Asylum: Human Smuggling and Bureaucracy at the Border*, Minneapolis: University of Minnesota Press.

MRCF (Migrant and Refugee Communities Forum) (2011) *Submission to the Leveson Inquiry into the culture, practices and ethics of the press*.

Mulholland, H. (2011) 'Duncan Smith blames riots on family breakdown and benefits system', *Guardian*, 3 October, www.guardian.co.uk/politics/2011/oct/03/duncan-smith-riots-benefits-system, accessed 1 May 2012.

Murray, C. (1986) 'White welfare, families, "white trash"', *National Review*, 38(5): 30–4.

— (1997) *What It Means to Be a Libertarian*, New York: Broadway Books.

— (2000) *Newsnight*, 10 May, BBC TV.

— (2001) *Underclass + 10: Charles Murray and the British Underclass 1990–2000*, London: Civitas/Sunday Times.

Murray, K. (2012) 'Views of the Aylesbury: one of Britain's most maligned estates', *Guardian*, 3 May.

Nayak, A. (2003) *Race, Place and Globalization: Youth Cultures in a Changing World*, Oxford: Berg.

— (2006) 'Displaced masculinities: chavs, youth and class in the post-industrial', *Sociology*, 40(5): 813–31.

Newburn, T., P. Lewis and F. Bawdon (2011a) 'Phase two of Reading the Riots: first rioters, next police and judges', *Guardian*, 9 December, www.guardian.co.uk/uk/2011/dec/09/phase-two-reading-the-riots, accessed 1 June 2012.

Newburn, T., A. Topping, B. Ferguson and M. Taylor (2011b) 'The four-day truce: gangs suspended hostilities during English riots', *Guardian*, 6 December, www.guardian.co.uk/uk/2011/dec/06/gang-truce-english-riots, accessed 6 June 2012.

Ngai, S. (2005) *Ugly Feelings: Literature, Affect, and Ideology*, Cambridge, MA: Harvard University Press.

NoBorders (2011) *Pease Pottage*, www.peasepottage.info/uk-borders-agency-detention-centre, accessed 10 June 2012.

Nussbaum, M. (2004) *Hiding from Humanity: Digust, Shame and the Law*, Princeton, NJ: Princeton University Press.

Nyers, P. (2003) 'Abject cosmopolitanism: the politics of protection in the anti-deportation movement', *Third World Quarterly*, 24(6): 1069–93.

— (2004) 'Introduction: what's left of citizenship?', *Citizenship Studies*, 8(3): 203–15.

— (2006) *Rethinking Refugees: Beyond States of Emergency*, New York: Routledge.

— (2008) 'No one is illegal between city and nation', in E. Isin and G. Nielsen (eds), *Acts of Citizenship*, London: Zed Books.

Observer (2005) 'Not just a city, a way of life', *Observer*, 27 February, www.guardian.co.uk/uk/2005/feb/27/theobserver.uknews1, accessed 1 June 2012.

OED (Oxford English Dictionary) (2012) *Oxford English Dictionary online*, www.oed.com.

O'Keeffe, A. (2008) 'Their right to liberty', *New Statesmen*, 18 December, www.newstatesman.com/uk-politics/2008/12/immigration-detention-children, accessed 10 June 2012.

Ong, A. (1999) *Flexible Citizenship: The Cultural Logics of Transnationality*, Durham, NC: Duke University Press.

Orwell, G. (2000) *My Country Right or Left 1940–1943: The Collected Essays, Journalism and Letters of George Orwell*, ed. S. Orwell and I. Angus, New Hampshire: Nonpareil.

O'Scumbag, P. (2011) 'Basildon Council sunk secret group appointed to solve Dale Farm crisis', 13 September, Dale Farm Solidarity, dalefarm.wordpress.com/2011/09/13/basildon-council-sunk-secret-group-appointed-to-solve-dale-farm-crisis/, accessed 9 June 2012.

Paglen, T. (2009) *Blank Spots on the Map: The Dark Geography of the Pentagon's Secret World*, New York and Toronto: Penguin.

Pahl, R. (1989) 'Is the emperor naked?

Some comments on the adequacy of sociological theory in urban and regional research', *International Journal of Urban and regional Research*, 13: 127–9.

Pakulski, J. and M. Waters (1996) 'The reshaping and dissolution of social class in advanced society', *Theory and Society*, 25(5): 667–91.

Panagia, D. (2010) '"Portage du sensible": the distribution of the sensible', in *Jacques Rancière Key Concepts*, Durham, NC: ACUMEN.

Papadopoulos, D., N. Stephenson and V. Tsianos (2008) *Escape Routes: Control and subversion in the 21st century*, London: Pluto Press.

Papastergiadis, N. (2006) 'The invasion complex: the abject other and spaces of violence', *Geografiska Annaler: Series B, Human Geography*, 88(4): 429–42.

Phillips, M. (2011) 'Britain's liberal intelligentsia has smashed virtually every social value', *Mail Online*, 11 August, www.dailymail.co.uk/debate/article-2024690/UK-riots-2011-Britains-liberal-intelligentsia-smashed-virtually-social-value.html, accessed 1 May 2012.

Pitcher, B. (2012) 'Race and capitalism redux', *Patterns of Prejudice*, 46(1): 1–15.

Plan B (2012a) 'Find out what kids are good at. It will change their lives', *Guardian*, 17 March, www.guardian.co.uk/commentisfree/2012/mar/17/plan-b-speech-british-youth-tedxobserver, accessed 1 June 2012.

— (2012b) 'Statement on Ill Manors', July, www.time4planb.co.uk/news/statement-on-ill-manors, accessed 11 September 2012.

Plant, R. (2010) *The Neo-Liberal State*, Oxford and New York: Oxford University Press.

Porter, B. (1979) *The Refugee Question in Mid-Victorian Politics*, Cambridge and New York: Cambridge University Press.

Powers, C. (2004) *Room to Roam, England's Irish Travellers*, London: Community Fund.

Prasad, R. (2011) 'English riots were "a sort of revenge" against the police', *Guardian*, 5 December, www.guardian.co.uk/uk/2011/dec/05/riots-revenge-against-police, accessed 5 December 2011.

Probyn, E. (2000) *Carnal appetites: food-sexidentities*, London: Routledge.

Puxon, G. (2010) 'Letter to the Essex Police Authority concerning the role of police vis-à-vis the direct action operation to evict the Gypsy and Traveller community at Dale Farm planned by Basildon District Council', 26 April, Dale Farm Housing Association/Gypsy and Traveller Community of Dale Farm/Human Rights Clinic of the University of Essex.

Raisborough, J. and M. Adams (2008) 'Mockery and morality in popular cultural representations of the white working class', *Sociological Research Online*, 13(2): 1–2.

Rancière, J. (1989) *The Nights of Labor: The Workers' Dream in Nineteenth-century France*, trans. J. Drury, Philadelphia, PA: Temple University Press.

— (1997) 'Democracy means equality: Jacques Rancière interviewed by *Passages*', *Radical Philosophy: A Journal of Socialist and Feminist Philosophy*, 82: 18–29.

— (1999) *Dis-agreement: Politics and Philosophy*, trans. J. Rose, Minneapolis and London: University of Minnesota Press.

— (2001) 'Ten theses on politics', *Theory and Event*, 5(3).

— (2004a) *The Philosopher and His Poor*, ed. A. Parker, trans. J. Drury, C. Oster and A. Parker, Durham, NC: Duke University Press.

— (2004b) *The Politics of Aesthetics:*

The Distribution of the Sensible, trans. G. Rockhill, London and New York: Continuum.

— (2011) *Staging the People: The Proletarian and His Double*, trans. D. Fernbach, London and New York: Verso.

Revel, J. and T. Negri (2011) 'The common in revolt', *Negri in English*, 14 August, antonionegriinenglish.wordpress.com/2012/01/30/the-common-in-revolt/, accessed 2 May 2012.

Richards, M. (2005) 'Sewing and sealing: speaking silence', in G. Coulter-Smith and M. Owen (eds), *Art in the Age of Terrorism*, London: Paul Holberton, pp. 34–48.

Richardson, J. (2010) 'Discourse dissonance: an examination of media, political and public discourse and its impact on policy implementation for Roma, Gypsies and Travellers at a local level', *Romani Mobilities in Europe: Multidisciplinary Perspectives, International Conference, 14–15 January 2010, University of Oxford*, Oxford: University of Oxford, pp. 166–96.

Riddell, M. (2012) 'London riots: the underclass lashes out', *Daily Telegraph*, 7 August, www.telegraph.co.uk/news/uknews/law-and-order/8630533/Riots-the-underclass-lashes-out.html, accessed 1 June 2012.

Rigby, J. and R. Schlembach (forthcoming) 'Impossible protest: NoBorders in Calais', *Citizenship Studies*.

Roberts, A. (2011) 'Stop blaming the wealthy', *Daily Beast*, 10 August, www.thedailybeast.com/articles/2011/08/10/london-riots-blame-the-feral-something-for-nothing-underclass.html, accessed 12 December 2011.

Robson, E. (2012) 'Dale Farm: the human cost of prejudice', March, www.redpepper.org.uk/dale-farm-the-human-cost-of-prejudice/, accessed 1 June 2012.

Rose, N. (1990) *Governing the Soul: The Shaping of the Private Self*, London: Routledge.

— (1999) *Powers of Freedom: Reframing Political Thought*, Cambridge: Cambridge University Press.

Roy, A. (2003) 'Instant-mix imperial democracy (buy one, get one free): speech presented in New York City at the Riverside Church', *Common Dreams*, 13 May, www.commondreams.org/views03/0518-01.htm, accessed 5 September 2012.

Royal Courts of Justice (2008) *McCarthy & Ors v. Basildon District Council*, London: Royal Courts of Justice.

Rushdie, S. (1982) 'The new empire within Britain', *New Society*, pp. 417–21.

Russell, A. (2011) *Boundaries of the Body: De/Constructing Boundaries in the Lives of Women who have been Trafficked for Sexual Exploitation*, PhD thesis, Leeds University.

Rutherford, J. (1990) 'The third space: interview with Homi Bhabha', in J. Rutherford (ed.), *Identity: Community, Culture, Difference*, London: Lawrence and Wishart, pp. 207–21.

Ryder, A., T. Acton, S. Alexande, M. Greenfields, J. Richardson et al. (2011) *A Big or Divided Society?: Final Recommendations and Report of the Panel Review into the Coalition Government Policy on Gypsies and Travellers*, Travellers Aid Trust.

Rygiel, K. (2010) *Globalizing Citizenship*, Vancouver: University of British Columbia Press.

Sassen, S. (2003) 'A universal harm: making criminals of migrants', openDemocracy, 20 August, www.opendemocracy.net/people-migrationeurope/article_1444.jsp, accessed 1 April 2009.

Sayer, A. (2002) 'What are you worth? Why class is an embarrassing subject', *Sociological Research Online*, 7(3).

— (2005) *The Moral Significance of Class*,

Cambridge: Cambridge University Press.

Schermerhorn, C. (dir.) (2010) *The Naked Option: A Last Resort*, Motion picture.

Sewell, B. (2009) 'How eugenics poisoned the welfare state', *Spectator*, 22 November.

Sheller, M. and J. Urry (2003) 'Mobile transformations of "public" and "private" life', *Theory, Culture and Society*, 20(3): 107–25.

Shepherd, S. (dir.) (2005) *CHAV!*, Motion picture.

Silverman, S. (2008) 'Redrawing the lines of control: political interventions by refugees and the sovereign state system', University of Edinburgh School of Law, 28 April, www.law.ed.ac.uk/festivaloflegaltheory/files/silverman.pdf.

Silvester, K. (2005) 'Tabloid scare headlines lead to Gypsies being bullied', *SecEd*, 28 April, www.sec-ed.co.uk/cgi-bin/go.pl/article/article.html?uid=32589;type_uid=1, accessed 10 June 2012.

Skartveit, H.-L. and K. J. Goodnow (2010) *Changes in Museum Practice: New Media, Refugees and Participation*, London: Museum of London and Berghahn Books.

Skeggs, B. (1997) *Formations of Class and Gender: Becoming Respectable*, London: Routledge.

— (2001) 'The toilet paper: femininity, class and misrecognition', *Women's Studies International Forum*, 24(2/3): 295–307.

— (2004) *Class, Self, Culture*, London: Routledge.

— (2005) 'The making of class and gender through visualizing moral subject formation', *Sociology*, 39(5): 965–82.

Slater, T. (2011) 'From "criminality" to marginality: rioting against a broken state', *Human Geography*, 3(4).

Smith, D. (2010) 'WikiLeaks cables: Shell's grip on Nigerian state revealed', *Guardian*, 8 December, www.guardian.co.uk/business/2010/dec/08/wikileaks-cables-shell-nigeria-spying.

Soguk, N. (2006) 'Splinters of hegemony: ontopoetical visions in international relations', *Alternatives: Global, Local, Political*, 31(4): 377–404.

Soldatic, K. and H. Meekosha (forthcoming) 'The place of disgust: disability, class and gender in spaces of workfare societies', *Societies*.

South Wales Evening Post (2008) 'Deportation decision goes against family', 5 May, www.highbeam.com/doc/1P2-16320027.html.

Souweine, I. (2005) 'Naked protest and the politics of personalism', in M. Narula, S. Sengupta, J. Bagchi, G. Lovink and L. Liang (eds), *Sarai Reader 05: Bare Acts*, trans. S. Sarda, Delhi: Sarai Media Lab.

Spivak, G. C. (1981) '"Draupadi" by Mahasveta Devi', trans. G. C. Spivak, *Critical Inquiry*, 8(2): 381–402.

— (1990) 'Questions of multiculturalism', in S. Harasym (ed.), *The Postcolonial Critic: Interviews, Strategies, Dialogues*, London: Routledge.

— (1992) 'Extreme Eurocentrism', *Lusitania*, 1(4): 55–60.

Stallybrass, P. (1990) 'Marx and heterogeneity: thinking the lumpenproletariat', *Representations*, 31: 69–95.

Stallybrass, P. and A. White (1986) *The Politics and Poetics of Transgression*, Ithaca, NY: Cornell University Press.

Stoddard, L. (1922) *The Revolt against Civilization*, New York: Scribner.

Stoler, A. L. (1995) *Race and the Education of Desire: Foucault's* History of Sexuality *and the Colonial Order of Things*, Durham, NC: Duke University Press.

— (2011) 'Colonial aphasia: race and disabled histories in France', *Public Culture*, 23(1): 63.

Stratton, A. (2011) 'David Cameron on riots: broken society is top of my political agenda', *Guardian*, 15 August, www.guardian.co.uk/uk/2011/aug/15/david-cameron-riots-broken-society, accessed 2 June 2012.

Sun (2003) 'Bogus asylum seekers are bringing HIV, TB and hepatitis B to our shores', *Sun*, 29 January, p. 2.

— (2005) 'Stamp on the camps', *Sun*, 9 March, www.thesun.co.uk/sol/homepage/news/104007/Stamp-on-the-camps.html, accessed 4 June 2012.

— (2011) 'Shop an Edwardian moron', *Sun*, 12 August, www.thesun.co.uk/sol/homepage/news/3758824/Edwardian-version-of-The-Suns-Shop-A-Moron-rogues-gallery.html, accessed 5 May 2012.

Sunderland Echo (2007) 'Ladettes on the rise', 8 May, www.sunderlandecho.com/news/local/all-news/ladettes-on-the-rise-1-1133881, accessed 5 May 2012.

Sutton, L. (2009) '"They'd only call you a scally if you are poor": the impact of socio-economic status on children's identities', *Children's Geographies*, 7(3): 277–90.

Swyngedouw, E. (2006) 'Governance Innovation and the citizen: the Janus face of governance-beyond-the-state', *Urban Studies*, 42(11): 1991–2006.

Tatchell, P. (2004) 'Iranian fearing deportation burnt himself to death', www.petertatchell.net/asylum/suicide.htm, accessed 10 June 2012.

Taylor, R. (2012) 'We need the tackiest dresses they have', *Time Out London*, 12–18 July, p. 10.

Telegraph and Argus (2007) 'Hundreds living "Vicky Pollard lifestyle"', *Telegraph and Argus*, 25 May, www.thetelegraphandargus.co.uk/news/1426821.hundreds_living_vicky_pollard_lifestyle/, accessed 4 May 2012.

Thatcher, M. (1977) 'The new Renaissance', Speech to the Zurich Economic Society, 14 March, www.margaretthatcher.org/document/103336, accessed 10 June 2012.

— (1978) TV interview for Granada's *World in Action* (G. Burns, interviewer), ITV, 27 January, Margaret Thatcher Foundation, www.margaretthatcher.org/speeches/displaydocument.asp?docid=103485, accessed 1 April 2009.

— (1981) Speech to the Indian parliament, New Delhi, 16 April, www.margaretthatcher.org/document/104625, accessed 10 June 2012.

Theodore, N. (2007) 'New Labour at work: long-term unemployment and the geography of opportunity', *Cambridge Journal of Economics*, 31(6): 927–39.

Thielemann, E. R. (2004) 'Why asylum policy harmonisation undermines refugee burden-sharing', *European Journal of Migration and Law*, 6(1): 47–65.

Thompson, E. P. (1980 [1963]) *The Making of the English Working Class*, Harmondsworth: Penguin.

Thompson, P. (2003) 'Asylum meltdown: you say end this madness', *Sun*, 30 January, www.thesun.co.uk/sol/homepage/news/154562/You-say-End-this-madness.html?print=yes, accessed 1 June 2012.

Thomson, A. (2012) 'Down on the farm nothing is simple', blogs.channel4.com/alex-thomsons-view/farm-simple/436, accessed 4 June 2012.

Times (1847) 'Editorial', *The Times*, 2 April, p. 4.

Topping, A. (2011) 'Dale Farm evictions signal end of Traveller lifestyle, say Gypsies', *Guardian*, 18 September.

Toynbee, P. (2011) 'Chav: the vile word at the heart of fractured Britain', *Guardian*, 31 May, www.guardian.co.uk/commentisfree/2011/may/31/chav-vile-word-fractured-britain, accessed 3 May 2012.

Traveller Solidarity Network (2011) *Principles*, travellersolidarity.org/about/principles/, accessed 10 June 2012.

Travis, A. (2000) 'Tabloids vent fury', *Guardian*, 12 February, www.guardian.co.uk/uk/2000/feb/12/stansted.theairlineindustry, accessed 1 June 2012.

Tricky (2008) 'Council Estate'.

Troughton, T. (2011) 'tabitha troughton writing and photography', 21 October, tabithatroughton.wordpress.com/2011/10/, accessed 9 June 2012.

Tyler, C. A. (2002) *Female Impersonation*, London and New York: Routledge.

Tyler, I. (2000) 'Reframing pregnant embodiment', in S. Ahmed, J. Kilby, C. Lury, M. McNeil and B. Skeggs (eds), *Transformations: Thinking through Feminism*, London: Routledge.

— (2001) 'Skin-tight: celebrity, pregnancy and subjectivity', in S. Ahmed and J. Stacey (eds), *Thinking through the Skin*, London and New York: Routledge, pp. 69–83.

— (2006) '"Welcome to Britain": the cultural politics of asylum', *European Journal of Cultural Studies*, 9(2): 185–202.

— (2008) '"Chav mum chav scum": class disgust in contemporary Britain', *Feminist Media Studies*, 8(1): 17–34.

— (2009a) 'Against abjection', *Feminist Theory*, 10(1): 77–98.

— (2009b) 'Why the maternal now?', *Studies in the Maternal*, 1(1).

— (2010) 'Designed to fail: a biopolitics of British citizenship', *Citizenship Studies*, 14(1): 61–74.

— (2011a) 'Pramface girls: the class politics of "maternal TV"', in H. Wood and B. Skeggs (eds), *Reality Television and Class*, London: BFI/Palgrave Macmillan, pp. 210–24.

— (2011b) 'Pregnant beauty: maternal femininities under neoliberalism', in R. Gill and C. Scharff (eds), *New Femininities: Postfeminism, Neoliberalism and Identity*, London: Palgrave.

Tyler, I. and L. Baraitser (forthcoming) *Private View: Public Birth: Maternal Commons*.

Tyler, I. and B. Bennett (2010) 'Celebrity chav: fame, femininity and social class', *European Journal of Cultural Studies*, 13(3): 375–93.

Tyler, I. and E. Loizidou (2000) 'The promise of Berlant: an interview', *Cultural Values*, 4(4): 497–511.

Tyler, I. and K. Marciniak (forthcoming) 'Immigrant protest: an introduction', *Citizenship Studies*.

UK Border Agency (2008) *If you were born in the UK or a qualifying territory*, www.ukba.homeoffice.gov.uk/britishcitizenship/othernationality/Britishcitizenship/borninukorqualifying territory, accessed 1 April 2009.

UK Delegation to the European Roma and Travellers (2005) 'Report: Evictions report of Roma and Irish Travellers', The Advocacy Project, December, www.advocacynet.org/resource/466, accessed 9 June 2012.

UNHCR (2012) 'Refugees', www.unhcr.org/pages/49c3646c125.html, accessed 20 June 2012.

United Nations (1997a) *UN Committee on ESC Rights General Comment No. 4 on adequate housing under Article 11(1) of the Covenant, para. 18*, United Nations.

— (1997b) *UN Committee on ESC Rights General Comment No. 7 on forced eviction Paragraph 16*, United Nations.

Ureche, H. and M. Franks (2007) *This Is Who We Are: A study of the experiences of Roma, Gypsy and Traveller children throughout England*, Children's Society.

Urry, J. (2010) 'Consuming the planet to excess', *Theory, Culture and Society*, 27(2/3): 191–212.

Valentine, G. and I. McDonald (2004) *Understanding Prejudice: Attitudes towards Minorities*, Stonewall.

Van Allen, J. (1972) '"Sitting on a man": colonialism and the lost political institutions of Igbo women', *Canadian Journal of African Studies*, 6: 65–182.

Van Zoonen, L. (2006) 'The personal, the political and the popular: a woman's guide to celebrity politics', *European Journal of Cultural Studies*, 9(3): 287–301.

Wacquant, L. (2008) *Urban Outcasts: A Comparative Sociology of Advanced Marginality*, Cambridge: Polity.

— (2010) 'Crafting the neoliberal state: workfare, prisonfare, and social insecurity', *Sociological Forum*, 25(2): 197–220.

Wajid, S. (2006) 'Murder she wrote', *Times Higher Education Supplement*, 26 March, www.timeshighereducation.co.uk/story.asp?storyCode=202164&sectioncode=26.

Walker, C. (2004) *Liminal Spaces within the Transgressive Body*, www.franko-b.com/text/cw_introduction.htm, accessed 1 June 2012.

Walker, P. (2012) 'Benefit cuts are fuelling abuse of disabled people, say charities', *Guardian*, 5 February, www.guardian.co.uk/society/2012/feb/05/benefit-cuts-fuelling-abuse-disabled-people, accessed 11 June 2012.

Walters, W. (2004) 'Secure borders, safe haven, domopolitics', *Citizenship Studies*, 8(3): 237–60.

— (2006) 'No border: games with(out) frontiers', *Social Justice*, 33(1): 21–39.

Watts, M. (ed.) (2008) *Curse of the Black Gold: 50 Years of Oil in the Niger Delta*, Powerhouse.

Waugh, M. (2010) *The Mothers in Exile Project: Women Asylum Seekers' and Refugees' Experiences of Pregnancy and Childbirth in Leeds*, Womens Health Matters.

Welch, M. and L. Schuster (2005) 'Detention of asylum seekers in the UK and USA: deciphering noisy and quiet constructions', *Punishment and Society*, 7(4): 397–417.

Welshman, J. (2006) *Underclass: A History of the Excluded: 1880–2000*, London: Hambledon Continuum.

West, E. (2011) 'There's nothing wrong with having a go at chavs', *Daily Telegraph*, 1 June, blogs.telegraph.co.uk/news/edwest/100090254/theres-nothing-wrong-with-having-a-go-at-chavs/, accessed 2 May 2012.

Westergaard, J. (1995) *Who Gets What? The Hardening of Class Inequality in the Late Twentieth Century*, Cambridge: Polity.

Wheldon, J. (2006) 'NHS health tourism is rife but I can't turn sick patients away', *Daily Mail Online*, 24 May, www.dailymail.co.uk/health/article-387538/NHS-health-tourism-rife-I-turn-sick-patients-away.html.

Williams, R. (1960) *Culture and Society 1780–1950*, New York: Anchor Books.

Williams, Z. (2011) 'The UK riots: the psychology of looting', *Guardian*, 9 August, www.guardian.co.uk/commentisfree/2011/aug/09/uk-riots-psychology-of-looting, accessed 11 September 2011.

Willms, J. (2004) *Conversations with Ulrich Beck*, Cambridge: Polity.

Wilson, M. and R. Home (1998) *A Directory of Planning Policies for Gypsy Site Provision in England*, Bristol: Policy Press.

Winter, B. (2008) *Hijab and the Republic: Uncovering the French Headscarf Debate*, Syracuse, NY: Syracuse University Press.

Wood, C. (2012) *Destination Unknown: Summer 2012*, London: Demos.

Young, I. M. (1990) 'The scaling of bodies and the politics of identity', in I. M. Young and D. S. Allen, *Justice and the Politics of Difference*, Princeton, NJ: Princeton University Press.

Yuval-Davis, N. (1996) 'Women and the biological reproduction of "the nation"', *Women's Studies International Forum*, 19(1/2): 17–24.

— (1997) 'Citizenship: pushing the boundaries', *Feminist Review*, 57: 4–27.

Yuval-Davis, N. and F. Anthias (eds) (1989) *Women, Nation, State*, London: Macmillan.

Ziarek, E. P. (2005) 'Kristeva and Fanon: revolutionary violence and ironic articulation', in T. Chanter and E. P. Ziarek (eds), *Revolt, Affect, Collectivity: The Unstable Boundaries of Kristeva's Polis*, New York: SUNY.

Žižek, S. (1999) *The Ticklish Subject: The Absent Centre of Political Ontology*, London and New York: Verso.

— (2006) *The Parallax View*, Cambridge, MA: MIT Press.

— (2008) *Violence: Six Sideways Reflections*, London: Profile Books.

— (2011) 'Shoplifters of the world unite', *London Review of Books*, 19 August, www.lrb.co.uk/2011/08/19/slavoj-zizek/shoplifters-of-the-world-unite, accessed 4 May 2012.

INDEX